Encyclopedia of North American Railroads

Encyclopedia of
NORTH AMERICAN
RAILROADS

Aaron E Klein

Exeter Books

NEW YORK

A Bison Book

Acknowledgments

The author and publisher would like to
thank the following people who have
helped in the preparation of this book:
Bill Yenne, who designed it; Mary Raho
and Sheila Byrd who did the photo
research; Thomas G Aylesworth, who
edited it.

Page 1: A front-end view of Santa Fe's
locomotive No. 3460, the *Blue Goose*.
Page 2-3: Great Northern No. 3040 and three
additional engines haul a long line of freight-
laden boxcars between the Great Lakes and the
West Coast.
Below: A sleek and streamlined Pennsylvania
Railroad steam turbine, with separate tender.

Picture Credits

Alaska Railroad 10 (both), 12–13
Algoma Central Railway 12 (bottom), 13 (bottom), 14, 14–15
Amtrak 82, 82–83, 131 (both), 132 (both), 132–33, 134 (both), 134–35, 136–37, 138 (both), 138–39, 140–41 (all 4), 160
Alan Anderson 198–99
Association of American Railroads 13 (top), 15, 16–17, 17 (top), 26 (top), 30, 30–31, 38–39, 51, 59 (top), 84 (right), 100–01, 101, 102, 149, 163, 175, 206, 224
Baltimore and Ohio Railroad Co 27 (bottom)
Baltimore and Ohio Railroad via Association of American Railroads 176, 208, 209 (top)
Bancroft Library, University of California, Berkeley 95 (top left), 108 (top)
Bay Area Rapid Transit (San Francisco) 28 (top)
British Columbia Railway 32, 33 (top)
H L Broadbelt 4–5, 24, 25, 26 (bottom), 27 (top), 28–29, 40 (bottom), 50–51, 56 (bottom), 70–71, 72–73, 104–05, 106 (both), 106–07, 108 (right), 112 (both), 114–15, 118–19, 120, 142–43, 162, 162–63, 164–65 (both), 166, 168–69, 192 (top), 205 (left), 236, 246–47, 248–49
Tom Brown 202
Burlington Northern 2–3, 34, 34–35, 36–37, 38 (bottom), 65 (bottom), 67, 74–75, 76–77, 78–79, 81, 91, 92 (both), 93, 94, 146–47, 148–49
California and Western Railroad 124–25
Canadian National 41 (both), 42–43, 43 (all 3), 122–23
Canadian Pacific Corporate Archives 44 (both), 45, 46–47, 47 (both), 48, 49, 90, 212–13 (both), 237
Chicago Transit Authority 54–55
City of Calgary Transportation Department 53
Collections of the Michigan State Archives, Department of State 120–21, 121
Conrail 55
Delaware River Port Authority 170–71
Electro-Motive Division, General Motors Corp 62–63, 97 (top), 113
Gulf Oil Co 59 (bottom), 206–07
Illinois Central Gulf 98–99
Illinois Central Railroad 97 (bottom)
Kathleen Jaeger 225 (top)
R H Kindig 226–27
Library of Congress 218–19

Maryland Department of Transportation 116–17 (top)
Massachusetts Bay Transit Authority 117, 116–17 (bottom)
Montréal Urban Community Transportation Commission 129 (both), 130–31
National Railway Historical Society 252–53
New York Public Library 56 (top), 72, 73, 84 (left), 86, 234, 235, 242
Norfolk and Western Railway 108–09
Northern Pacific 126–27
Ontario Northland 150–51 (all 3), 152–53 (all 5)
PHMC Railroad Museum of Pennsylvania 166–67 (both)
Vic Reyna 110–11
Richmond, Fredericksburg and Potomac Railroad 177
Santa Fe Southern Pacific Corporation 1, 8–9, 18–19, 19, 20 (both), 20–21, 22–23, 65 (top), 161, 178–79, 256
Sierra Railroad 181, 182–83
Southern Methodist University via De Golyer Library 174–75
Southern Pacific 69, 88, 89, 95 (top right and bottom), 103, 108 (left middle 2), 158–59, 184–85, 186–87, 188–89 (both), 190–91, 192 (bottom), 193, 194 (top), 195 (top), 196–97 (both), 200–01 (both), 202–03, 220–21, 250–51 (all 3)
Southern Pacific via Association of American Railroads 108 (bottom left), 214–15 (both)
Stevens Institute of Technology 205 (right 2)
Toronto Transit Commission 209 (bottom)
Union Pacific 228–29, 230–31 (all 3), 232–33 (both)
Union Pacific Railroad Museum Collection 226
Union Pacific via Association of American Railroads 17 (bottom), 156–57, 216–17, 222–23, 225 (bottom)
VIA Rail 6 (top), 238–39, 242–43
Washington Metropolitan Area Transit Authority 240–41, 244–45
© **Bill Yenne** 6 (bottom 2), 7, 11 (both), 33 (bottom), 38 (middle), 40 (top), 52, 57 (all 4), 61–62, 64, 75, 93, 96 (both), 144, 145, 148, 154–55, 159, 180, 194 (bottom), 195 (bottom), 204, 254, 255

CONTENTS

Above: A VIA Rail passenger train in the heart of the Canadian Rockies. The company was established in 1978 to run Canadian National and Canadian Pacific Rail passenger trains. Travel by VIA Rail offers superb scenery.

Overleaf: The Santa Fe diesel-servicing facility in Barstow, California. The Santa Fe route structure covers much the same territory as Southern Pacific with whom it merged in 1983 and has 12,319 miles of track.

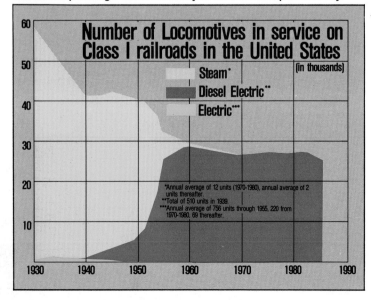

Number of Locomotives in service on Class I railroads in the United States

[in thousands]

Steam*
Diesel Electric**
Electric***

*Annual average of 12 units (1970-1980), annual average of 2 units thereafter.
**Total of 510 units in 1939.
***Annual average of 756 units through 1955, 220 from 1970-1980, 69 thereafter.

60
50
40
30
20
10

1930 1940 1950 1960 1970 1980 1990

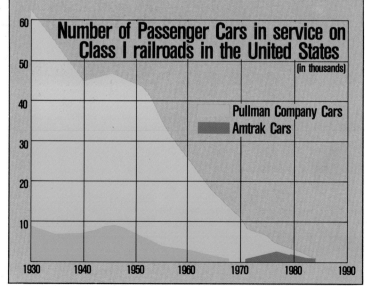

Number of Passenger Cars in service on Class I railroads in the United States

[in thousands]

Pullman Company Cars
Amtrak Cars

60
50
40
30
20
10

1930 1940 1950 1960 1970 1980 1990

Introduction

Attempting to produce a work on the current status of North American railroads is very much like trying to hit a moving target. The past quarter century has been one of great change for railways, both in Canada and the United States. The years in which this volume was in preparation were particularly turbulent. For example, as press time approached, the sale of Conrail to the Norfolk Southern Corporation had been approved by the Interstate Commerce Commission but not yet completed. This sale, if finalized, will make the Norfolk Southern system the largest in the country, displacing the CSX Corporation lines. The proposed merger of the Southern Pacific and the Atchison, Topeka and Santa Fe was still being held up by litigation. Every effort has been made, right up to press, to make the information in this volume as up-to-date as possible.

Information on the number of freight cars, passenger cars, locomotives and route mileage is provided in the entries on individual railroads. However, a railroad's complement of locomotives and rolling stock changes almost daily, so these figures can be regarded only as approximations. All extant Class I United States railroads, as well as major Canadian railways are included. A number of Class II railroads, which in the judgment of the author, are of particular interest, are also discussed. Some lines that are no longer in existence but which are of historical significance are included.

Individually named trains are discussed in the entry on Passenger Trains, The Great Ones, and not in separate entries. Items printed in small capital letters are cross references and indicate that the topic is discussed in a separate alphabetical entry.

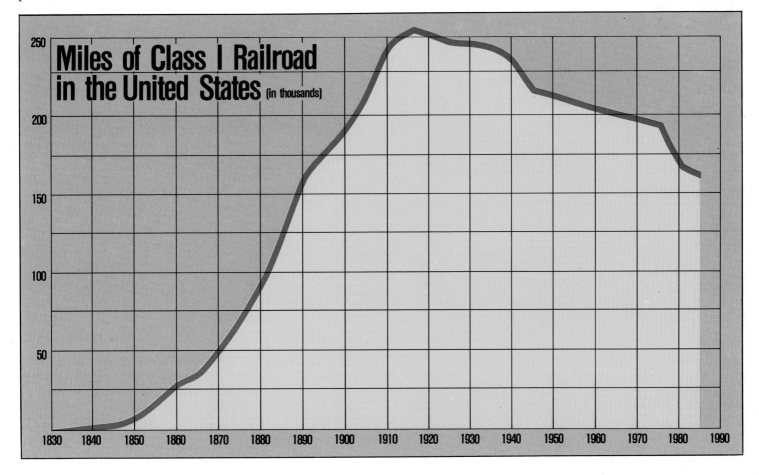

Miles of Class I Railroad in the United States (in thousands)

Aberdeen and Rockfish Railroad.

The Aberdeen and Rockfish Railroad runs between Aberdeen and Fayetteville, North Carolina. Incorporated in 1892, the line opened in sections, achieving full operations in 1913. The A&R is principally a carrier of building materials, chemicals, feed grains and animal byproducts.

Locomotives: 3
Freight cars: 224
Miles operated: 47
(as of January 1984)

Alaska Railroad.

The Alaska Railroad runs between Seward and Fairbanks. The single-track main line serves Whittier, Anchorage and Denali Park. Branch lines serve Eielson Air Force Base, Fairbanks International Airport and the Sutrana coalfield. The present Alaska Railroad was authorized by Congress in 1912. Prior to that time, two railroads, the standard gauge Alaska Northern and the narrow gauge Tanana Valley, operated in the territory. The Alaska Northern built northward from Seward, while the Tanana Valley connected Fairbanks with the head of navigation on the Tanana River. It was felt that a continuous line from the coast to the interior was needed, but the lack of population discouraged private invest-

ment. In a rider to the 1912 act granting self-government to the territory, the Alaska Engineering Commission was authorized to take over the Alaska Northern and Tanana Valley and to lay track connecting these two lines. When the line was completed in 1923, it was named the Alaska Railroad, and placed under the direct ownership of the Federal Government. Legislation authorizing transfer of the line from the US Department of Transportation to the State of Alaska was passed by Congress in 1983. The actual transfer took place in January 1985.

Profits from traffic generated by the construction of the trans-Alaska pipeline in the 1970s allowed investment in upgrading track, equipment and roadbed. A drop in traffic following completion of the pipeline resulted in a temporary period of deficit operations. However, 1982 revenues of $58.8 million set a new record, surpassing the previous record set in 1976 during the pipeline boom. Major commodities carried include coal,

An Alaska Railroad diesel locomotive in 1983 (*above*) and caboose (*below*).

The Alaska Railroad 1984

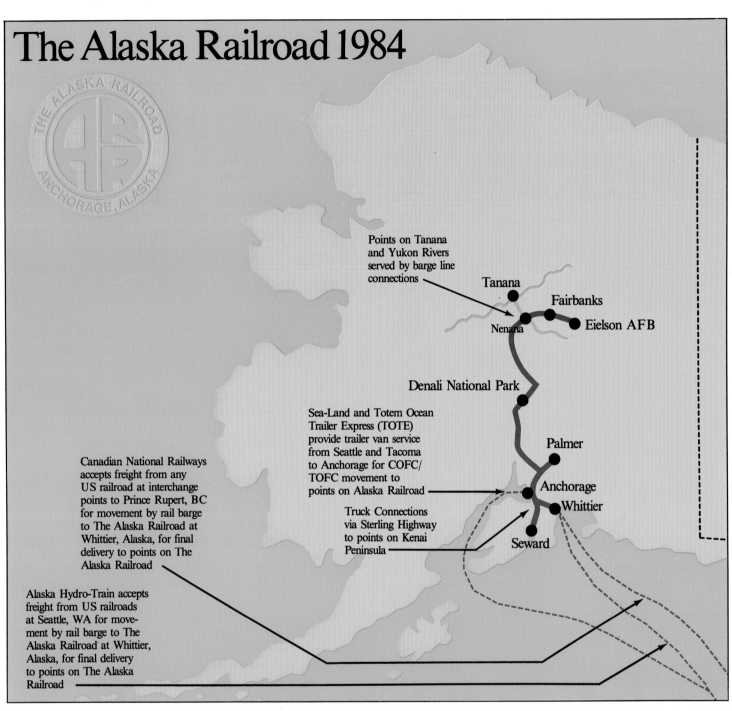

Points on Tanana and Yukon Rivers served by barge line connections

Tanana

Fairbanks

Nenana

Eielson AFB

Denali National Park

Sea-Land and Totem Ocean Trailer Express (TOTE) provide trailer van service from Seattle and Tacoma to Anchorage for COFC/TOFC movement to points on Alaska Railroad

Palmer

Anchorage

Whittier

Truck Connections via Sterling Highway to points on Kenai Peninsula

Seward

Canadian National Railways accepts freight from any US railroad at interchange points to Prince Rupert, BC for movement by rail barge to The Alaska Railroad at Whittier, Alaska, for final delivery to points on The Alaska Railroad

Alaska Hydro-Train accepts freight from US railroads at Seattle, WA for movement by rail barge to The Alaska Railroad at Whittier, Alaska, for final delivery to points on The Alaska Railroad

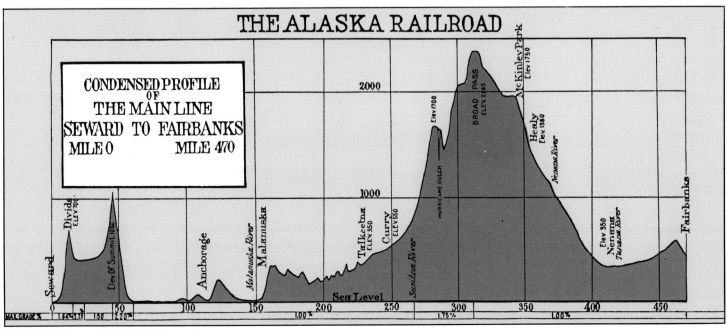

THE ALASKA RAILROAD

CONDENSED PROFILE OF THE MAIN LINE SEWARD TO FAIRBANKS
MILE 0   MILE 470

petroleum, sand and gravel, and iron and steel products. The Alaska Railroad still runs passenger service, and much of its ridership is on special tourist trains.

Locomotives: 65
Freight cars: 1251
Passenger cars: 42
Miles operated: 322
(as of January 1984)

Algoma Central Railway. The Algoma Central Railway runs through the Ontario wilderness between Sault Ste Marie and Hearst. Chartered in 1899, the original intention was to build to Hudson Bay; the road was called the Algoma Central and Hudson Bay Railway until 1965. The principal commodities carried are iron ore and forest products. The Algoma Central runs an actively promoted passenger excursion service, maintaining a wilderness park at the Agawa River Canyon. The company also has extensive real estate, trucking and forest interests.

Locomotives: 34
Freight cars: 1223
Passenger cars: 42
Miles operated: 322
(as of January 1984)

Allegheny-type locomotive. These 2-6-6-6 articulated locomotives were built by the Lima Locomotive Company for the CHESAPEAKE AND OHIO RAILROAD. Among the last steam locomotives made for a main-line North American railroad, the first unit was delivered late in 1941. Some 60 were built, the last locomotive being delivered in 1948. To many observers

the 600-ton Allegheny appeared to be larger than the much heavier and longer BIG BOY. The Alleghenies had large trailing trucks and two sand domes, each of 5-ton capacity. Replacing 2-10-4s, they proved to be successful in handling heavy war-time loads on the C&O's mountain runs.

Allen, Horatio (10 May 1802–31 December 1899). This civil engineer, inventor and entrepreneur was born in Schenectady, New York. He was the son of educated parents, and he received a superior education for the time. Graduating from Columbia College in 1823 with honors, he became interested in engineering, and worked on various Delaware canals in that capacity.

While with the Delaware and Hudson Company, the necessity for the use of steam locomotives at the western end of that company's canal became apparent, and Allen was chosen to go to England to investigate and purchase such new devices. The very first use of any railroad locomotive on American tracks was the STOURBRIDGE LION, one of Allen's acquisitions. It was operated for the Delaware and Hudson Company at Honesdale, Pennsylvania, on 9 August 1829 by Allen himself. The round trip included 3 miles

of track, for which the locomotive proved almost too heavy. However, the experiment proved that the future of locomotives as an adjunct to canal travel was feasible.

A month later, Allen became chief engineer of the South Carolina Railroad Company, for whom he advocated steam locomotive power over horse power with the prophetic words, 'There is no reason to expect any material improvement in the breed of

Above: An Alaska Railroad FP-7 locomotive and express passenger train. *Right:* Horatio Allen introduced steam locomotives in the US. *Below:* Two examples of steam engine once a part of the Algoma Central Railway fleet.

Left: Two generations of locomotives: an Algoma Central steam engine and a modern diesel (*above*).

a flatcar,' spurred the invention of locomotive mounted headlights.

Among the many honors accorded to Allen was the presidency of the American Society of Civil Engineers in 1872.

Alton and Southern Railway. A belt line serving the East St Louis, Illinois area, the Alton and Southern transfers cars of railroads entering its area. Incorporated in 1913, it was controlled by the Aluminum Company of America for a number of years. The MISSOURI PACIFIC petitioned the Interstate Commerce Commission for permission to buy the A&S in 1966. Following an ICC recommendation for joint ownership of the A&S by several roads, the line was purchased by the MP and the CHICAGO AND NORTH WESTERN in 1968. The C & NW's share was purchased by the St Louis Southwestern in 1973.

Locomotives: 20
Miles operated: 32
(as of January 1984)

American Civil War railroads. The American Civil War (1861–65) was the first major conflict in which

horses in the future while, in my judgment, the man is not living who knows what the breed of locomotive is to place at command.' In December of 1830 the line's historic BEST FRIEND OF CHARLESTON became operative under his direction and at his instigation. It was the first locomotive built in the United States. Thanks to the *Best Friend*, the South Carolina Railroad Company became the first scheduled steam railroad in the country. In 1833, its 136-mile-long track, built by Allen, became, for a time, the longest in the world.

Over the course of a long life, Allen went from one civil engineering challenge to another. He was associated with the Croton (New York) Aque-duct, the New York and Erie Railroad Company (as its president in 1843) and was a consultant on the construction of the Brooklyn Bridge, among many other projects. As a businessman, he was part owner of one of the country's biggest steamship engine companies of the era.

Allen was also known for his ingenious railroad inventions and improvements. He initiated many safety measures, both for their practical and public relations values. The first attempt at night runs of locomotives was his idea, for which he improvised a lighting car comprised of a wood fire trundled along a flat bed full of sand and pushed ahead of the locomotive. This 1831 device, called a 'bonfire on

railroads played a significant role in the outcome. At the outset of the war, the North possessed some 22,000 miles of railroad compared to the South's 9000 miles. While there were scores of foundries and locomotive works in the North, the South had only the Tredegar Iron Works in Richmond.

Railroads in the border states, such as the BALTIMORE AND OHIO, suffered disruption and destruction during the war. Most other railroads, North and South, prospered. In 1861, the Confederate General Stonewall Jackson raided the B&O yards at Martinsburg Virginia (now West Virginia), destroyed 42 locomotives and hauled 14 back to Confederate lines for use by the South. In the latter days of the war, railroads in the South were subject to massive destruction at the hands of advancing Union armies. Both the Union and the Confederacy commandeered lines and equipment as was deemed necessary. In the South, entire railroads were ripped up from Florida, Texas and other areas considered to be nonessential and rein-

stalled in more strategic areas. As the Union advanced into the Confederacy, many seized lines were operated as the United States Military Railroads.

The military of both sides were slow to realize the importance of railroads. When Union General William Rosecrans was put under seige at Chattanooga, he appealed for reinforcements. The closest available troops, some 16,000 men, were near Washington, more than 1000 miles away. According to military thinking of the time, at least three months would be required to move the troops. The chief of the Army Telegraph Corps, who had railroad experience, suggested that the men could be moved by railroad in about two weeks. Disbelieving generals were opposed to even trying, even though Rosecrans had been attacked by troops deployed quickly by rail. The doubting generals were overruled by Secretary of War Stanton and President

Below: Engines were stored in Washington DC during the Civil War, out of reach of the rebels.

Below: A United States Military Railroad 4-4-0
engine crosses a troop-guarded bridge on the
Orange and Alexandria Railroad during the Civil
War. *Far right:* Confiscated Orange and
Alexandria Railroad locomotive *General Haupt*
was named for the first chief of the Military
Railway Service. It was built in 1863.

Lincoln, who ordered the movement. By the time the deployment started, the troops had increased to 25,000 men. The troops and their equipment, including several batteries of artillery, were transported from Virginia to Tennessee in less than 11 days.

Great feats of railroad civil engineering were performed during the war. Of General Herman Haupt, who was put in charge of military railroad construction and repair in the eastern war theater, President Lincoln commented, '. . . That man Haupt has built a bridge across Potomac Creek about 400 feet long and nearly 100 feet high, over which loaded trains are running every hour, and . . . there is nothing in it but beanpoles and cornstalks.' The bridge had been constructed in less than two weeks with inexperienced labor. When it had to be destroyed because of Union setbacks, it was rebuilt—three times.

Andrew's raid, in which a locomotive, the *General*, was seized by Union raiders, was one of the war's more spectacular exploits. The purpose of the raid was to run the locomotive north along the tracks of the

Below: Union Pacific No. 1, *General Sherman*, was a 4-4-0 'American-type' engine.

Western & Atlantic Railroad, destroying tracks and telegraph lines behind them as they traveled. Spectacular as it was, the raid had little military significance.

'American type' (4-4-0) engine. The 4-4-0, or 'American type,' engine became the most widely used type of locomotive in nineteenth-century North America. The original 4-4-0 was built and patented by HENRY R CAMPBELL of Philadelphia. In the patent description, Campbell stated that the axles of the 54–inch-diameter wheels were placed in front of and behind the firebox 'in order to distribute the weight of the engine upon the rails more completely.' Campbell's patent was secured on 5 February 1836, and an engine was completed in May of 1837 by James Brook of Philadelphia. Intended for use on the Philadelphia, Germantown and Norristown Railway, the engine was not entirely successful. Although it had greater tractive force than the Baldwin 4-2-0s commonly in use at the time, the suspension of Campbell's engine was rigid, lacked in stability and tended to derail. The major problem was not having a means of equalizing the weight on the drivers.

The firm of Garrett and Eastwick completed a 4-4-0 engine in 1837 called *Hercules*. The 15-ton engine had a flexible running gear and could adapt to track irregularities. An equalizing lever, designed by Harrison, allowing a three-point suspension, is considered to be one of the most significant innovations in locomotive design. There is some evidence that Campbell attempted to sue Garrett and Eastwick for patent infringement. A later dispute with the Philadelphia and Reading Railroad was settled for 40 shares of Reading stock.

After 1840, production of 4-4-0s increased sharply. The typical 4-4-0 of the early 1840s was a small machine weighing about 12 tons. It was not until after the mid-1840s that the 4-4-0 began to take on the familiar appearance of the typical American locomotive of the nineteenth century. Boilers were lengthened, resulting in greater separation of the truck and drivers. Engines tended to become larger through the 1850s, and most

were built with cabs. Increasing concern over high centers of gravity resulted in low-set boilers.

The emergence of the 'modern' 4-4-0 stemmed largely from the influence of THOMAS ROGERS and his associates. Rogers machines were characterized by leading trucks with spread wheels, 'wagon-top' boilers and Stephenson link motion. By the mid-1850s, practically every American locomotive builder was producing machines based on what was widely referred to as the 'Rogers pattern.' Except for increases in size, they changed little over the next 30 years.

The 4-4-0, or eight-wheeler, continued as undisputed master of American and Canadian rails until the 1880s when the introduction of heavier rolling stock and the demand for faster schedules created a need for engines of greater capacity. The 4-4-0 was considered obsolete by 1900. However, it continued to be built in small numbers until the advent of diesels in the late 1940s.

Amtrak. See National Railroad Passenger Corporation.

Apalachiola Northern Railroad ('Port St Joe Route'). Operating in the western Florida panhandle, and the southeastern and southwestern corners of Alabama and Georgia respectively, the Apalachiola Northern was incorporated in 1903. The line was bought by the St Joe Paper Company in 1936. Principal commodities carried are lumber, pulpwood, paper products and coal. Much of the latter is hauled from Port St Joe, Florida, the deepest natural harbor on the Gulf of Mexico, to Chattahoochee, Florida, where connection is made with the SEABOARD SYSTEM for forwarding.

Locomotives: 11
Freight cars: 261
Miles operated: 96
(as of January 1984)

Atchison, Topeka and Santa Fe Railway Company (Santa Fe). The Atchison, Topeka and Santa Fe Sys-

tem extends through the western United States from Chicago to the Gulf of Mexico and the Pacific Coast. Pending ICC approval of the merger with the SOUTHERN PACIFIC, the Santa Fe and the Southern Pacific continue to operate as independent railroads owned by the SANTA FE SOUTHERN PACIFIC CORPORATION.

The Santa Fe was started at Topeka, Kansas, in 1872. By 1887, the rails had reached Los Angeles and a few years later the system had spread to San Francisco Bay and the Gulf of Mexico at Galveston. The Santa Fe set a standard of passenger service previously unknown in the West. Fred Harvey, an Englishman, obtained the catering concession for the Santa Fe in 1869. His restaurants soon became widely known for the excellence of their food and service and the charm and beauty of the girls who worked in them. 'Harvey Girls' had impeccable reputations in all respects. Many of them married Santa Fe customers and settled in the Southwest.

Above: The first Santa Fe *California Limited* into Los Angeles. *Below:* Generations of Santa Fe locomotives, from steam to diesel.

Top: Santa Fe EMD locomotives in Chicago.
Above: Santa Fe's rotary snowplow.
Right: The *Super Chief* was Santa Fe's daily all-Pullman streamliner between Chicago and Los Angeles.

The Santa Fe merged briefly with the San Francisco and St Louis Railroad in the 1900s. The Santa Fe was known as a company willing to experiment with new types of steam locomotives. It was one of the first western lines to make use of articulated locomotives, including a 2-10-10-2 with a hinged boiler. The 4-8-4 locomotives used for passenger service could run without change between Kansas City

and Los Angeles. The Santa Fe was one of the first railroads to change to diesel locomotives. The first diesel units were put into service in 1935 for hauling the *Super Chief*. Freight units followed in 1941. By 1943, two divisions were completely dieselized. The last steam locomotive on the Santa Fe was retired in 1959.

The Santa Fe's reputation for excellence in passenger service continued through the first half of the twentieth century. The *Super Chief* service between Chicago and Los Angeles became one of the best-known trains in the world. It succeeded the *Chief*,

an all-Pullman Chicago–Los Angeles service started in 1923. The *El Capitan*, an all-coach streamliner between Los Angeles and Chicago, was started in 1938. Santa Fe surrendered all passenger service to AMTRAK in 1973.

The Santa Fe is one of the leading intermodal shippers in North America. Most of its intermodal traffic is obtained from arrangements with third-party carriers such as trucking companies and shipping agents. These arrangements enabled Santa Fe to reduce the number of intermodal terminals to 38 from a peak of about 100 by the end of 1983. In the mid-

Evolution of the Santa Fe Logo

| 1888-1895 | 1895-1896 | 1896-1899 | 1899-1901 | 1901-Present |

Santa Fe's ten-pack train near Victorville, California, enroute to Chicago.

1980s, Santa Fe developed a new type of freight car called the 'fuel foiler' container. The 45-foot aerodynamically shaped containers are built in a configuration somewhat like a letter 'A.' The legs of the 'A' allow the cars to be stacked in pairs on Santa Fe's 'fuel foiler' skeletal frame cars. The design allows a low center of gravity, and reduces the wind drag encountered with ordinary boxcars.

A merger with Southern Pacific to form the Santa Fe Southern Pacific Corporation occurred on 23 December 1983. (See maps on pp 254–55.)
Locomotives: 2000
Freight cars: 62,610
Miles operated: 12,079

Arkansas and Louisiana Missouri Railway.

Operating between Monroe, Louisiana, and Crossett, Arkansas, the Arkansas and Louisiana Missouri was incorporated in 1920 with the absorption of the Arkansas and Louisiana Midland Railway. The line is owned by the Olin Corporation through its Olinkraft Inc subsidiary. Most of the A&LM's business is carrying fertilizer, pulpwood and paper products.
Locomotives: 4
Freight cars: 374
Miles operated: 54
(as of January 1983)

Ashley, Drew and Northern Railway.

Operating in Arkansas between Crossett, Fordyce and Monticello, this line carries paper products, pulpwood and other pine-tree derived products. The origins of the line stem from the 1905 incorporation of the Crossett Railway, intended to service the Crossett Lumber Company. This line was bought by the Crossett, Monticello, and Northern Railway in 1912. Plans to extend the line north to connect with the St Louis, Iron Mountain, and Southern (now part of the MISSOURI PACIFIC) were never carried out due to lack of money. The operation was purchased by the AD&N in 1913, which in turn, was leased to the Arkansas, Louisiana, and Gulf between 1914 and 1920. The AD&N and the Crossett Lumber Company were purchased by the Georgia Pacific Corporation in 1963, which also owns the neighboring Fordyce and Princeton Railroad.
Locomotives: 6
Freight cars: 2076
Miles operated: 41
(as of January 1984)

Atlanta and St Andrews Bay Railway (The Bay Line).

Organized in 1906 as a logging railroad, the original intent was to link Panama City (on St Andrews Bay), Florida, and Atlanta. Although the company never laid track north of Dothan, Alabama, Atlanta has remained in the railroad's name. The line was once owned by the United Fruit Company, which had plans to make Panama City a major banana port. In 1931 it was sold to the International Paper Company. The present owner is Southwest Forest Industries. The major commodities hauled are grain, paper products, pulpwood and chemicals.
Locomotives: 13
Freight cars: 828
Miles operated: 89
(as of January 1984)

Atlantic and Western Railway.

Incorporated in 1927, the Atlantic and Western originally ran 26 miles between Lillington and Sanford, North Carolina. Most of the line was abandoned in 1962, and its present terminus is Jonesboro, some 3 miles from Lillington. The railroad is notable for having a fleet of freight cars considerably larger than railroads with many more locomotives and miles of track. With only two locomotives operating on 3 miles of track, the Atlantic and Western has more than 1600 freight cars. The Atlantic and Western is mainly a carrier of sand and gravel, scrap iron and furniture.

Atlantic Coast Line.

The earliest predecessor of the Atlantic Coast Line was the Petersburg Railroad, which opened in 1833 between Petersburg, Virginia, and Weldon, North Carolina, on the Roanoke River. The name Atlantic Coast Line of Virginia, assumed in 1898, was changed to Atlantic Coast Line in 1900. The begin-

This 4-8-4 locomotive was built by Matthias Baldwin for the Atlantic Coast Line.

ning of the new century saw a period of expansion through the acquisition of several small lines in Virginia, North Carolina and South Carolina, which resulted in extending the ACL from Richmond to Charleston, South Carolina. The Plant system, a combined rail-steamship operation, was acquired in 1902, extending AC rails to Tampa, Florida, via Waycross, Georgia, and to Jacksonville, Florida, and Mongomery, Alabama. Control of the Louisville and Nashville was obtained at about the same time, and the two lines jointly leased the Georgia Railroad and the Clinchfield Railroad. Mergers with the Atlanta, Birmingham and Coast Railroad and the Charleston and Western Carolina occurred in 1945 and 1959, respectively. At its peak, ACL extended from Richmond to Florida, and westward to Alabama, and profited from the New York–Florida passenger business. ACL merged with SEABOARD AIR LINE RAILROAD in 1967, becoming the SEABOARD COAST LINE. When the Seaboard Coast Line became part of CSX CORPORATION in 1980, the name was changed to SEABOARD SYSTEM RAILROAD.

Atlantic-type locomotives. See Locomotive wheel arrangements.

Baird, Matthew (1817–1877). An American locomotive builder, Baird was born in Ireland, the son of a coppersmith. From 1834 to 1836 he was apprenticed to the New Castle Manufacturing Company in Delaware, where he learned the basics of building locomotives. He served briefly as superintendent of the Newcastle and Frenchtown Railroad shop before being hired by MATTHIAS BALDWIN as foreman of the boiler and sheet metal shop in 1838. He became a full partner of Baldwin in 1854.

Baird is generally credited with the innovation of using a firebrick arch, although the patent was taken out by GEORGE GRIGGS in 1854. In 1842, Baird designed a widely used spark arrester.

Baldwin Locomotive Works. See Baldwin, Matthias W.

Baldwin, Matthias W (10 November 1795–7 September 1866). A railroad designer, manufacturer and inventor, Baldwin was one of the most significant figures in early American locomotive development. He was born in Elizabeth, New Jersey. His father had been a successful carriage maker, but financial reverses led to Matthias' early apprenticeship to a manufacturing jeweler in Philadelphia.

At age 30, with a partner, Baldwin set up a manufacturing business of his own in which tool-making played a large part. An interest in engine design led him to fashion and exhibit an improved model of an English loco-

Pennsylvania Railroad's No. 212 was Matthias Baldwin's 1000th locomotive.

motive. As a result, he was asked to help assemble the first working locomotive in the Philadelphia area imported from England, the *Delaware*.

Baldwin was an excellent combination of pragmatic designer and practical entrepreneur. In order to begin manufacturing his own locomotives, he devised tools for the job and made thoughtful improvements in the design. His first engine, called OLD IRONSIDES, was completed in 1832. His company began to manufacture railroad engines on a large scale, and it prospered through several subsequent depressions.

Baldwin was most noted for his significant locomotive inventions and improvements. In 1842, his 'flexible-beam-truck' locomotive was patented. This design was an engineering breakthrough in overcoming the lack of traction on a curve. Baldwin had attempted to cure the problem in 1839 with a design of geared leading wheels, but the 1842 model was the successful solution. So many railroads wanted this locomotive that by 1835 Baldwin's Philadelphia firm employed 300 men to meet the demand. About 300 of these locomotives were manufactured overall. Although by 1859 production of them ceased, in 1911 in Cuba such a locomotive was still in operation.

Some of Baldwin's other inventions and improvements included a smokestack steam heater (1852) and a variable cutoff gear (1853) both of which enhanced his reputation as a pioneer.

Matthias Baldwin (*right*) founded the Baldwin Locomotive Works of Philadelphia, Pennsylvania in 1831 (*below*). He designed and built locomotives and was known for his various locomotive inventions. *Far right:* Baltimore and Ohio's No. 7400, photographed in 1931, was an articulated 2-6-6-2. *Far right, below:* The 7-ton *Atlantic* was the prototype grasshopper, vertical-boiler locomotive designed and built by Phineas Davis in York, Pennsylvania, in 1831. The locomotive went into service on the Baltimore and Ohio Railroad the following year. Shown here pulling two double-decked Imlay coaches, this engine is still in working order.

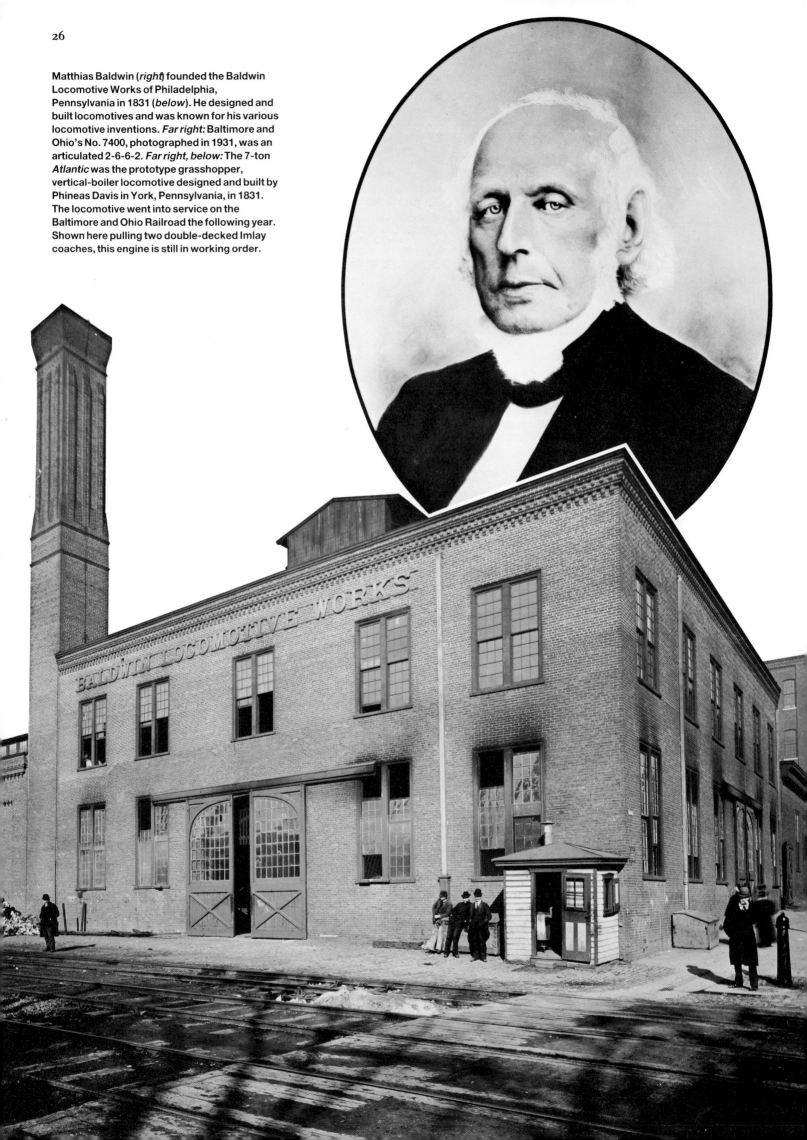

Baldwin was extremely successful as a businessman. In his lifetime his firm produced 1500 locomotives. In keeping with the time, Baldwin's conservative approach to locomotive innovation was well received by his customers. His firm was a large supplier to the Union Army during the CIVIL WAR.

Personally, Baldwin was religious and philanthropic. In addition to his many church charities, as an abolitionist he was generous to the black freedom cause and in the forefront of philanthropy for education of blacks.

Baltimore and Ohio Railroad. Incorporated in 1827 to build westward from Baltimore, the Baltimore and Ohio was one of the first railroads incorporated in North America. Originally intended to be a horse-powered line, the directors were convinced to change to steam after PETER COOPER's successful demonstration of the TOM THUMB. The Ohio River was reached in 1853, and expansion continued through the rest of the century with acquisitions and construction. The CHESAPEAKE AND OHIO obtained control of the B&O in the early 1960s. (See also Chessie System.)

Bangor and Aroostook Railroad. Incorporated in 1891, the Bangor and Aroostook runs between Searsport on

the Maine Coast and Fort Kent, Van Buren and Caribou, Maine. Rail passenger service was discontinued in 1961, but the BAR runs a bus service between Bangor and points north. The road is almost entirely owned by the Amoskeag Company. Pulpwood and other forest products are the major commodities hauled.

Locomotives: 45

Freight cars: 3590
Miles operated: 494
(as of January 1984)

Bay Area Rapid Transit (BART) (San Francisco). The BART system boasts some spectacular engineering feats, including a 4-mile underwater tunnel and a 3.2-mile tunnel bored through solid rock. One of the most

Above: The train on the right pulls into the Bay Area Rapid Transit System (BART) Rockridge Station in Oakland, California, heading for Oakland and then San Francisco. The train on the left leaves the station on its way to Concord. This photograph was taken in 1978, after the BART commuter line had been in service for two years. Using the median of the freeway limits the impact on traffic and the environment. *Below:* Samuel Vauclain of the Baldwin Locomotive Works poses with his family in front of a Baltimore and Ohio 2-6-6-2 during the 1920s.

ambitious rapid transit projects ever undertaken in North America, BART had to be locally funded since it was built before the 1974 URBAN MASS TRANSPORTATION ASSISTANCE ACT. The entire system, including train controls, signals, fare collection and crowd control, is automated. Trains operate at speeds as high as 80 mph.

Electrification system: 1000V DC, third rail
Gauge: 6ft 7in
No. of stations: 34
Rolling stock: 439
Route mileage: 72

Bay Colony Railroad. Incorporated in 1982, the Bay Colony Railroad operates on sections of ex-CONRAIL and NEW YORK, NEW HAVEN AND HARTFORD track now owned by the state of Massachusetts. Areas served include the Cape Cod Peninsula between Hyannis, Falmouth, Buzzards Bay and Middleboro, a section between Plymouth and Braintree, a section between Westport and Watuppa in the Fall River area, a section between Medfield Junction and Needham Junction southwest of Boston, and short sections from Taunton and Hingham. Included on the Bay Colony's line is a vertical lift bridge spanning the Cape Cod Canal at Buzzard's Bay. The Bay Colony transports a variety of goods including food products, salt, grain and building materials. A limited passenger service is operated between Falmouth and Hyannis on tracks of the Cape Cod and Hyannis Railroad.

Locomotives: 5
Freight cars: 47
Miles operated: 124
(as of January 1984)

Belt Railway of Chicago. Built between 1880 and 1882 as the Belt Division of the Chicago and Western Indiana Railroad, the purpose of this line was to provide connections between line-haul railroads in an area away from the congestion of inner-city Chicago. The major feature of the BRC is the Clearing Yard, which was the largest freight yard in the world when it opened in 1902. It was also one of the first three hump yards in the United States. The BRC currently connects with all line-haul roads serving Chicago. The line has been jointly owned by various railroads since its founding. As of 1983, the owners were:
ATCHISON, TOPEKA AND SANTA FE
BURLINGTON NORTHERN
CHESAPEAKE AND OHIO
CONRAIL
GRAND TRUNK WESTERN
ILLINOIS CENTRAL GULF
MISSOURI PACIFIC
NORFOLK AND WESTERN
SEABOARD SYSTEM
SOO LINE
Number of locomotives: 41
Miles operated: 48
(as of January 1984)

Berkshire-type locomotive. Developed by the Lima Locomotive Works, the prototype of this 2-8-4 locomotive was tested on the Boston and Albany Railroad in 1925. The four-wheel trailing truck was used to support a large firebox that had 337 feet of evaporating surface, more than the largest articulated locomotives of the time. Baker valve gear rather than the more widely used Walschaerts design was used. On a trial run of 55 miles hauling a 2296-ton train through the Taconic Mountains from Albany to North Adams, Massachusetts, it arrived ten minutes ahead of a MIKADO locomotive, pulling a 1691-ton train that had started the same trip 47 minutes earlier. The name Berkshire was applied by the Boston and Albany when it ordered 55 of the machines. Used primarily for freight on several railroads, more than 750 Berkshire-type locomotives were built. In addition to Lima, Berkshires were also built by Baldwin and the American Locomotive Company. Berkshires used by the Texas and Pacific Railroad and the ILLINOIS CENTRAL RAILROAD were equipped with small two-cylinder auxilliary engines powering the rear axle of the trailing truck. These engines provided an additional 12,000 pounds of tractive force.

Bessemer and Lake Erie Railroad. Since its inception in 1865 as the Bear Creek Railroad, this line has operated under a number of names and organizational schemes. Operating in western Pennsylvania, the B&LE runs between North Bessemer and the cities of Erie, Pennsylvania, and Conneaut, Ohio, on the Lake Erie shore. It is primarily a

hauler of coal, coke, iron ore and limestone. Historically, the road has been closely associated with the development of the American steel industry. An 1896 agreement with the Carnegie Steel Company and the Union Railroad to build a line from Butler, Pennsylvania, east to Pittsburgh gave Carnegie control of all companies involved in transporting iron ore to the Pittsburgh steel mills, a circumstance instrumental in the forming of the United States Steel Corporation in 1901. Running through hilly coun-

try, the B&LE line includes two of the longest railroad bridges in North America—a 1724-foot viaduct near Osgood, Pennsylvania, and a 2327-foot bridge over the Allegheny River near Pittsburgh. The Western Allegheny, purchased from the PENNSYL-VANIA RAILROAD in 1967, is operated as a separate division. Still owned by United States Steel, the B&LE also operates a 3.9-mile stretch of track between Renton and Unity Junction, Pennsylvania, called the Unity Railroad.

Locomotives: 64
Freight cars: 9556
Miles operated: 205
(as of January 1984)

The Best Friend of Charleston.
Built in 1830, this four-wheel locomotive was the first to haul a train in North America. Bought by the Charleston and Hamburg Railroad, later known as the South Carolina Railroad, the *Best Friend of Charleston* was designed by E L Miller of Charleston and built by the West Point Foundry of New York.

The *Best Friend of Charleston* weighed 4.5 tons and was equipped with a vertical boiler. The cylinders were six inches in diameter and had a bore of 16 inches. Its driving wheel was 54 inches in diameter, and it generated 50 pounds of steam pressure and developed a tractive force of 400 pounds.

The first trial run was on 2 December 1830, and on 14 and 15 December of that year it pulled some 50 passengers riding in four or five cars at speeds up to 21 miles an hour. The locomotive went into regular service hauling three-car trains on 15 January 1831. In June of 1831, the fireman, annoyed with the sound of escaping steam from the safety valve, closed it either by tying or holding it down. The boiler exploded, fatally injuring the fireman and seriously scalding the engineer. The engine was later rebuilt and renamed *Phoenix*.

Big Boy locomotives (4000 Class).
These 4-8-8-4 articulated locomotives were made for the UNION PACIFIC RAILROAD by the American Locomotive Company. Among the largest steam locomotives ever made, Big Boys weighed 1,104,200 pounds (over 552 tons) and were 133 feet long. Built for hauling heavy loads up mountain grades, the engine developed 135,375 pounds of tractive effort and were capable of 80 miles per hour. Under heavy load on steep grades a Big Boy could consume 22 tons of coal and 22,000 gallons of water in an hour. The first Big Boy was delivered in 1941, and some 25 were built.

Bipolar locomotive. See Electric locomotives.

Birmingham Southern Railroad.
Owned by the United States Steel Corporation, the Birmingham South-

Above left: This drawing of the *Best Friend of Charleston* pulling a special excursion train in January 1830 includes the directors of the South Carolina Canal and Rail Road Company, now part of the Southern Railway System. *Below:* The wood-burning *Best Friend of Charleston* was the first locomotive built in North America for regular service on a railroad.

ern hauls steel, iron ore and other raw materials between Port Birmingham, Alabama, on the Warrior River and steel mills in Fairfield and Bessemer. It is also engaged in general terminal service in Birmingham. Barges transport iron ore to Port Birmingham where it is transferred to ore cars for shipment to the US Steel plant at Fairfield. Incorporated in 1899, the line was soon purchased by the SOUTHERN RAILWAY and the LOUISVILLE AND NASHVILLE. A few years later it was bought by the Tennessee Coal, Iron, and Railroad Company, which was bought by US Steel in 1906.

Locomotives: 22
Freight cars: 796
Miles operated: 91
(as of January 1984)

Blood, Aretas (1816–97). An American locomotive maker, Blood was born in Vermont. At age 17, he was apprenticed to a blacksmith. After his apprenticeship he worked as a machinist for the Locks and Canal machine shop in Lowell, Massachusetts. In 1849, he was at the Essex Machine Shop of Lawrence, Massachusetts, making locomotive parts. With capital gained from this venture, he bought into the newly formed Manchester Locomotive Works in 1853. For the first few years after its founding, the Manchester works did poorly, primarily because the locomotives it produced were too light. Blood became the chief supervisor in 1857 and began producing heavier machines that were favorably received. Becoming the chief owner of the Manchester shops, Blood acquired the fire engine division of the Amoskeag Manufacturing Company in 1872. The Manchester Works produced some 1800 locomotives before it closed in 1901.

Boston and Maine Corporation. Dating from 1833, the Boston and Maine today operates in all the New England states except Rhode Island, and to Mechanicsville, New York, near Albany, through the 4.7-mile Hoosac Tunnel. Although it is primarily a freight line, it operates a commuter service to Boston under contract with the MASSACHUSETTS BAY TRANSPORTATION AUTHORITY (MBTA).

When the line declared bankruptcy in 1970, it chose to reorganize rather than join CONRAIL. Lines in eastern Massachusetts were sold, as was its fleet of Budd rail diesel cars, which

A British Columbia Railway diesel-electric locomotive traveling inland beside the spectacular Howe Sound.

was the largest in the world. Many of these cars are still in service on the MBTA commuter lines operated by B&M.

In 1982, the Interstate Commerce Commission approved the purchase of the B&M by Guilford Transportation Industries (GTI) which also owns the DELAWARE AND HUDSON and the MAINE CENTRAL. In that same year, in conjunction with the CENTRAL VERMONT RAILWAY, B&M started an overnight trailer on flat car (TOFC) service between Boston and Montreal. Called 'Rocket,' the service operates up to 15 cars with a two-man crew and no caboose. The success of this service encouraged the opening of a similar service called 'East Wind' between Bangor, Maine and New Haven, Connecticut.

Locomotives: 162
Freight cars: 3226
Diesel rail cars: 51
Miles operated: 1393
(as of January 1984)

British Columbia Hydro and Power Authority. Owned by the province of British Columbia, the British Columbia Hydro and Power Authority (BCHPA) supplies electric power and gas to much of British Columbia and Victoria. The rail service was reorganized from an electric interurban and street railway that operated in Vancouver and environs starting in 1897. Passenger service was discontinued in 1958. The BCHPA now operates a diesel-powered freight service between Vancouver and Chilliwick. Major commodities carried include automobiles, food and forest products.

Locomotives: 22
Freight cars: 231
Miles operated: 104
(as of January 1984)

British Columbia Railway. The British Columbia Railway operates in that province between Vancouver and Fort Nelson. Chartered in 1912 as the Pacific Great Eastern, the railroad started with a 12-mile line from Vancouver to Horseshoe Bay where connection was made with a bankrupt line that ran from Squamish. The provincial government of British Columbia acquired the PGE in 1918 and continued construction northward, reaching Prince George in 1952, Dawson Creek in 1958 and Fort Nelson in 1972. The BCR is primarily a hauler of forest products and coal. A limited passenger service with rail-diesel cars is operated between Vancouver and Prince George ('Cariboo Dayliner'). A summer steam service between Vancouver and Squamish hauled by a former CANADIAN PACIFIC *Royal Hudson* is a popular tourist attraction. Electrification of the so-called Tumbler Ridge branch is underway.

Locomotives: 125

Railroads of Western Canada

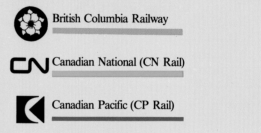

British Columbia Railway

Canadian National (CN Rail)

Canadian Pacific (CP Rail)

Canadian National *and* Canadian Pacific

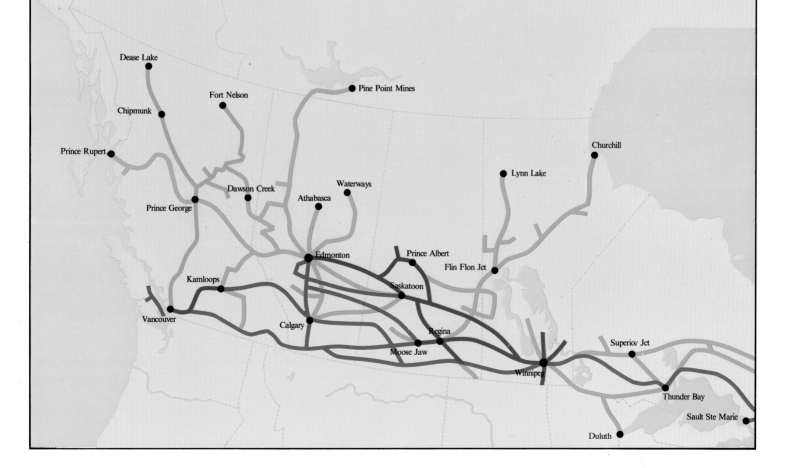

Dease Lake

Pine Point Mines

Fort Nelson

Chipmunk

Prince Rupert

Churchill

Lynn Lake

Waterways

Dawson Creek

Athabasca

Prince George

Edmonton

Prince Albert

Flin Flon Jct

Kamloops

Saskatoon

Vancouver

Calgary

Regina

Superior Jct

Moose Jaw

Winnipeg

Thunder Bay

Sault Ste Marie

Duluth

A Burlington Northern unit train, carrying 11,000 tons of low-sulfur coal (*left*) approaches a tunnel shortly after leaving a mine near Gillette, Wyoming. Another freight train (*below*) prepares to leave the rail yard.

Freight cars: 9790
Miles operated: 1261
(as of January 1984)

Brother Jonathan. See The Experiment.

Buffalo, Bayou, Brazos and Colorado. See South Pacific Company.

Burlington Northern. The Burlington Northern (BN) started its corporate existence in March 1970 with the merger of four railroads: CHICAGO BURLINGTON AND QUINCY RAILROAD; GREAT NORTHERN RAILWAY; NORTHERN PACIFIC RAILWAY and the Spokane, Portland, and Seattle Railway. In 1980 the St Louis–San Francisco Railway (the Frisco) was added. The Colorado and Southern Railway Company, and the Denver Railway Company, previously owned by the CB&Q, were fully absorbed in 1981. With the addition of these three roads, the BN became the largest single railroad in North America. While the csx railroads have more route mileage, the various component companies retain a degree of autonomy. The BN is a 29,200-mile system operating in 25 states and two Canadian provinces extending from the Gulf Coast at Houston and Pensacola through the Midwest to the northern tier of states, and westward to the Pacific Coast of Oregon and Washington. The BN includes the first- and second-longest railroad tunnels in North America, the 7.79-mile Cascade Tunnel in Washington, and the 7.75-mile Flathead Tunnel in Montana.

Burlington Northern operates as a subsidiary of Burlington Northern Inc, a holding company which also has interests in logging, oil and gas

Great Northern's *Empire Builder* heads for the summit of the Continental
Divide near Glacier Park in 1947. The Great Northern merged with the
Chicago, Burlington and Quincy Railroad, the Northern Pacific Railway
and Spokane, Portland, and Seattle Railway in 1970 to form Burlington
Northern. The *Empire Builder* now operates as an Amtrak train between
Spokane, Washington, and Portland, Oregon.

Chicago, Burlington & Quincy
Fort Worth & Denver
Colorado & Southern
Great Northern
Northern Pacific
Spokane, Portland & Seattle
St. Louis & San Francisco (The Frisco)

Burlington Northern

Above: Burlington Northern's *Pioneer Zephyr*, America's first diesel streamlined train.
Below left: A BN unit coal train near Marsland, Nebraska, enroute to the mine near Gillette, Wyoming.

exploration, coal and mineral mining and real estate. BN is primarily a hauler of coal, grain and forest products. Direct TOFC and COFC service is provided between the Great Lakes to the Pacific Northwest, the Canadian border and the Gulf Coast. BN includes a number of AMTRAK routes, including the Chicago–Denver *California Zephyr*, the St Paul–Seattle and Spokane–Portland *Empire Builder* and the Seattle–Portland *Coast Starlight*. BN also operates commuter service between Chicago and Aurora, Illinois, for the REGIONAL TRANSPORTATION AUTHORITY. (See maps on pp 254–55.)

products for the Union Lumber Company, which is the owner. The *Skunk* carries passengers in the fall, winter and spring, while diesels take over for the summer months. (See photo, pg 40.)

Locomotives: 6
Freight cars: —
Passenger cars: 11
Miles operated: 40
(as of January 1984)

Caltrans. Caltrans is operated by the state of California in conjunction with the SOUTHERN PACIFIC to provide commuter rail service between San Francisco and San Jose, and Los Angeles and Oxnard. Locomotives and cars are leased from the Southern Pacific. Caltrans also subsidizes the operations of several Amtrak trains and connecting buses.

Cambria and Indiana Railroad. Serving the towns of Colver, Nanty Glo and Manver in western Pennsylvania, the Cambria and Indiana started as a logging road around the turn of the century. Incorporated as the Blacklick and Yellow Creek Railroad in 1904, it became a coal carrier. The present name, assumed in 1911, refers to the counties in which it operates. Since 1950, the line has been owned by the Bethlehem Steel Corporation.

Locomotives: 18
Freight cars: 955
Miles operated: 57
(as of January 1983)

Camden and Amboy Railroad. See Stevens, Robert L.

Camel locomotive. The camel class of locomotive, designed by ROSS WINANS and put in service on the BALTIMORE AND OHIO RAILROAD in 1848, was one of the most powerful locomotives of its time. It was also one of the most unusually designed locomotives ever built. The name 'camel' stemmed from the placement of the cab on top of the boiler of these 0-8-0 locomotives. The prototype camel had a large steam dome placed ahead of the firebox rather than above it. Its weight was 45,000 pounds and it had 17-by-22-inch cylinders and 43-inch driving wheels. Most later versions had 19-by-22-inch cylinders and weighed from 50,000 to 58,000 pounds. Camels proved to be quite successful on the B&O's tough '17-mile grade,' a rise of almost 2000 feet west of

Locomotives: 3205
Freight cars: 108,600
Miles operated: 29,200
(as of January 1984)

Butte, Anaconda and Pacific Railway. Operating between Butte and Brown, Montana, the Butte, Anaconda and Pacific was opened in 1893 to serve copper mines and smelters in the Butte–Anaconda area. Copper ore remains the major commodity carried. In 1911, the BA&P, owned by the Anaconda Copper Mining Company, electrified the line. Mixed diesel and electric operation continued until 1967, when the line converted to all-diesel operation.

Locomotives: 9
Freight cars: 411
Miles operated: 43
(as of January 1983)

California and Oregon Railroad. See Southern Pacific Company.

California and Western Railroad. The California and Western Railroad operates between Fort Bragg and Willits, California. The origins of the C&W stem from the redwood lumber operations of Charles R Johnson in the 1880s. In 1885 Johnson put together an operation called the Fort Bragg Railroad to haul logs to a mill in that town. The railroad, under various names, reached its present eastern terminus of Willits in 1911. The C&W received a gasoline-engine Mack railbus in 1925. Called the *Skunk*, because of the exhaust smell, the railbus became a tourist attraction in the 1950s. In addition to carrying tourists through its scenic route, the C&W also continues as a carrier of forest

Piedmont, Virginia. Of the more than 200 camels produced, 119 were used by the B&O. In addition to the B&O, camels were used on the PENNSYL-VANIA RAILROAD and the Erie Railroad, among others. Camels were the subject of bitter controversy when the B&O decided to adopt 4-6-0 locomotives. Regarding the decision as a personal affront, Winans published pamphlets defending his locomotives, and the B&O countered with pamphlets attacking them.

Campbell, Henry R (1810?–1870?). An inventor and manufacturer, Campbell is best known for his 1836 patent of a 4-4-0 locomotive, which was the precursor of what came to be known as the AMERICAN-TYPE LOCOMOTIVE. Very little is known of Campbell's early history. He was chief engineer of the Philadelphia, Germantown and Norristown Railroad and chief engineer of the CENTRAL VERMONT in the late 1840s to mid-1850s. He was involved in litigation with the Philadelphia and Reading Railroad and the firm of Garrett and Eastwick for alleged infringement of his patent.

Canadian National (CN Rail). CN Rail, the national railway of Canada, is the largest operating division of Canadian National, a company owned by the Canadian Government. In addition to CN Rail, Canadian National operates telecommunications, trucking, hotel, shipping and petroleum interests. While CN Rail is

Above: The California and Western Railroad *Skunk* locomotive is a tourist attraction.
Below: A 2-8-0 camel in service with the North Carolina and St Louis Railway.

Canada's national railway, the name Canadian National Railways is no longer official. The GRAND TRUNK CORPORATION is a Canadian National subsidiary that controls three US railroads: CENTRAL VERMONT; DULUTH, WINNIPEG, AND PACIFIC and GRAND TRUNK WESTERN.

Canadian National Railways was established in 1922 to assume control of several financially distressed railways including the Canadian Northern, GRAND TRUNK RAILWAY, and the Grand Trunk Pacific. The 3ft 6 in gauge Newfoundland Railway was added in 1949 when that province joined the Canadian Confederation. The Northern Alberta Railroad, which had been organized to take over several lines previously under provincial control, was also added to the CN system. The CN Rail system today extends from the Maritime Provinces to the Pacific Coast, and northward to Hudson Bay. As of 1984, CN Rail operated about 1780 standard gauge locomotives and some 50 narrow gauge locomotives. About 79,460 standard gauge freight cars and 1230 narrow gauge cars operated on some 22,520 miles of track.

Since passenger services were taken over by VIA RAIL in 1978, CN Rail has been a freight operation. The only passenger service is an electrified Montréal commuter service operated under contract for the MONTREAL URBAN COMMUNITY TRANSPORTATION COMMISSION (Commission de Transport

Above: Six Canadian National Rail engines at Railway Week in Belleville, Ontario.
Below: A Canadian National 4-8-4 builds up steam for departure.

de la Communauté Urbaine de Montréal). 'Laser' piggyback service is actively promoted as an economical alternative to shipping by truck on highways. Containerized service and computerized traffic control have been expanded since the 1970s. The prototype computerized traffic control system went into operation in Winnipeg in 1978, and the main system went online in Edmonton in 1982.

Throughout the 1980s, an intensive double-tracking program was under way in the western provinces. Track over the entire system was improved with the laying of concrete sleepers. The Victoria Bridge built over the St Lawrence River was one of the first long railway bridges in the world. The first Victoria Bridge, opened in 1859, employed the tubular structure designed by the British engineer Robert Stephenson. It was a single-track structure, almost two miles long. The original bridge was replaced in 1898 by a double-track, steel structure named the Victoria Jubilee Bridge.

CN's No. 9000 diesel-electric locomotive, put into service in 1929, is widely regarded as the world's first successful passenger locomotive.
Locomotives: 1830
Freight cars: 80,690
Miles operated: 22,520

Canadian Northern. See Canadian National.

Canadian Pacific (CP Rail). Incorporated in 1881 as the Canadian Pacific, the original intent of the organization was to build a transcontinental railroad in Canada. CP Rail today is the rails division of Canadian Pacific Limited, which also has extensive interests in shipping, airlines, trucking, telecommunications and other enterprises. The SOO LINE is an American subsidiary of CP rail. Passenger equipment and operations were turned over to VIA RAIL in 1978. However, CP Rail operates commuter rail services under contract for the MONTREAL URBAN COMMUNITY TRANS-

PORTATION COMMISSION (Commission de Transport de la Communauté Urbaine de Montréal) and the GOVERNMENT OF ONTARIO TRANSIT in Toronto.

The transcontinental line from Callender, Ontario, to the Pacific Coast, as completed in 1885, included 4.5 percent grades at the Kicking Horse Pass crossing of the Rockies. Operations on the eight-mile section between Field and Hector, called the 'Big Hill,' were difficult and dangerous. A partial solution to these operating problems came with the building of the 'spiral tunnels' in 1907–08 through Cathedral Mountain and Mount Ogden. Expansion to Ottawa and Montréal was accomplished in the early 1880s with the absorption of the Canada Central. The leasing of the Ontario and Québec gained access to Toronto, and in 1884, rails were laid to Windsor, Ontario, opposite Detroit. By 1890, the Canadian Pacific was a true coast-to-coast railway from New Brunswick to Vancouver.

Political considerations and the dis-

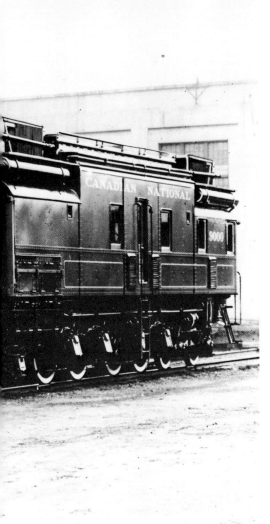

Left: CN's oil electric double unit No. 9000 was photographed in 1928, the year before entering service. *Top:* Diesel locomotive No. 6500 passenger train was built in 1954. *Above:* A new CN diesel in London, Ontario, and a unit coal train (*below*) in Alberta.

covery of silver in British Columbia led to expansion in that province in the late 1880s. Because of the expense of construction and operations in this area, the Canadian Government provided money grants in exchange for a permanently low rate for shipping grain. The 1897 Crowsnest Pass Agreement set the rate at approximately 0.5 cents a ton-mile. This so-called 'crow' rate proved to be inadequate almost from the start. By the 1980s, the actual cost of shipping grain was about 6 cents a ton-mile. The rate was not changed until the passage of the Western Grain Transportation Act of 1983, which provides for the Canadian Government to share the cost of transporting grain with grain producers.

CP Rail today operates in all Canadian provinces except Newfoundland and Prince Edward Island. Major commodities carried include grain, coal, potash, sulfur, copper, iron and nickel ores, forest products, liquid petroleum gas, oil, gasoline and chemi-

Above: A CP Rail freight train enroute to Banff, Alberta. *Below:* The 3000hp CP No. 6028

Right: A CP Rail westbound train near Field, British Columbia.

cals. CP Rail was one of the first railways to introduce unit train systems for handling bulk materials. Unit trains are seldom uncoupled, moving as a unit almost continuously from loading facility to destination. CP Rail was also one of the innovators in intermodal services. In 1979, a domestic container service was initiated, using general purpose dry van, 44-foot, 3-inch-long containers designed to fit on 45-foot piggyback trailers. Although the containers are slightly shorter than those used previously, their use has increased efficiency. Another first for CP Rail in Canada is a computerized system which allows

Above: The station at Sudbury Junction in Ontario, photographed around 1900. **Top:** The CP Rail station at Revelstoke, British Columbia, and Banff, Alberta (*left*), in the heart of the Canadian Rockies. CP also built hotels to accommodate the many visitors who came by train to enjoy the exceptional beauty of the region.

customers to receive daily car reports on their computer terminals.

In 1983, CP Rail initiated the Rogers Pass Project. This $600 million project is the largest single building project undertaken by CP Rail since the building of the transcontinental line in the 1880s. The major components of the project are double tracking and the building of a nine-

48

Above: CP Rail No. 6024 came out of the shop in 1981. *Right:* CP Rail passenger train *The Canadian* follows the Bow River out of Lake Louise, Alberta.

mile tunnel through the Selkirk Mountains in British Columbia. Expected to be completed in 1989 or 1990, the tunnel will be the longest in North America. A one-mile tunnel under the Trans-Canada Highway is also planned. The project will reduce the approach grade for westbound trains on the east slope of the Selkirks about one percent from the current 2.2 percent average grade on the steepest parts of the line. Operating capacity in the Selkirks will increase, with a new ventilation system in the tunnels to allow about twice the former train frequency.
Locomotives: 1178
Freight cars: 55,300
Miles operated: 21,500

Central Pacific. See Southern Pacific Company; Transcontinental railroad (United States).

Central Vermont Railway. The Central Vermont operates between New London, Connecticut, and several points in extreme northern Vermont and New York. It was opened under its present name in 1849 with a line between Windsor and Burlington, Vermont. It achieved its greatest extent in the 1870s with lines extending from New London to Ogdensburg, New York. It was reorganized in 1898 into a system that is much the same as it is today. CVR operates a fast piggyback service, 'The Rocket,' between New Haven, Connecticut, and St Albans, Vermont, with the Boston and Maine.
Locomotives: 29
Freight cars: 549
Miles operated: 377
(as of January 1984)

Chesapeake and Ohio. The earliest precursor of the Chesapeake and Ohio was the Louisa Railroad, incorporated in 1836 to serve Louisa County, Virginia. The name Chesapeake and Ohio was assumed in 1867. Tidewater was reached at Newport News in 1881 and extension westward was accelerated in 1910 with the acquisition of the Chicago, Cincinnati and Louisville line that traversed Indiana. In the 1930s the C&O became part of the Van Sweringen railroad complex, which fell apart during the Great Depression. In 1947 C&O merged with Pere Marquette and became the New York Central's largest stockholder. This stock was sold in the 1950s. In an attempt to resist the trend to dieselization, C&O invested in the development of a steam turbo-electric locomotive in the late 1940s and early 1950s. Three of these 'M-1' locomotives were built, but they proved to be unreliable and expensive to run and maintain. Control of the BALTIMORE AND OHIO RAILROAD and the CHICAGO, SOUTH SHORE AND SOUTH BEND was obtained in the 1960s. The latter road is not part of the CHESSIE SYSTEM.

Chicago, Burlington and Quincy Railroad. See Burlington Northern.

Chessie System Railroads. The Chessie System, one of the rail components of the CSX CORPORATION, operates in the northeastern United States, providing service between mid-Atlantic states and the coal and industrial areas of Kentucky, Ohio, western Pennsylvania, Michigan, Indiana, Illinois and Missouri. Lines also extend to Rochester, Buffalo and southern Ontario. The BALTIMORE AND OHIO RAILROAD and the CHESAPEAKE AND OHIO RAILWAY operates as affiliates within the Chessie organization. The Western Maryland Railway operated as an affiliate until 1983, when it was fully absorbed into the Baltimore and Ohio. The combined Chessie System railroads are the largest coal-hauling system in the United States. (See map on pg 57.)
Locomotives: 1964
Freight cars: 108,230
Diesel rail cars: 6
Passenger cars: 6
Miles operated: 16,300
(as of January 1984)

Chicago and Illinois Midland Railway. The Chicago and Illinois Midland Railway operates between Peoria and Cimic and Taylorville in southern Illinois. Its earliest precursor was the Pawnee Railroad, incorporated in 1888. The present name was assumed in 1905 after the railway was purchased by the Illinois Midland Coal Company. The C&IM is primarily a coal-carrying railroad, delivering coal to power stations near Pekin, and to Peoria for shipment by barge to Chicago. This coal is primarily low-sulfur coal from Wyoming and Colorado received from the BURLINGTON NORTHERN and the CHICAGO AND NORTH WESTERN rather than the low-sulfur coal of southern Illinois, formerly the line's major source of revenue.
Locomotives: 20
Freight cars: 1076
Miles operated: 121
(as of January 1984)

Chicago and North Western Transportation Company. The Chicago and North Western serves Wisconsin, the grain-producing areas of Minnesota, Iowa, South Dakota and Nebraska, and the coal-mining country of Wyoming. Service is also provided to St Louis and Kansas City. The earliest ancestor of the C&NW was the Galena and Chicago Union Railroad, chartered in 1836. A later precursor was the Chicago, St Paul and Fond du Lac, chartered in 1855 to build northward from Chicago through Wisconsin and Minnesota. This road was organized as the Chicago and North Western Railway in 1859, and in 1864 it merged with the Galena and Chicago Union. A road called the Chicago and Milwaukee was leased in 1866. Expansion continued steadily through the rest of the nineteenth century. In the late 1950s and early 1960s, C&NW embarked on a program of acquisition of several small lines, including the Minneapolis and St Louis, Des Moines and Central Iowa and the Chicago Great Western. In March 1970 the C&NW was bought by its employees, incorporated in Delaware as the North Western Employees Transportation Corporation. The present name was adopted in 1972. The Chicago and North Western can claim a number of 'firsts,' including first railroad in

A Chesapeake and Ohio steam turbo-electric locomotive of the late 1940s and early 1950s, one of three that were built.

Chicago and Northwestern's *Pioneer* was the first locomotive in Chicago.

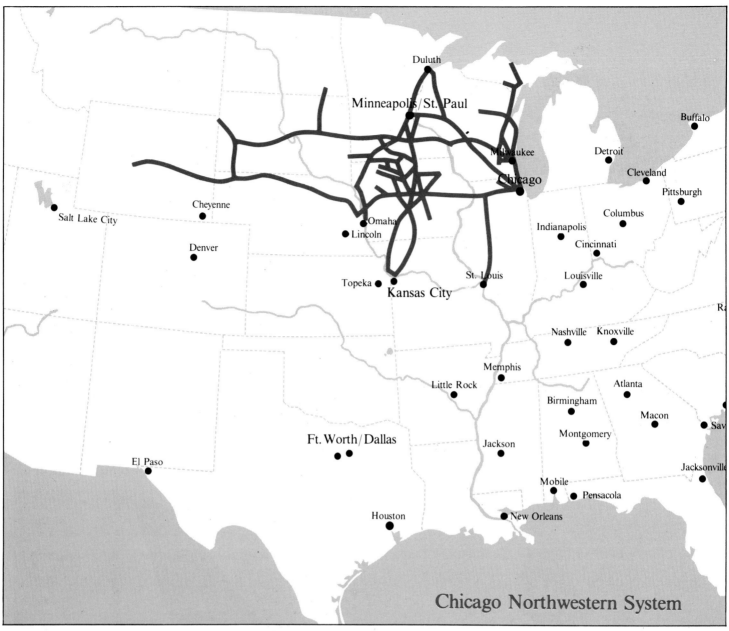

Chicago Northwestern System

Chicago, first locomotive in Chicago (the *Pioneer*—out on the tracks in 1848), first railroad to utilize steel rail (1865) and the first Class I railroad to be owned by its employees. The C&NW is primarily a carrier of grain, coal and food products.
Locomotives: 1103
Freight cars: 33,269
Passenger cars: 18
Miles operated: 6899
(as of January 1984)

Chicago, Milwaukee and St Paul. See Chicago, Milwaukee, St Paul and Pacific Railroad Company.

Chicago, Milwaukee, St Paul and Pacific Railroad Company (The Milwaukee Road). At its peak, the Milwaukee Road operated more than 9800 miles of routes in 16 states. After entering reorganization proceedings in 1977, the railroad embargoed some

6000 miles of routes, including all lines west of Miles, Montana. Operations are now limited to lines extending from Chicago northward to Milwaukee, through Wisconsin to Minneapolis and Duluth, westward to Sheldon, Iowa, southwestward to Kansas City, and southward to Terre Haute and Louisville. The earliest precursor of the Milwaukee Road was the Milwaukee and Mississippi Rail Road, incorporated in 1847. The Mississippi River was reached in 1857, and by the end of the 1860s it had expanded into Wisconsin through the purchase of several small lines. In 1874, the name was changed to Chicago, Milwaukee and St Paul. The Missouri River was crossed in 1882 and Kansas City was reached in 1887. A decision to build to the Pacific Coast at Seattle was made in 1905. This line was completed in 1909. Portions of this line in Montana, Idaho and

Washington were electrified. The Milwaukee Road's passenger service included the crack Hiawathas. In the early 1980s, a number of companies, including the GRAND TRUNK CORPORATION and the CHICAGO AND NORTH WESTERN made bids to take over the Milwaukee Road in the 1980s. The Milwaukee Road is primarily a carrier of food products, wood, lumber and coal.
Locomotives: 327
Freight cars: 12,489
Miles operated: 3200
(as of January 1984)

Chicago, South Shore and South Bend Railroad. The Chicago, South Shore and South Bend operates commuter rail service between Chicago and South Bend, Indiana. It also provides freight service. The company started in 1901 as the Chicago and Indiana Air Line Railway. In 1904 the

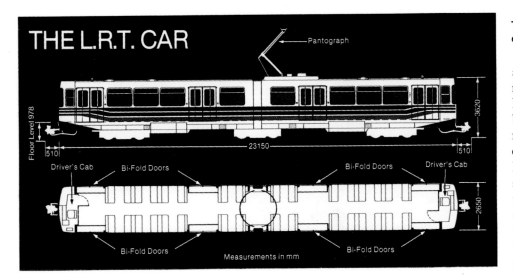

THE L.R.T. CAR

Pantograph

Floor Level 978

3620

23150

510 510

Driver's Cab   Bi-Fold Doors   Bi-Fold Doors   Driver's Cab

2650

Bi-Fold Doors   Measurements in mm   Bi-Fold Doors

The City of Calgary Transportation Department operates light-rail transit trains.

name was changed to Chicago, Lake Shore and South Bend. By 1908 service was offered from Hammond to South Bend and the line was electrified at 6600V AC. Samuel Insull bought the line in 1925, and reorganized it under its present name. He embarked on a modernization plan that involved changing the electrification to 1500V DC, purchase of modern steel cars and operation of part of the line over ILLINOIS CENTRAL's newly electrified suburban line. Insull lost control when the line went bankrupt in 1932. The CHESAPEAKE AND OHIO obtained control in 1967.

Locomotives: 10
Passenger cars (electric): 50
Freight cars: 27
Miles operated: 76

Chicago Transit Authority. One of the most extensive transit systems in North America, the Chicago Transit Authority System operates on six lines (North-South, West-Northwest, West-South, Ravenswood, Evanston, Skokie). A 4.5-mile extension on the West-Northwest line to O'Hare International Airport was started in 1983. 'Park-and-Ride' stations are being constructed along this line, which runs along the median strip of the Kennedy Expressway. An extensive rehabilitation of the 85-year-old downtown tracks was underway in the 1980s. (See photo on pg 54–55.)

Electrification system: 600V DC, third Rail
Gauge: 4ft 8in
No. of stations: 142 (20 in tunnel, 64 elevated)
Rolling stock: 1200
Route mileage: 95.5

City of Calgary Transportation Department. An all light rail system, the first section (south) was completed in 1981. The 6-mile Northeast section was started in 1982.

Electrification system: 600V DC, overhead wire
Gauge: 4ft 8in
No. of stations: 0
Rolling stock: 30
Route mileage: 7.8

Civil War. See American Civil War Railroads.

Class D locomotive. See Electric locomotives.

Class EP-2 locomotive. See Electric locomotives.

Class S locomotives. See Electric locomotives.

Colorado and Wyoming Railway. Owned by the Colorado Fuel and Iron Company, the Colorado and Wyoming Railway is a coal-hauling line operating in Colorado between Pueblo and Allen Mine, via Trinidad and Jansen. It was started at the turn of the century after the discovery of iron ore in the region.

Locomotives: 18
Freight cars: 168
Miles operated: 110

Columbus and Greenville Railway. The Columbus and Greenville Railway operates in Mississippi between Greenville and Columbus. It was incorporated in 1878 as a narrow gauge road. When it became associated with the Georgia Pacific Railroad it was changed to standard gauge (1889). When Georgia Pacific became part of the Southern Railway System, the C&G became independent because of a Mississippi law requiring

any railroad operating in that state to maintain its headquarters there. The line went bankrupt in 1920 and was bought by A G Stovall. In 1972 the road became part of ILLINOIS CENTRAL GULF. When ICG closed part of the line after floods in 1973, businesses served by the road petitioned the state public service commission to encourage purchase by local interests. The purchase was effected in 1975. The C&G carries a variety of commodities, including agricultural products, steel, furniture, pulpwood and coal.

Locomotives: 19
Freight cars: 1160
Miles operated: 168

Commission de Transport de la Communauté Urbaine de Montréal. See Montréal Urban Community Transportation Commission.

Conrail (Consolidated Rail Corporation). Conrail operates in 15 states of the northeastern United States and in two Canadian provinces. The industrial belt from New York and New Jersey westward through Pennsylvania, Ohio, West Virginia, Indiana, Michigan and Illinois as well as southern New England, the Washington DC and Delmarva Peninsula areas are served. Conrail was created by an act of Congress passed largely in response to the collapse of the Penn Central in 1970. In that same year, Congress established the United States Railway Association to determine what should be done with the Penn Central. The result was the Rail Revitalization and Regulatory Reform Act of 1975 which established the Consolidated Rail Corporation—Conrail. Conrail was authorized to take over the operation of the following bankrupt eastern railroads: CENTRAL OF NEW JERSEY, Erie Lackawanna, Lehigh and Hudson River, LEHIGH VALLEY, Penn Central, Reading and the Pennsylvania-Reading Seashore Lines. With the help of more than $2 billion in federal subsidies, operations began on 1 April 1976 when most of the properties of the bankrupt roads were turned over to Conrail. Soon after its formation, Conrail sold the Northeast Corridor lines (Boston–New York–Washington; New Haven–Springfield; Philadelphia–Harrisburg) to AMTRAK.

Above: A Conrail freight train laden with coal. Conrail operates in the industrial states from New York as far west as Michigan. *Left:* Chicago Transit Authority trains enter and leave the busy Loop 'L' at Lake and Wells Junction.

Various other lines were sold or abandoned; others were run with state subsidies. Although it was organized to be primarily a freight line, Conrail ran commuter rail services when it was first started. The Northeast Rail Services Act of 1981 enabled Conrail to shed the commuter services at the end of 1982. These were taken over by various state, local and regional agencies. The act also specified that Conrail had to pass two profitability tests in 1983 if it were to remain in operation. It had to demonstrate that it could become profitable, and that it actually was profitable between June and October of 1983. The Board of Directors of the United States Railway Association determined that both criteria had been met. Several large investor groups expressed interest in Conrail. In 1984 NORFOLK AND WESTERN received preliminary approval to purchase Conrail.

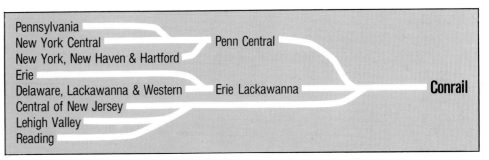

Pennsylvania
New York Central → Penn Central
New York, New Haven & Hartford
Erie
Delaware, Lackawanna & Western → Erie Lackawanna → **Conrail**
Central of New Jersey
Lehigh Valley
Reading

The principal commodities carried by Conrail are coal, coke, iron ore, iron and steel, food products, chemicals, automobiles and automobile parts. Conrail is one of the leading TOFC shippers in the United States. An average of 34 Conrail TrailVan trains a day operate in dedicated point-to-point service between the Midwest and Atlantic ports.

Locomotives: 3572
Freight cars: 104,640
Miles operated: 14,967
(as of January 1983)

Consolidation-type locomotive.

The prototype of the 2-8-0 Consolidation-type locomotive was designed by ALEXANDER MITCHELL of the LEHIGH VALLEY RAILROAD and built, somewhat reluctantly, by MATTHIAS BALDWIN. When asked to bid on its construction, Baldwin at first declined, believing the machine would be a failure. Completed in 1866, the locomotive performed well, hauling a 340-ton train up a 1.5 percent grade. The engine was named Consolidation to commemorate the merger of the Lehigh Valley with the Beaver Meadow Railroad. More than 33,000 Consolidation type engines were constructed in North America over the next 50 years.

Cooper, Peter

(12 February 1791–4 April 1883). An inventor, manufacturer and philanthropist, Peter Cooper was born in New York City, the son of John and Margaret Campbell Cooper. As a boy, he learned a variety of skills and trades from his father who engaged in many trades, including hat-making, brewing and brick-making. At age 17, he was apprenticed to a coach-maker. Following his apprenticeship, he followed the example of his father and tried a number of things, including running a grocery store, until he bought a glue factory. The glue factory was highly successful to the point where he had a virtual monopoly on this product. He obtained several patents on inventions related to glue-making. A prolific inventor, he obtained patents for a wide variety of contrivances, including a washing machine, a mechanical rocking cradle and a hub-mortising machine.

In 1828, he built an iron works in Baltimore. The fledgling BALTIMORE AND OHIO RAILROAD attracted his interest, since the value of his land

Peter Cooper built the first US locomotive.

holdings depended to, a large degree, on the success of the railroad. Cooper was among those who believed that the future of American rails lay with steam power rather than horses. However, it was widely believed that no locomotive could safely negotiate the many hills and curves of the B&O. Cooper announced that he could 'knock together' an engine that would pull carriages at 10 miles an hour. His engine, called the TOM THUMB, was a small vertical boiler engine. It pulled a load of more than 40 passengers at a speed in excess of 10 miles an hour. In a race with a horse, the engine was well ahead until a fan which provided draft broke down. The B&O directors were convinced, and all horses were soon replaced by steam locomotives.

When he sold the iron works, he accepted B&O stock in payment at

$45 a share, which he was able to sell shortly afterwards for $230 a share. He expanded his interests to include wire, blast furnaces, iron mines and telegraph companies.

Crocker, Charles.

See Southern Pacific Company; Transcontinental railroad (United States).

CSX Corporation.

The CSX Corporation was formed with the 1980 merger of the CHESSIE SYSTEM and Seaboard Coast Line Industries, the parent company of the SEABOARD SYSTEM RAILROAD. While the component railroads continue to operate independently, the operations are coordinated to provide service over an area covering 22 states, the District of Columbia and one Canadian province. The rail operations of CSX include some 27,156 miles of track, making it the largest rail system under the control of one corporation in the United States. Although CSX is involved in several enterprises other than rails, railroad operations generate more than 90 percent of the corporation's revenue.

Davis, Phineas.

See Grasshopper; The York.

Delaware and Hudson Railway.

One of the first railroads in North America, the Delaware and Hudson was incorporated in 1823 as the Delaware and Hudson Canal Company to build a canal from Honesdale, Pennsylvania, to Kingston, New York, to carry coal from the Pennsylvania mines to New York City. Rail operations on the D&H began with a gravity railroad and stationary steam engines to pull trains up grades. The first steam locomotive to be operated

This 1945 diesel-powered Seaboard Air Line railroad locomotive had two engines and eight motors.

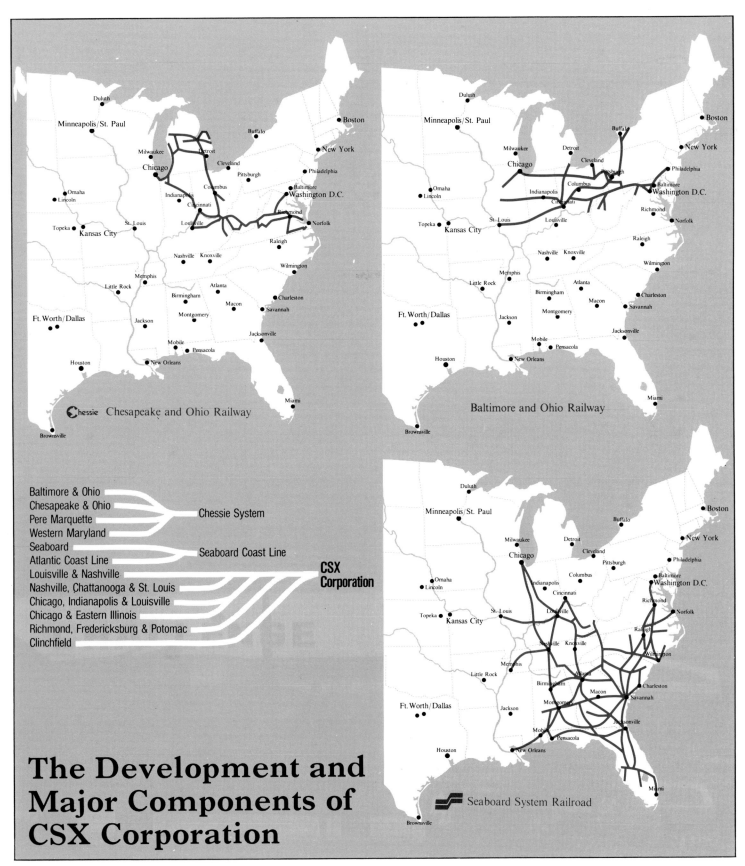

Chessie Chesapeake and Ohio Railway

Baltimore and Ohio Railway

Baltimore & Ohio
Chesapeake & Ohio
Pere Marquette
Western Maryland
Seaboard
Atlantic Coast Line
Louisville & Nashville
Nashville, Chattanooga & St. Louis
Chicago, Indianapolis & Louisville
Chicago & Eastern Illinois
Richmond, Fredericksburg & Potomac
Clinchfield

Chessie System

Seaboard Coast Line

CSX Corporation

Seaboard System Railroad

The Development and Major Components of CSX Corporation

on American rails, the STOURBRIDGE LION, was run down D&H tracks in 1829. The canal was sold in 1899 and abandoned in 1904. Rapid expansion took place after the Civil War. Access to Lake Champlain was gained in the 1870s. In 1968 a subsidiary of NORFOLK AND WESTERN obtained control of D&H and the ERIE LACKAWANNA. However, neither D&H nor EL were ever considered to be part of the N&W system. EL entered CONRAIL in 1976, but D&H chose to remain independent, and expanded through purchase of former PENNSYLVANIA RAILROAD trackage rights from Conrail. Today D&H operates in New York, Pennsylvania, New Jersey, Maryland, the District of Columbia, Vermont and Québec. Service is pro-vided to a number of important centers including Philadelphia, Washington DC, Buffalo–Niagara Falls, Albany–Schenectady, Scranton–Wilkes Barre, Newark and Montréal. In 1983 D&H was bought by Guildford Transportation Industries, and it carries a variety of commodities including iron, pulp, paper and agricultural products. Locomotives: 136

Freight cars: 4764
Miles operated: 1709
(as of January 1984)

Denver and Rio Grande Railroad.
See Denver and Rio Grande Western Railroad Company.

Denver and Rio Grande Western Railroad Company. Today's Denver and Rio Grande Western operates between Denver and Pueblo, Colorado and Salt Lake City/Ogden, Utah. The road was incorporated in 1870 as the Denver and Rio Grande by WILLIAM JACKSON PALMER. Palmer's intention was to build south from Denver along the eastern side of the Rockies to El Paso. Built in 3-foot gauge for reasons of economy, the line reached Colorado Springs in 1871, and coal areas near Canon City, Colorado a few years later. In the late 1870s, Palmer fought battles, both physical and legal, with the SANTA FE for control of important mountain passes. The Raton Pass was lost to the Santa Fe, but litigation over the Royal Gorge of the Arkansas

River continued for some time. The D&RG was leased to Santa Fe for a year, returning to independent status in 1879 under the management of Palmer and JAY GOULD. In 1882 D&RG joined with the Denver and Rio Grande Western, a line it had leased, to form a line between Denver and Salt Lake City. A standard gauge line was completed in 1890 over Tennessee Pass, the highest point on a standard gauge main line in North America. The Denver and Rio Grande went bankrupt in 1910, following the bankruptcy of Western Pacific, a line in which D&RG had made heavy investments. When it was sold in 1920, it became the Denver and Rio Grande Western.

Coming out of receivership in 1947, D&RGW merged with the Denver and Salt Lake. Shortly afterward, it began operation of the *California Zephyr* service from Chicago to San Francisco in conjunction with Western Pacific and the CHICAGO, BURLINGTON AND QUINCY. D&RGW abandoned most of its narrow gauge passenger

lines. Some were retained, notably the Durango–Silverton line, which is a popular tourist attraction. D&RGW refused to join AMTRAK in 1971, continuing to operate the Rio Grande *Zephyr* passenger service between Denver and Salt Lake City. This service was discontinued in 1983, when D&RGW finally joined Amtrak. D&RGW is primarily a carrier of coal. (See maps on pg 254–55.)
Locomotives: 284
Freight cars: 740
Miles operated: 1840
(as of January 1984)

Detroit and Mackinac Railway.
The Detroit and Mackinac operates in the northern two-thirds of Michigan's Lower Peninsula. Its earliest predecessor was the Lake Huron and Southwestern, a 38-in gauge logging railroad started in 1878. It was converted to standard gauge in 1888 and the present name was assumed in 1895. Portions of former NEW YORK CENTRAL line were obtained in 1976, providing a route between Bay City and Mackinaw City. This acquisition practically doubled the size of the D&M. The D&M carries a variety of commodities including gravel, shale, wood products and gypsum.
Locomotives: 12
Freight cars: 1320
Miles operated: 405
(as of January 1984)

DeWitt Clinton. The *DeWitt Clinton* was the first locomotive used on the MOHAWK AND HUDSON, the earliest predecessor of the NEW YORK CENTRAL. Built by the West Point Foundry of New York, New York, the *DeWitt Clinton* was a four-wheeled engine weighing some 6750 pounds. It was 11.5 feet long and rated at 10 horsepower. On its first run on 9 August 1831, between Albany and Schenectady, New York, it achieved an average speed of 15 miles per hour. Later, it was reputed to have reached the astonishing speed of 30 mph on some of its runs. The *DeWitt Clinton* was retired after a few years of service.

Diesel power and the decline of steam. The move to diesel engines on North American railroads was rapid and complete. The first successful diesel locomotive was put into service on the CANADIAN NATIONAL in 1928. By 1958, steam locomotives had all but disappeared from North American

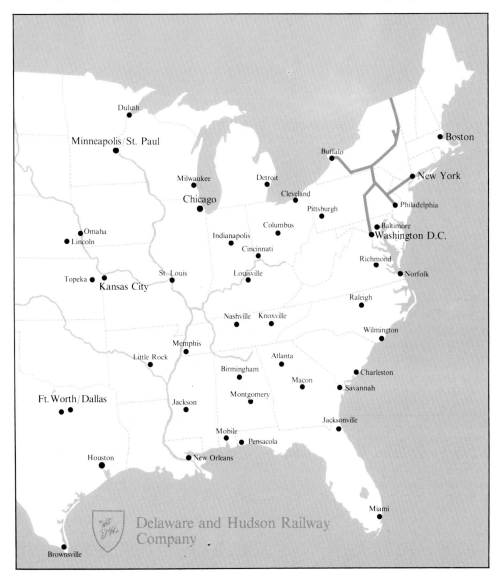

Delaware and Hudson Railway Company

rails. Except for the electrified portions of the Northeast Corridor, a few small feeder lines and museum lines operated for steam engine aficionados, the triumph of the diesel locomotive was complete. Almost all diesel locomotives in use in North America are diesel electric. That is, diesel engines turn dynamos supplying electric current to motors that are geared to the wheels. As such, it is an electric locomotive carrying its own power supply. A number of operational and economic factors contributed to the rapid conversion to diesel.

During the period from the 1930s to the 1950s, when the diesel conversion took place, oil was cheaper than coal. Diesels eliminated the necessity of maintaining water facilities for steam locomotives, a factor that was (continued on page 70.)

The *DeWitt Clinton* was the third locomotive built in the US. It was ordered by the Mohawk and Hudson and engineered by David Matthew. The first excursion with passengers (*above*) was made from Albany to Schenectady on 9 August 1831.

A Southern Pacific diesel locomotive in the San Francisco yard, one of a new breed of powerful and versatile locomotives capable of express speeds when carrying large volumes of heavy tonnage.

APTCO
DISTRIBUTORS, INC.
合泰興公司
590 TOWNSEND ST. 626-4200

This Chicago Great Western locomotive was built by General Motors, one of the major builders of diesel locomotives.

A NEW DAY DAWNS IN RAILROADING

A crack "Express Train" of 1865 as pictured by Currier & Ives. Four years later an important new era began when the first railroad linked the Atlantic and Pacific.

War traffic has more than doubled the volume of freight hauled by the Western Pacific Railroad from Salt Lake City to San Francisco. Wherever the going is toughest on this rugged route, General Motors Diesel freight locomotives have kept this vast stream of vital munitions moving steadily.

Throughout history, wars have set up new milestones of transportation progress. And with this war, it is the General Motors Diesel Locomotive that is ushering in the new era. What advances the future will bring are already apparent in the present performance of these locomotives and the way they are helping to meet the abnormal demands upon the railroads today.

War building is being rushed ahead with reliable General Motors Diesel power. In the days to come this dependable, economical power will be ready to do the hard jobs of peace.

KEEP AMERICA STRONG • BUY MORE BONDS

GENERAL MOTORS

DIESEL POWER

LOCOMOTIVES....................ELECTRO-MOTIVE DIVISION, La Grange, Ill.

ENGINES..150 to 2000 H.P...CLEVELAND DIESEL ENGINE DIVISION, Cleveland, Ohio

ENGINES.....15 to 250 H.P......DETROIT DIESEL ENGINE DIVISION, Detroit, Mich.

Above: A modern 2800hp Santa Fe locomotive No. 7906 built by General Electric. Santa Fe was one of the first western railroads to make the transition to diesel. *Below:* A new Burlington Northern diesel with a low nose for good visibility.

A Great Northern freight train hauls a long line of boxcars along the Little Spokane River in Washington in 1966.

Two 1940s-era streamlined passenger locomotives. The *City of San Francisco*, on the left, which began service between San Francisco and Chicago in 1936, was Southern Pacific's first diesel train. It also operated on Union Pacific, Chicago West and Northern Pacific lines.

Matthias Baldwin was a great steam locomotive builder who couldn't make the transition to diesel. This demonstrator was later scrapped.

Matthias Baldwin was a great steam locomotive builder who couldn't make the transition to diesel. This demonstrator was later scrapped.

particularly advantageous on western lines running through desert areas. Although electric locomotives would have accomplished the same end, the cost of electric power systems was much higher than that of diesel locomotives. Diesel locomotives are much more versatile than steam. Any number of diesel units can be coupled to provide the power required for different loads and terrain.

Steam engines could also be 'double-headed,' but each engine required its own crew, while coupled diesel units can be operated with only one crew. Diesels are much easier to operate than steam locomotives; less time is needed to train people to run them. By the end of World War II, the steam locomotive fleets of many roads had fallen into disrepair. In general, most banks preferred to make loans on new diesels rather than on the repair of old steam locomotives. The smoother starting characteristics of diesels resulted in less damage to rolling stock and freight. Steam-hauled trains were made up with considerable slack between the cars to give the locomotive a chance to get speed before it was pulling a full load. When the cars near the head were first put into the motion, those at the rear were still stationary. Generally, the rear cars were pulled into motion in a violent, jerking manner, sometimes causing damage to cars and contents. Diesels have higher starting pull than a steam locomotive of equal power, eliminating the need for slack and its potential for damage.

The manufacture and marketing of diesel locomotives in North America began with the purchase of the Electromotive Company and the Winton Company by General Motors. The Electromotive Company had manufactured small gasoline-electric railcars, while the Winton Company had supplied the engines. This division of General Motors began to make diesel locomotives to order in the early 1930s after achieving a design breakthrough that reduced the weight/horsepower ratio from about 80 pounds to 20 pounds of engine weight per horsepower. This company made the pioneer high-speed trains sets such as the *Pioneer Zephyr*. In 1937 the company began to market standard locomotives, available as cab units and booster

Major General Grenville Mellen Dodge.

rank of major general of volunteers. Seriously wounded during the Atlanta campaign, he had to retire temporarily from active service. In addition to his combat service, he carried out a number of engineering projects, including the building of railroads and a 710-foot bridge across the Chattahoochee River in Georgia. His military engineering feats earned him a commendation from General Ulysses S Grant. In 1863, President Lincoln asked Dodge to advise him on where to locate the eastern terminus of the Union Pacific. Lincoln accepted Dodge's suggestion of Omaha.

Upon leaving the Army in 1866, he assumed duties as chief engineer of the Union Pacific, replacing Peter Dey. Dodge refined much of the route previously surveyed by Dey. He had serious disagreements with the Union Pacific management, who wanted the route to be as long as possible in order to qualify for more government money. Dodge, on the other hand, wanted the line to be short and economical. Ulysses S Grant was called in to arbitrate, and he decided in favor of Dodge. The work was completed on 10 May 1869 with the nailing of the golden spike at Promontory, Utah. Dodge somehow found time to serve as Republican congressman from Iowa's Fifth District from 1866–68.

He left the Union Pacific to become chief engineer of the Texas and

units without cabs, to be used for assembling locomotives of varying power. General Motors and General Electric remain the leading suppliers of diesel locomotives in North America. The future of the diesel locomotive is dependent to a great extent on the supply and price of petroleum. Steam locomotives could make a comeback as the supply of petroleum dwindles.

Dodge, Grenville Mellen (12 April 1831–3 January 1916). A civil engineer and railroad builder, Dodge was born at Danvers, Massachusetts, the son of Sylvanus and Julia Phillips Dodge. His boyhood jobs included store clerking, driving a butcher's cart and working on farms. He attended Norwich University, obtaining training in military and civil engineering. He became interested in railroads during his college years, which were an intense period of railroad building.

In 1852, a year after graduating from college, he joined the ILLINOIS CENTRAL as a surveying engineer. Two years later, he was chief assistant to Peter A Dey, in a survey for the Rock Island Railroad. At this time he met Thomas Durant who was beginning to assemble preliminary plans for a transcontinental railroad. Durant asked Dodge to survey the route westward from Council Bluffs, Iowa to the foot of the Rockies, which was designated as that of the UNION PACIFIC by the Pacific Railroad Act of 1862. Dodge spent some five years exploring the Platte River Valley, both for Durant and for himself. He returned to Council Bluffs in the late 1850s and produced a map of the Emigrant Trail, which was widely used by people traveling west.

Dodge served with distinction in the Civil War as colonel of the 4th Iowa Regiment, advancing to the

Pacific in 1871. When that road failed in 1873, he joined JAY GOULD in his southwest railroad enterprises.

Dripps, Isaac (1810–1892). A mechanic and locomotive builder, Dripps was born in Belfast, Ireland, and brought to the United States as an infant. Apprenticed to a shipwright at age 16, he was hired away from the shipwright by ROBERT L STEVENS of the Camden and Amboy Railroad. One of Dripps's first tasks was the assembly of the locomotive JOHN BULL, which had been shipped disassembled from England. Dripps was responsible for a number of improvements to the *John Bull*, including the addition of a pilot and cow catcher mechanism that greatly reduced the incidence of derailments. He designed an eight-wheel locomotive and contributed to the design of spark arrester smokestacks. In 1847, at Steven's request, but against his better judgment, he designed a high-wheel locomotive based on the European Crampton design. Although the machine was very fast, it lacked hauling capacity.

Dripps left the Camden and Amboy in 1854 to become a partner in the Trenton Locomotive Works. During his tenure there, he designed the first arch-bar trucks.

Duluth, Missabe and Iron Range Railway. A carrier of iron ore from northeastern Minnesota mines to ports on Lake Superior, the Duluth, Missa-

Above: Thomas C Durant built the Union Pacific, for which Grenville Dodge was engineer.

Below: A Duluth Missabe and Iron Range 2-8-8-4 steam locomotive.

be, and Iron Range is descended from a number of smaller ore-carrying lines of the region. The earliest of these was the Duluth and Iron Range Rail Road, incorporated in 1874. Another was the Duluth, Missabe and Northern, incorporated in 1891. Both of these lines were bought by United States Steel in 1901. The present name was assumed in 1937 when the merger of the DM&N with the Spirit Lake Transfer Railway was completed. The DM&IR, leased since 1930, was absorbed in 1938. Still owned by US Steel, it is the largest carrier of iron ore in the United States. In recent years, as high-grade ore deposits have been depleted, the line has carried more taconite, a low-grade ore that is processed into pellets. The taconite is carried in small four-car unit trains called 'miniquads.'

Locomotives: 66

Great Northern once operated what was one of the world's two largest single-cab electric locomotives designed for heavy mountain duty.

Freight cars: 7405
Miles operated: 357
(as of January 1984)

Duluth, Winnipeg and Pacific Railway (the 'Peg'). Operating between Fort Frances, Ontario, and Duluth, Minnesota, the Duluth, Winnipeg and Pacific started in 1901 as the Duluth, Virginia and Rainy Lake, a logging railroad running from Virginia, Minnesota to Silver Lake. Soon after its opening it was bought by the Canadian Northern Railway, and the name was changed to Duluth, Rainy Lake and Winnipeg. The road was extended northward to Fort Frances in 1908 and to Duluth in 1912. The present name was assumed in 1909. When CANADIAN NATIONAL took over Canadian Northern in 1918, control of the DW&P passed to that organization. The line is operated today by the GRAND TRUNK CORPORATION. The DW&P is primarily a carrier of lumber, paper and potash.

Locomotives: 13

Freight cars: 2430
Miles operated: 167
(as of January, 1983)

Durant, Thomas. See Dodge, Grenville Mellen; Transcontinental railroad (United States).

Eddy, Wilson (1813–1898). An American machinist and locomotive builder, Eddy was born in Vermont. At age 19 he went to work for the Locks and Canal machine shop. In 1840 he became foreman of the Western Railroad's locomotive repair shops, becoming master mechanic of that road some ten years later. Eddy was a strong advocate of large fireboxes. His first locomotive, the Addison Gilmore, had an unusually large heating surface. He designed a plate frame which permitted very wide between-the-frame grates. As was the case with most American locomotive manufacturers in the mid- to late nineteenth century, Eddy built eight-wheel locomotives. His machines were notable

for a number of innovations, including a sliding connection at the cylinder saddle, a perforated dry pipe and a large-diameter straight boiler that lacked a steam dome. Eddy's engines were widely referred to as 'clocks,' an allusion to their high quality.

Edmonton Transit (Alberta). Work on a one-mile extension in the center of the city was started in 1983. Plans call for an eventual 15.6-mile extension to the south. Completion of an extension to the University was expected by 1986.

Electrification system: 600 V DC, overhead
Gauge: 4ft 8in
No. of stations: 8
Rolling stock: 37
Route mileage: 6.56

Electric locomotives. The principle of electromagnetic propulsion was demonstrated by the American Joseph Henry as early as 1829. Thomas Davenport of Vermont took out a patent on an electric motor in 1835, and two years later had constructed a small electrically driven vehicle which he operated on a short section of track. In 1842, Davenport ran an electric locomotive in Scotland. In 1850, Charles Page was directed by the United States Congress to build an electric locomotive. Although Page completed a prototype that actually hauled a train, it could not develop sufficient power to be used for regular service. Neither the Davenport nor the Page locomotives could compete with rapidly developing steam engines because at the time there was no dependable source of electricity.

Development of electric generators and motors with sufficient output to power locomotives began in the 1860s and 1870s. In 1879, at the Berlin Exhibition, Siemens and Halske demonstrated a small electric locomotive that could pull a load of 30 passengers around a circular track at a speed of 4 miles an hour. Interest in electric locomotives and railways was intense around the turn of the century, both in Europe and North America. However, electric railway development was limited in North America compared to the extensive development in Europe. Down to the present day, electrified main line mileage in North America is only a small percentage of the extensive networks that cross the European continent.

Baltimore and Ohio No. 1 to 3 (Bo + Bo) This machine was the first locomotive to be used on an electrified main line in North America. Put into use in 1895, they were used to haul trains, including the steam locomotive, through a tunnel into Baltimore's Mount Royal Station in accordance with a Baltimore ordinance forbidding operation of steam locomotives within the city limits. Built by General Electric, the locomotives operated on 675 volt direct current (DC) picked up from a rigid overhead conductor. Current was fed to four gearless 360hp (270kW) motors. Power was trans-

Great Northern electrified the Cascade Tunnel approaches to avoid problems with smoke. Electrification ceased when a ventilation system was built in the tunnel. Shown *below* is an electrified passenger locomotive and *overleaf* a freight locomotive at Skykomish, Washington.

mitted to the wheels through rubber block, flexible drives. These locomotives were used until 1912.
Length: 27ft 1½in
Weight: 192,000lb
Tractive effort: 45,000lb
Maximum speed: 60 mph

Class S 1-Do-1

The Class S machines were the first electric locomotives to be used in the tunnel to New York's Grand Central Terminal. Built by General Electric, the prototype (No. 6000) was completed late in 1904. They operated on 660V DC that was picked up from a third rail. Current was fed to four 550hp (410kW) gearless traction motors mounted on the frames. The locomotives were designed by Asa Batchelder, a GE engineer, who employed a number of innovations, including the use of bipolar motors with poles hung on the frame. The armatures were mounted on the axle and the frames were outside the wheels to accommodate the armatures. The locomotives could develop short-term horsepower of 3000 and the continuous rating was 2200hp. These locomotives were the first to be equipped with Frank Sprague's multiple-unit control allowing the operation of two or more units from one control station.

The NEW YORK CENTRAL ordered 34 machines, designated 'T.' These were delivered in 1906. After a derailment of a train hauled by two T-class locomotives resulted in 23 fatalities, they were redesigned with end trucks. The redesigned 2-Do-2 locomotives were redesignated 'S.'

The machines proved to be more economical than steam locomotives both in operating and maintenance costs. In operation for more than 50 years, some class S machines were still being used for switching in the 1970s.
Length: 37ft
Weight: 142,000lb adhesive, 205,500lb total
Tractive effort: 32,000lb
Maximum speed: 70 mph

Class DD 2-B + 2-B

The first electric locomotives to be used in the Hudson and East River tunnels which gave the PENNSYLVANIA RAILROAD access to New York City, these machines were designed and built at the Pennsylvania Railroad's Altoona shops. They ran on a

660V, DC system, and were designed to pick up current from both overhead wires and third rail. Current was fed to two 1065hp (795kW) motors. Each motor drove two main axles via a jackshaft and connecting rods. Composed of two 2-B units coupled back-to-back, the wheel arrangement of each unit resembled that of a 4-4-0 steam locomotive. Put into regular service in 1910, these locomotives were used for passenger service into and out of Pennsylvania Station until the mid-1930s. After that time they were used for moving empty trains. Several assigned to the Long Island Railroad remained in service on that line until the early 1950s.

Length: 64ft 1in
Weight: 99,000lb adhesive,
    319,000lb total
Tractive effort: 49,400lb
Maximum speed: 80 mph

Class EP-2 1-B-D-D-B-1 'Bipolar'
These locomotives were built for use on the CHICAGO, MILWAUKEE, ST PAUL AND PACIFIC RAILROAD ('Milwaukee Road') electrified main line from St Paul to Seattle. Operating on a 3000V, DC overhead wire system, current was fed to twelve 370hp (275kW) gearless motors mounted directly on the axles. Built by the General Electric Company, the first units were delivered in 1919. The name 'bipolar' stemmed from the use of two-pole motors in an attempt to simplify the machine. Articulated into three sections connected by four-axle trucks, the rounded ends gave the machines a considerably more streamlined appearance than other electric locomotives of the period. Bipolars were used to haul the Milwaukee Road's premier train, the *Olympian Hiawatha*, as late as the 1950s, long after more powerful and efficient locomotives had been added to the railroad's fleet. All electric operations on the Milwaukee Road came to an end in 1973.

Length: 76ft
Weight: 457,000lb adhesive,
    530,000lb total
Tractive effort: 123,500lb
Maximum speed: 70 mph

GG1 2-Co-Co-2
The GG1 was adopted by the PENNSYLVANIA RAILROAD to fill the need for a fast, powerful, passenger locomotive to use on its electrified New York–Washington route. The Pennsylvania started to electrify many of its eastern

routes in 1928, installing a 15,000V, 25cps alternating current (AC) overhead catenary system. The New York–Washington section was completed in 1934. Based on a boxy 2-Co-Co-2 that had been used by the NEW YORK, NEW HAVEN AND HARTFORD RAILROAD, the GG-1 featured a streamlined casing designed by Raymond Loewy.

Power from the overhead wires was directed via a step-down transformer to twelve 410hp single-phase traction motors. Pairs of motors drove a main axle via gearing and a quill-type flexible drive. This mechanical arrangement, which had been well tried on the New Haven, proved to be more than adequate for the Pennsylvania's needs. Widely regarded as one of the most successful and dependable electric locomotives in the world, 139 GG1s were built between 1935 and 1943. Some were constructed at the Pennsylvania Railroad's Altoona shops, while others were made by Baldwin or General Electric with electrical equipment supplied by the latter or Westinghouse. Coded information on track conditions were sent over circuits to a small signal display system in the cab, which was very advanced technology for that time.

Most GG-1s were still in operation in 1970, when the PENN CENTRAL, the result of the merger of the Pennsylvania and NEW YORK CENTRAL, went into bankruptcy. These were distributed to successor organizations such as AMTRAK, CONRAIL and the New Jersey Department of Transportation, which became NEW JERSEY TRANSIT. A few were still in use on the latter in the mid-1980s.

Length: 79ft 6in
Weight: 303,000lb adhesive,
    477,000lb total
Tractive effort: 70,700lb
Maximum speed: 100 mph

W1 Bo-Do-Do-Bo
The first 2.6-mile Cascade Tunnel of the GREAT NORTHERN RAILWAY was completed in 1900. Serious problems with smoke were encountered in tunnel operations, a situation that encouraged the Great Northern to electrify the tunnel and its approaches in 1909. The electrification was extended when the tunnel length was increased to 7.6 miles in 1927. The W1 was a low-speed high-tractive effort machine designed to haul heavy loads through the tunnel and its approaches. Power was picked up from a 11,500V, 25cps AC system

and fed to two motor-generator sets which converted the current to DC. The DC was directed to twelve 275hp (205kW) traction motors suspended on the nose, and motion was transferred to the axles via gears. After the Cascade Tunnel was equipped with a ventilation system, all electrified operations on the Great Northern were discontinued.

Length: 101ft
Weight: 527,000lb
Tractive effort: 180,000lb
Maximum speed: 65 mph

Metroliner Two-car trainset
These trainsets were intended to enable the PENNSYLVANIA RAILROAD to compete with airlines for short-haul passenger business, in particular on the electrified New York–Washington route. A trial of the Budd MP85 car was started in 1958. The City of Philadelphia acquired Budd 'Silverliners' in 1963 for the Pennsylvania to use on commuter runs. Federal grants were obtained in the mid-1960s for acquiring trains and improving track. The Metroliners obtained in 1966 from the Budd Company were stainless steel, two-car trainsets. The 11,500V, 25cps AC is fed to step-down transformers and rectifiers to eight 300hp (224kW) motors suspended in the nose of the car. Each pair of wheels is geared to a motor. Although the train sets are capable of speeds of 160 miles per hour, track conditions keep actual speeds well below that figure. A variety of problems kept the Metroliner from entering regular service until 1969, after the Pennsylvania–New York Central merger. When AMTRAK took over operation of the Metroliner in 1971, 14 trips daily at average speeds as high as 95 miles per hour were scheduled. The trainsets were supplanted on the New York–Washington run by AEM-7 locomotives hauling coaches in the early 1980s. Metroliner trainsets now run on the Harrisburg–Philadelphia–New York route.

Length: 170ft
Weight: 328,400lb
Maximum speed: 160 mph

Electrification. Although electrification was considered in the United States long before it was seriously investigated in Europe, electrified main line mileage in North America is only a small fraction of that in Europe. Thomas Davenport of Vermont de-

A 5000hp Great Northern Railway electric locomotive hauls a freight train through the 7.79-mile Cascade Tunnel near Berne, Washington.

monstrated electric traction in 1837 when he ran a small electrically powered vehicle down a short stretch of track. In 1850, Charles Page was authorized by Congress to build an electric locomotive, but the result was not particularly impressive; no further funds were appropriated. One of the first practical demonstrations of electric traction was at the Berlin Exhibition of 1879, where a small electric locomotive designed by Siemens and Halske pulled carriages around a circular track.

The latter quarter of the nineteenth century saw renewed interest in elec-

tric traction. In 1880 Thomas Edison demonstrated an electric locomotive that could reach 40 miles an hour. The Richmond Union Passenger Railway was electrified in 1885, and there was rapid growth in the electric streetcar industry. In that same year, Frank J Sprague took out a patent on a system which allowed several electrically powered cars or locomotives to be controlled from one master controller in the lead car. This system is now used on practically every electric commuter railroad and rapid transit system in the world.

The first electrification of a main line railroad in North America occurred in 1895 on the BALTIMORE AND OHIO RAILROAD. A city ordinance forbade the operation of steam loco-

motives within the Baltimore city limits, and for years horses had pulled trains through the city. Four miles of track, including a mile-long tunnel under the Patapsco River, were electrified, using a 600 volt direct current (DC) system. Small General Electric Locomotives were used to haul trains, including steam locomotives, into and out of Baltimore's Mount Royal Station.

In 1903, New York City passed an ordinance forbidding the use of steam locomotives south of the Harlem River after 1908. The NEW YORK CENTRAL RAILROAD responded by electrifying track between its Grand Central Terminal and Croton, New York, a project that was completed in 1913. Electrification made it possible to

preference for DC. In the early days of electrification, the proponents of AC and DC were in sharp competition. AC is more easily and economically transmitted over long distances than is DC. However, traction motors that run on DC are simpler and less expensive than AC motors. The electric locomotives used on the New Haven were among the first equipped to use both AC and DC. The development of the thyristor greatly simplified the technology required for the running of DC motors on current supplied from AC lines. Most electric locomotives used on the extensive electrified lines of Europe are equipped to run on all the various AC and DC systems in use there.

The GREAT NORTHERN RAILWAY electrified the first Cascade Tunnel in 1909 to alleviate the smoke problems encountered operating steam locomotives through the 2.6-mile structure. In 1927, the new 7.8-mile Cascade Tunnel, the longest railway tunnel in North America, and its approaches were electrified. Electrified operations were discontinued after a new ventilation system was installed in the tunnel in 1956.

The CHICAGO, MILWAUKEE, ST PAUL AND PACIFIC RAILROAD began electrifying the route between St Paul and Seattle in 1914. Eventually 902 miles of this route were electrified with a 3000 volt, overhead wire, DC system powered with current supplied by hydroelectric generators. Heavy (521,000 pounds) 3840hp locomotives called BIPOLARS were used on this line. After World War II the electric system was scrapped in favor of diesels.

In 1928 the PENNSYLVANIA RAILROAD began a massive electrification project. By 1938, all main lines east of Harrisburg, Pennsylvania, including the heavily traveled Washington–New York route, were under the wires, using a 25cps, AC system similar to that installed on the New Haven. Some 670 route miles, comprising 2200 miles of track, were electrified. The highly successful GG1 locomotive was designed for use on these routes. First put into operation in 1934, some were still being used by AMTRAK in the 1980s.

The Pennsylvania Railroad project was the last major main line electrification in North America. The Northeast Corridor between Washington and New Haven, Connecticut, is the

only major electrified railroad operation in North America. The BRITISH COLUMBIA RAILWAY planned to electrify the 80-mile Tumbler Ridge branch, started in 1981, to eliminate ventilation problems in the many tunnels on this route.

Elgin, Joliet and Eastern Railway. (Chicago Outer Belt). The Elgin, Joliet and Eastern Railway runs between Waukegan, Illinois, and Porter, Indiana, in a somewhat semicircular route around Chicago, about 30 to 40 miles from the city center. Intersecting with every railroad entering Chicago, it also has a branch line between Griffith, Indiana, and South Chicago that serves the Gary steel mill area. Owned by United States Steel, the line is primarily a carrier of iron, coal and steel.
Locomotives: 100
Freight cars: 10,190
Miles operated: 231
(as of January 1983)

Erie Lackawanna. See Conrail.

Escambia and Lake Superior Railroad. Operating in Northern Wisconsin and Michigan's Upper Peninsula, the Escambia and Lake Superior runs between Ontonagon and Escanaba, Michigan, and Green Bay, Wisconsin. The line forms an asymmetrical X with Channing, Michigan, at the intersect and Green Bay, Escanaba, Onantagon and Republic, Michigan at the ends. Incorporated in 1898, the E&LS took over and purchased a number of lines from the MILWAUKEE ROAD in 1980. Major commodities carried include iron ore, paper and pulpwood.
Locomotives: 8
Freight cars: 130
Miles operated: 325
(as of January 1983)

Evans, Oliver (1755–1819). An early American inventor and industrialist, Evans was born in New Castle County, Delaware, the son of a farmer, Charles Evans. At age 14, Evans apprenticed himself to a wagon maker. His mechanical aptitude was soon evident, and he embarked on a program of self-education in mechanics and mathematics. During this period, he developed a life-long interest in steam engines.

By the time he was 20, Evans was manufacturing teeth for wool cards.

Amtrak's heavily traveled Washington-Boston corridor is being rebuilt to accommodate a new generation of passenger equipment (*left*), including the latest AEM-7 electric locomotives (*above*).

operate trains in a tunnel under Park Avenue leading to the terminal. This third-rail, DC system still operates.

The first alternating current (AC) electrification project in North America was completed on the NEW YORK, NEW HAVEN AND HARTFORD RAILROAD in 1907. This 11,000 volt, 25cps, overhead wire system was still in use in the mid-1980s, although plans had been made to convert to 60cps.

The New Haven system was built by the Westinghouse Corporation, which favored and promoted AC, while the New York Central electrification was carried out by the General Electric Corporation, which at the time, still reflected Thomas Edison's

Oliver Evans was a prolific inventor.

He devised a machine that could turn out some 1500 cards a minute. In 1780 Evans and his brothers started construction of a completely mechanized flour mill operated by water power. In 1786 and 1787, respectively, he petitioned the Pennsylvania and Maryland legislatures for exclusive rights to use his 'improvements in flour mills and steam carriages' in those states. While Maryland granted permission for both the mill and steam carriages, Pennsylvania would permit only the flour mill improvements. He temporarily put aside his experiments with steam carriages to concentrate on stationary steam engines. Convinced that the atmospheric steam engines in use at the time were inadequate for powering machinery, he concentrated on high-pressure steam engines. By the early 1800s he had developed a high-pressure engine. Evans attempted to sell these engines at a time when high-pressure engines were widely regarded as dangerous. Nevertheless, some 50 were in use in the United States by 1820.

In 1804 he received a contract to construct a steam dredge for use around the Philadelphia docks. The dredge, a steam engine mounted in a 15-ton, 30-foot scow, was completed in Evans' shop which was about two miles from the river. When it was completed, he solved the problem of getting it to the water by mounting wheels on its sides. A belt transmitted power to the wheels. In so doing, Evans made the first steam-powered road vehicle in the United States. Called the *Orukter Amphibolos* by Evans, he drove it through the streets of Philadelphia to the river.

Evans' last large project was the construction of engines and boilers for Philadelphia's Fairmount Water Works in 1817. Although he never built a steam carriage as such, he predicted the development of high-speed steam locomotives.

The Experiment. This machine, later renamed the *Brother Jonathon*, was the first 4-2-0 locomotive built in North America. Designed by John Jervis in 1831, the engine was built for the MOHAWK AND HUDSON RAILROAD. Jervis employed a radical departure from the typical British practice of the period in his design of the running gear. He equipped the Experiment with a swiveling leading truck and a long wheel base. The intention was to improve performance on the twisting, uneven tracks of early American railroads, on which British locomotives, with their rigid, short wheel bases, tended to derail. The swiveling truck design proved to be highly successful on American rails, and it set the trend for future locomotive construction in North America. The locomotive itself was not an immediate success since it would not make steam. Intended at first to burn anthracite, the shallow firebox could not produce enough heat. Rebuilt later as a wood-burner, the engine ran well and was in use for many years. It was converted to an eight-wheeler some years after its original construction.

The 7-ton Experiment had 9.5-inch diameter cylinders with a 16-inch stroke. The driving wheels, placed in back of the firebox, were 60 inches in diameter.

Fisk, James (1 April 1834– 7 January 1872). An American financier and speculator, Fisk was born in Bennington, Vermont, the son of James and Love B Fisk. In his early years he was, among other things, a waiter, a circus barker and a salesman for his father's 'traveling emporium,' an enterprise he later bought. In 1860, he went to work for the Boston firm of Jordan and Marsh, managing large Civil War contracts. After the war, he bought cotton in the south, making enough money to open a dry-goods jobbing

John B Jervis supervised the building of the Mohawk and Hudson line and designed the *Experiment* for that company.

business in Boston, which failed in the postwar deflation. He then went to work for Daniel Drew, selling steamboats. With Drew's help, he set up a brokerage firm in New York—Fisk and Belden.

Fisk became a director of the Erie Railroad. In collaboration with Drew and JAY GOULD, he ravaged the railroad through embezzlement, stock frauds and other tactics. In the 1868 'Erie Wars' against CORNELIUS VANDERBILT, he thwarted Vanderbilt's attempt to take the Erie by printing 50,000 counterfeit Erie stock certificates, almost all of which were bought by Vanderbilt. Fisk, Drew and Gould— the 'Erie Ring'—fled to New Jersey with some $6 million, where they stayed in a heavily guarded hotel in Jersey City until the New York legislature could be bribed to legalize the bogus stock. In 1868, after settling with Vanderbilt, the Erie Ring increased the value of Erie stock from $34,265,000 to $57,766,000. Much of the proceeds were used in wild speculations. Their 1868 conspiracy to raise the price of gold had a disastrous effect that caused the ruin of thousands. Erie stock was dropped from New York Stock Exchange. They also launched stock raids on the United States Express Company and the Albany and Susquehanna Railroad. The latter involved pitched battles between rival railroad gangs. Another attempt to corner the gold market in 1868 again caused financial ruin for thousands and caused a severe economic recession.

Fisk's personal life was flamboyant and brassy. He bought Pike's Opera House in New York City, fitting it out with opulent offices and producing operas and dramas. He designated himself 'Admiral' of the Fall River and Bristol steamboat line he controlled, often wearing a uniform of his own design. He had many mistresses, but singled out an actress, Josie Mansfield, as his favorite. He was shot to death on 6 January 1872, by Edward Stokes, a rival for Josie Mansfield's affections.

Flagler, Henry M (2 January 1830–20 May 1913). An American financier, Flagler was born at Hopewell, New York, the son of a Presbyterian minister. Flagler had very little formal education. He started working in a general store at the age of 14, and by age 21 had established himself as a grain dealer in Bellvue, Ohio. John D Rockefeller was his selling agent in this venture. With $50,000 made in grain dealing, he went into salt processing and lost his fortune. He recouped it with grain dealing, and with those funds and some money borrowed from relatives, he went into partnership with John D Rockefeller and several others who owned a number of oil refineries. These companies were the nucleus of the Standard Oil Company, which Flagler helped to organize. Flagler started to invest in Florida properties in the 1880s. He built hotels in St Augustine, Florida, and acquired additional hotels in other Florida cities. In 1883, he bought the narrow gauge St Augustine and Halifax Railroad, changed it to standard gauge, and began to build southward, reaching Miami in 1896. His major motivation in building the railroad, which became the FLORIDA EAST COAST RAILWAY, was to bring customers to his hotels. In 1905 he began to extend the railroad across the Florida Keys to Key West. This 'railroad over the sea,' as it was called, was completed in 1912. Flagler was also a director of the Chicago, Rock Island and Pacific Railway, the Duluth and Iron Range Railroad and the Western Union Company. He remained in the directorship of the Standard Oil Company until 1911.

Florida East Coast Railway. The origins of the Florida East Railway stem from the 1883 purchase of a small narrow gauge line called the Jacksonville, St Augustine and Halifax by the millionaire oil magnate HENRY M FLAGLER. Flagler immediately changed the line to standard gauge, built a bridge over the St Johns River and began to push southward from Jacksonville, reaching Palm Beach in 1894 and Miami in 1896 at a time when much of this area could still be described as wilderness. After reaching Miami, he continued to build across the Everglades and across the Florida keys to Key West. The 57-mile Key West extension, which included some 17 miles of bridges over open water, was completed in 1912 shortly before Flagler's death. Although the line prospered in the Florida boom of the 1920s, the depression and competition from the SEABOARD AIR LINE contributed to the FEC falling into receivership in 1931. A hurricane in 1935 destroyed the Key West line. The remains were rebuilt as a highway—US Route 1. Offers to buy the line came in the 1940s from the ATLANTIC COAST LINE, Seaboard, and the SOUTHERN RAILWAY. These offers were rejected largely due to local pressures to keep ownership of the line in Florida. In 1960 the line was reorganized when the St Joe Paper Company assumed control. A bitter strike, which started in 1963, was not settled until 1971. Management ran freight service during the strike, which was marked by bombings and other acts of destruction. During the strike period, passenger service was discontinued, more efficient work rules were instituted and extensive upgrading and rebuilding of lines and equipment was undertaken. The FEC today is primarily a carrier of agricultural products, operating between Jacksonville and a few miles south of Miami. A branch extends from Fort Pierce to Lake Harbor on Lake Okechobee.
Locomotives: 60
Freight cars: 2500
Miles operated: 554
(as of January 1984)

Forney, Matthias Nace (28 March 1835–14 January 1908). An American inventor and editor, Forney was born in Hanover, Pennsylvania, the son of Matthias Nace and Amanda Forney. At the age of 17, he was apprenticed to ROSS WINANS. For three years he was a draftsman for the BALTIMORE AND OHIO RAILROAD, went into business for himself for a while, and then became a draftsman for the ILLINOIS CENTRAL RAILROAD. In 1865 he was at the Hinkley and Williams Works, supervising the building of locomotives for the Illinois Central.

In the 1860s, Forney turned his attention to the development of an improved locomotive for use in and around cities. These engines were generally called 'tank' engines because they had reservoirs at the sides or wrapped around the boilers. The major problem of these machines was that as the coal and water were used, weight over the drivers was reduced, with a consequent loss of tractive effort. Forney's tank engine was a 0-4-4T ('T' is for tank) designed so that the variable load was entirely over the trailing truck. Forney engines were not widely adopted by city railway systems until the 1870s. Their adoption was encouraged by an epidemic of equine distemper that killed thousands of horses and by Forney's editorializing in his publications. Forney engines, which were constructed by several companies, were used on elevated railroads in Chicago, New York and on a number of railroads including the NEW YORK CENTRAL and NEW YORK, NEW HAVEN AND HARTFORD.

In 1870, Forney became an associate editor of the *Railroad Gazette*. In 1872, he bought a half interest in the publication, serving as editor until 1883, when he resigned because of ill health. In his writings he expressed opposition to the use of narrow gauge, even though many Forneys were built to narrow gauge. In 1886, recovered from his illness, he bought the *American Railroad Journal* and *Van Nostrand's Engineering Magazine*, which he combined into one publication called *Railroad and Engineering Journal* until 1893, and *American Engineer and Railroad Journal* from 1893 to 1896, when he sold it.

He also published the *Railway Gazette* and a book *Catechism of the Locomotive*. Other works include *The Car Builders' Dictionary*, and *Memoir of Horatio Allen*. An organizer of the American Society of Mechanical Engineers, he was also an honorary member of the American Railway Master Mechanics' Association.

Galveston, Harrisburg and San Antonio Railroad. See Southern Pacific Company.

The *George Washington*. Built by William Norris of Philadelphia, this small 7.5-ton, 4-2-0 engine is noted for dispelling the belief that locomotives could not pull heavy loads up an incline of any consequence. Many of the earliest railroads used stationary engines to haul trains up grades with cables. On 10 July 1836 the *George Washington* pulled a 19,200-pound load up the 1 in 14 grade Belmont inclined plane of the Philadelphia and Columbia Railroad, attaining a speed of 15 miles an hour in the process. MATTHIAS BALDWIN had supplied the Philadelphia and Columbia with locomotives that were quite similar to the *George Washington*, but did not have its hauling capacity. The major difference was in the position of the driving wheels. They were placed behind the firebox by Baldwin, while they were forward of the firebox in the Norris machine. The Norris placement resulted in greater weight on the driving wheels and increased traction. The Baldwin engines, however, had steadier riding characteristics, a circumstance that encouraged their use as passenger engines, while Norris engines were more often used for freight.

GGI locomotive. See Electric locomotives.

Gould, Jay (27 May 1835–2 December 1892). A financier and speculator, Gould was born in Roxbury, New York, the son of John and Mary Moore Gould. As a young man Gould worked for a blacksmith and clerked in a country store. He obtained a sketchy education in an academy, and learned a little surveying, going into this work when he was age 18. He contributed to the mapping of several counties in New York, Ohio and Michigan. In 1865, he published a book, *History of Delaware County, and Border Wars of New York*.

By the time he was age 21, he had saved $5000, and with that sum he opened a large tannery in Pennsylvania. In the early 1860s he left the leather business and started to speculate in stocks and bonds of small rail lines. He made a great deal of money, and for a while was manager of the Rensselaer and Saratoga Railroad.

In 1867, he and JAMES FISK assumed seats on the board of the Erie Railroad, of which Daniel Drew was treasurer and controlling agent. These three

Jay Gould let nothing interfere with his passion for moneymaking.

men, widely called the 'Erie Ring,' manipulated stock, embezzled funds, and used Erie resources for wild speculations, while generally neglecting the running and maintenance of the railroad. In 1868, an attempt by CORNELIUS VANDERBILT to take over the Erie was thwarted when Gould and his colleagues issued 50,000 shares of counterfeit stock. The three conspirators fled to Jersey City to avoid arrest. Gould, however, in defiance of the threat of arrest, traveled to Albany carrying a satchel full of cash with which he hoped to bribe the New York

Legislature into legalizing the stock issue. One house passed the legislation, but a settlement was reached with Vanderbilt before the legislation was completed.

Gould and Fisk, joined by Tammany politicians Peter B Sweeney and William M 'Boss' Tweed, who were on the Erie board, then forced Drew out of the Erie, and commenced a spectacular series of frauds and complicated financial dealings that made millions of dollars, but ruined many others in the process. They looted the Erie with huge stock-watering schemes, raided the credit, export, and produce markets, and in 1869, attempted to corner the gold

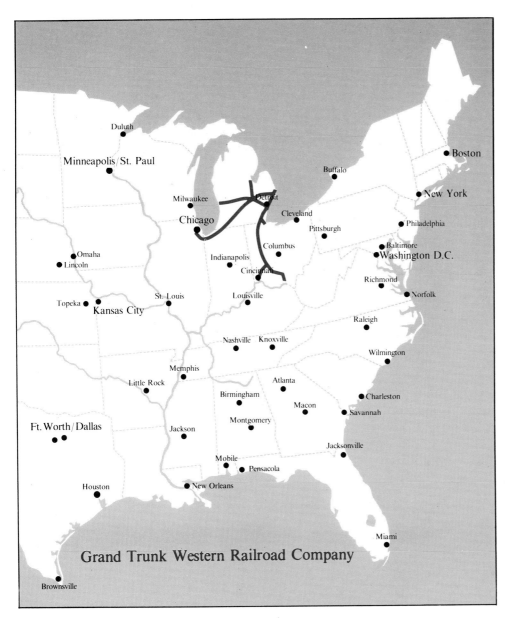

Duluth

Minneapolis/St. Paul

Boston

Buffalo

Milwaukee
Detroit
New York

Chicago
Cleveland
Philadelphia

Pittsburgh

Omaha
Columbus
Baltimore

Lincoln
Indianapolis
Washington D.C.

Cincinnati

Richmond

Topeka
St. Louis
Louisville
Norfolk

Kansas City

Raleigh

Nashville Knoxville

Memphis
Wilmington

Little Rock
Atlanta

Birmingham
Charleston

Macon
Savannah

Ft. Worth/Dallas
Jackson
Montgomery

Jacksonville

Mobile

Pensacola

Houston
New Orleans

Miami

Grand Trunk Western Railroad Company

Brownsville

market. The latter scheme brought on the financial panic known as Black Friday. Public outcry and litigation followed. With the death of Fisk and fall of the 'Tweed Ring,' Gould was ousted from the Erie on 10 March 1872.

With a personal fortune estimated at $25,000,000, Gould had no difficulty continuing his career as a stock speculator. He bought large blocks of UNION PACIFIC stock, becoming a director in 1874. He maintained control of that railroad for the next four years, buying control of the Kansas Pacific Railroad in the interim. In 1879, he added the Western Pacific to the list of railroads under his control. He forced the Union Pacific to consolidate with the Kansas Pacific at par by threatening to extend the Kansas Pacific to Salt Lake City, connecting with the CENTRAL PACIFIC to form a new transcontinental railroad. He later sold his Kansas Pacific stock, clearing about $10,000,000. By 1890, he con-

trolled almost one half of all the railroad mileage in the Southwest through ownership of the Missouri Pacific, Texas and Pacific, St Louis Southwestern and the International and Great Northern. Other interests included the *New York World*, which he owned from 1879 to 1883, New York elevated railways and the Western Union Telegraph Company.

Government of Ontario Transit. Government of Ontario Transit operates commuter rail service in and around Toronto. In 1959 CANADIAN NATIONAL started to build a freight classification yard northeast of Toronto, freeing the tracks along Lake Ontario for commuter traffic. CN, however, did not wish to run this service. The province began operating Government of Ontario Transit in 1967 between Toronto, Pickering and Hamilton. Service to Georgetown, Richmond Hill and Milton was added in 1974, 1978 and 1981, respectively.

In 1982 GO took over operation of two trains from VIA RAIL; these ran between Toronto and Stouffville, and Toronto and Bradford. Many of GO's commuter coaches are bilevel cars.
Locomotives: 45
Passenger cars: 270
Miles operated: 212
(as of January 1984)

Grand Trunk Corporation. The Grand Trunk Corporation is a holding company wholly owned by CANADIAN NATIONAL for the operation of CN's subsidiary lines in the United States. Incorporated in 1971, GTC runs the CENTRAL VERMONT RAILWAY, GRAND TRUNK WESTERN RAILROAD and THE DULUTH, WINNIPEG AND PACIFIC RAILWAY.

Grand Trunk Railway. See Grand Trunk Western Railroad.

Grand Trunk Western Railroad. Owned by CANADIAN NATIONAL through its wholly owned subsidiary GRAND TRUNK CORPORATION, the Grand Trunk Western operates from Port Huron, Michigan, to Chicago, southward from Port Huron to Detroit, Toledo, Cincinnati and other Ohio points, and westward to Bay City, Muskegon, Lansing and other points in central Michigan. The Grand Trunk Western is a descendant of the Grand Trunk Railway, which was started in 1852 to connect Montreal and Toronto. The line crossed the border at the St Clair River into Port Huron from Sarnia, Ontario, in 1858. Until a tunnel was completed, cars were ferried across the St Clair. Extension through Michigan and Indiana to Chicago was accomplished by 1880. Financial troubles led to absorption by the Canadian Government in 1923 and incorporation into the Canadian National System. The name Grand Trunk Western was assumed in 1928 following a reorganization. The Detroit, Toledo and Ironton was purchased in 1980. GTW shared ownership of the Detroit and Toledo Shoreline with the NORFOLK AND WESTERN until 1981, when GTW bought out N&W's half-interest. The GTW is a major carrier of automobiles and automobile parts in this major industrial area.
Locomotives: 262
Freight cars: 11,870
Miles operated: 1515
(as of January 1984)

Grasshopper. These vertical-boiler locomotives were used by the BALTIMORE AND OHIO RAILROAD from the 1830s to the mid-1890s. Although they were, in general, successful on the B&O, they had little, if any, influence on locomotive development. The name 'grasshopper' stemmed from the drive mechanism, which consisted of overhead walking beams and long rods that turned a pair of cranks on countershafts. The attitude and motion of the walking beams and rods reminded railroad workers of grasshopper legs. The prototype grasshopper was the 7-ton *Atlantic*, designed by Phineas Davis in 1831. In that same year Davis had won a $4000 prize offered by the B&O for the design of his locomotive, the YORK. Davis turned out 18 grasshoppers at the B&O Mount Clare shops.

Great Western Railway. Owned by the Great Western Sugar Company, the Great Western carries sugar beets, sugar and molasses for the parent company in central Colorado. It also carries coal. Incorporated in 1901, it was expanded as more sugar refineries were built. GWR operated steam engines well into the 1960s. One of these engines, Decapod No. 900, is operated on the Strasburg Railroad in Strasburg, Pennsylvania, a preservation line.
Locomotives: 4

Freight cars: 150
Miles operated: 58
(as of January 1984)

Greater Cleveland Regional Transit Authority. This rapid transit line links downtown Cleveland with Hopkins Airport.
Electrification system: 600V DC, overhead
Gauge: 4ft 8in
No. of stations: 18
Rolling stock: 100
Route mileage: 19

Great Northern Railway. See Burlington Northern.

Green Bay and Western Railroad (Green Bay Route). The Green Bay and Western Railroad is a paper-carrying line operating between the Mississippi River at Winona, Minnesota, and Kewaunee, Wisconsin, on Lake Michigan, via Green Bay. Chartered in 1866 as the Green Bay and Lake Pepin, it was built to provide an outlet for the region's wheat and lumber. It also provided connecting service with Lake Michigan ferries. From time to time, BURLINGTON NORTHERN has expressed interest in buying GB&W.
Locomotives: 19
Freight cars: 2060
Miles operated: 255
(as of January 1984)

Green Mountain Railroad. The Green Mountain Railroad started with the closing of the Rutland Railway. When F Nelson Blount, operator of the Steamtown USA Museum, proposed extending his excursion trains over portions of Rutland track between Bellows Falls and Rutland, Vermont, the state of Vermont asked if he would also operate a freight service on the line on an as-needed basis. The freight service began in 1965, a year after Steamtown USA moved across the Connecticut River from a New Hampshire location to a site north of Bellows Falls. Blount had originally agreed to run a freight service on 27 miles of track between Bellows Falls and Ludlow. After the move, the service was extended to Rutland. After Blount died in 1967, the Green Mountain became an employee-owned railroad. The GMR took over operation of the BOSTON AND MAINE yard at Keene, New Hampshire, and in 1982 began operations on a section of B&M line between Keene and Brattleboro, Vermont. The GMR is primarily a carrier of talc.
Locomotives: 6
Freight cars: 500
Miles operated: 50

Griggs, George S (1805–70). A mechanic and locomotive builder, Griggs designed locomotives which greatly influenced other locomotive

manufacturers, particularly in New England. Before going into locomotive making, Griggs worked as a millwright at the Locks and Canal machine shop. In 1834 he was appointed master mechanic of the Boston and Providence Railroad; he remained with that road for his entire career. His first locomotive, the *Norfolk*, was built in 1845. It had a riveted frame, a Stephenson boiler, and was inside connected, features which became characteristic of New England 4-4-0 locomotives for many years. He obtained patents for a number of inventions, including car brakes, wooden cushion driving wheels and a firebrick arch. He also experimented with steam brakes and coal-burning fireboxes.

Harriman, Edward H (20 February 1884–9 September 1909). An American railroad builder and financier, Harriman was born in Hempstead, New York, the son of Benjamin and Hannah Flanders Harriman. Harriman's formal education ended when he was 14. However, by the time he started to work on Wall Street as an office boy at age 21, he had already demonstrated that he had the skills and acumen to succeed in stock speculations. Harriman's interest in the transportation industry began with his marriage to Mary Averell, the daughter of William J Averell, president of the Ogdensburg and Lake Champlain Railroad Company. This interest led him to undertake the rehabilitation of a small bankrupt line, the Lake Ontario Southern. After rescuing this line, he sold it to the PENNSYLVANIA RAILROAD for a handsome profit. In 1883, he became affiliated with the ILLINOIS CENTRAL, becoming president of this line in 1887. In 1897, he became a director of the UNION PACIFIC, which was in receivership. By the turn of the century he had restored the road to a sound financial condition. He became president of the Union Pacific in 1903, and was given virtual carte blanche in the running of the company. In 1900, when COLLIS P HUNTINGTON died, the Union Pacific board authorized the issue of $100,000,000 of convertible bonds, giving Harriman the discretion to use these funds 'as his judgment may be practicable and desirable.' Harriman used much of this money to buy Huntington's share of the SOUTHERN PACIFIC. The purchase gave Union Pacific a 46 percent share of

SP president E H Harriman (*far left and above*), helped to set up a soup kitchen in San Francisco after the 1906 earthquake.

Southern Pacific and ownership of the Central Pacific. Harriman then proceeded to improve the line between Ogden and San Francisco with the building of the Lucin cutoff across the Great Salt Lake, an engineering feat that had been considered impossible.

Harriman next turned his attention to gaining access to Chicago, a move that put him into direct conflict with JAMES J HILL. For this he needed the CHICAGO, BURLINGTON AND QUINCY. However, Hill outmaneuvered him and secured control of the CB&Q. Harriman then began to buy stock in the NORTHERN PACIFIC, which had a half-interest in the CB&Q. The battle

between Harriman and Hill precipitated the panic of 1901. A compromise was reached with the formation of the Northern Securities Company, a holding company for the GREAT NORTHERN and Northern Pacific. In 1904 the Supreme Court declared the Northern Securities Company to be engaged in restraint of trade, and was ordered to divest itself of the stock in the two railroads. Subsequent court decisions on distribution of the stock resulted in the Hill interests being in control of both railroads. Harriman, no longer able to wield any influence in northern railroads, sold his stock.

Harriman then began to buy stocks in roads all over the country, ostensibly to establish a Union Pacific community of interests. This policy led to an investigation by the Interstate Commerce Commission in 1906–07.

The report of the ICC stated that Harriman's using of the Union Pacific as a holding company for the stock of other companies was not in the public interest.

Hill, James J (16 September 1838–29 May 1916). A railroad executive and financier, Hill was born in Ontario of Irish ancestors who had been among the first of Ontario's settlers.

His early education was interrupted by the necessity for his help with the family income after his father's death. However, young Hill showed such academic promise that the head of the Rockwood Academy, his former school, gave him free help and tuition. By age 18, Hill, a life-long enthusiast for things Far Eastern, was determined to set out for the Orient. Having no luck obtaining passage on the East Coast, he made his way to St Paul where he hoped to join a band of trappers traveling to the West Coast. However, circumstances forced him to take whatever work was available while waiting, and those early jobs gave Hill a good grounding in the problems of freight transportation with which he was always to be involved. He served as clerk for a steamboat line, determining freight rates and learning steamboat operation. Later, he became an independent freight agent and commodities broker.

In 1867, Hill, who saw the future of coal as a desirable fuel for railroads, began supplying the St Paul and Pacific line, but soon expanded his business with former competitors as partners in the Northwestern Fuel Company. Hill's familiarity with steamships also led him into partnership with Norman Kittson in the operation of a fur-transport steamship line in successful competition with the Hudson's Bay Company.

Hill returned to his interest in the St Paul and Pacific railroad when, through a complicated financial crisis, it went into receivership. Hill saw an opportunity to acquire and rehabilitate this and other railroads in similar crises. With his friends, Kittson, Donald Smith and George Stephen, all prominent Canadians, Hill wangled credit and backing, and, in 1878, purchased the St Paul and Pacific. Under Hill's leadership, the railroad was

Left: George Stephen was the first president of the Canadian Pacific, from 1881-88.
Right: James J Hill put together the Great Northern Railway.

Right: Donald Smith (1820-1914) provided
financial backing for James Hill's railroad
ventures. *Below:* James Hill assumed control of
the Oregon Trunk Railway, and drove the golden
spike in the finished line in 1911.

reconstructed and expanded westward to Seattle and Portland. Under
its new name—St Paul, Minneapolis
and Manitoba—new branch lines were
taken under control and new methods
of financing created. Eventually, in
1880, Hill-controlled lines and companies became the GREAT NORTHERN
RAILWAY, of which Hill served succes-
sively as manager, president and chairman of the board.

As an intercontinental railroad, the
Great Northern was uniquely well
managed and solvent, a particularly
remarkable circumstance since it had
had no government grant or aids.

Right: Donald Smith (1820-1914) provided financial backing for James Hill's railroad ventures. *Below:* James Hill assumed control of the Oregon Trunk Railway, and drove the golden spike in the finished line in 1911.

James Hill's Great Northern Railway hauling empty freight cars crosses Two Medicine Bridge near present-day Glacier National Park in 1891.

When the competing NORTHERN PACIFIC was on the verge of bankruptcy, Hill led efforts for its reorganization, which included plans to promote co-operation between the two giants, and a policy to guarantee, not interrupt, service. A working plan of financial reconstruction, with the Great Northern to guarantee and acquire Northern Pacific stock, was stopped by a Minnesota law prohibiting consolidation of parallel railroads. Nevertheless, Hill and his associates, acting as individuals, purchased enough Northern Pacific stock to save the line. In conjunction with J P Morgan, Hill also acquired enough of the CHICAGO, BURLINGTON AND QUINCY stock to give the Great Northern and the Northern Pacific access to Chicago and St Louis.

Hill was also closely associated with the beginnings of the CANADIAN PACIFIC RAILWAY, again, in conjunction with Smith and Stephens. His personal contribution included selection of routes and methods of construction. He continued as a director until differences of philosophy with WILLIAM VAN HORNE, another director, over whether the Canadian railroad should compete or cooperate with American

lines, forced his resignation.

Hill's motives, though solicitous for his stockholders, were often centered around his concern for the stability of the railroad industry as a whole. His rivalry with railroad tycoon EDWARD HARRIMAN were often of this nature. Eventually, Hill took steps to insure a kind of stock status quo by initiating the Northern Securities Company, a kind of overall railroad trust company, of which he became president. However, the state of Minnesota, and later the Supreme Court, enjoined the company from operation under the Sherman Anti-Trust Act of 1890. Interestingly, Hill and others had not believed the statute applied to railroads.

Hill's failure to secure the economic structure of his empire did not deflect his interest in railroad operations. After his resignation from Northern Securities, Hill devoted the rest of his life to lecturing and writing about railroad transportation—its policies and the goods it carried. He early advocated advanced agricultural reforms and the conservation of natural resources, forward-looking policies that came into their own much later.

James J Hill was, in many respects, a Renaissance Man. He found time, in the 1880s and 1890s, to explore the underdevelopment of western export

to the Orient through western ports (and the railroad transportation that could serve it). Hill developed the Great Northern Steamship Company to expedite such commerce, and, for a while, export of American raw materials and steel flourished from the West Coast.

Hill is also considered to have been, railroad operations aside, a financier of the first rank. He served for many years as a director of the Chase National Bank, among many other national and local banks. His ideas of the development of the West through railroad expansion brought much growth to large undeveloped areas of the United States and Canada.

In 1915, at the Panama–Pacific Exposition in San Francisco, at a states' hall of fame event, Hill was named by the State of Minnesota its 'greatest living citizen.' He was also active in Democratic Party politics and as a patron of the arts and literature.

Hillsdale County Railway. The Hillsdale County Railway operates between Steubenville, Indiana, and Litchfield, Michigan. The line started operations in 1976 on former NEW YORK CENTRAL track that had not been included in CONRAIL. Industries in the area had stated they could not stay if

A gallery of railroad barons: James Hill (*left*) was founder of the Great Northern. Three of the Big Four include Leland Stanford (*right*), president of the Central Pacific and later Southern Pacific; Collis Huntington (*far right*), Stanford's replacement as president of SP; and Charles Crocker (*below*), surrounded by his family, construction supervisor of the CP.

Rush, but gave up prospecting after a day or so and set up a general store in Sacramento, eventually going into partnership with Mark Hopkins.

In 1860, Huntington and Hopkins, along with LELAND STANFORD and CHARLES CROCKER (the 'Big Four') agreed to finance a survey of a possible railroad route across the Sierra Nevada mountains proposed by THEODORE JUDAH. With the passage of the Pacific Railroad Acts of 1862 and 1864, federal money and land grants were made available and construction could begin. Organized as the CENTRAL PACIFIC RAILROAD, Huntington's group built eastward across the Sierra while the UNION PACIFIC RAILROAD pushed westward from Omaha. Internal conflicts between Judah and Huntington's group delayed construction and ended only with Judah's death in 1863. After the completion of the transcontinental railroad in 1869, Huntington and his associates built and acquired lines in southern and western California which ultimately were joined with the SOUTHERN PACIFIC RAILROAD. Huntington became the first vice-president of the Southern Pacific, remaining as general agent of the Central Pacific and serving on the board of directors of both organizations.

Illinois Central Gulf Railroad. The Illinois Central Railroad operates in 11 states from the Gulf Coast to the Great Lakes, including most states bordering the Mississippi River. Major cities served include Chicago, St Louis, Omaha, Kansas City, Indianapolis, Louisville, Memphis, Birmingham, Mobile and New Orleans. Its predecessor, Illinois Central, was chartered in 1851 to build a north-south line through Illinois from Cairo to Galena, with a branch to Chicago. Aided by federal land grants, the line was completed in 1856. In the 1860s, the IC expanded westward into Iowa by building and leasing lines, and reached Sioux City in 1870. Southern extension to New Orleans was accomplished

rail service was not restored. The Indiana Public Service Commission and the Michigan State Highway Commission purchased the line and operations began shortly afterward. The Hillsdale County carries grain and other agricultural products as well as manufactured goods from several factories on the line. It also operates the Little River Railroad as a passenger service tourist attraction.

Locomotives: 3
Freight cars: 60
Miles operated: 62

Hinkley, Holmes (1793–1866). An American locomotive manufacturer, Hinkley was born in Maine where he worked as a carpenter before he went to Boston to become a machinist. In 1841 he and Gardener P Drury and Daniel P Childs opened a small machine shop which grew into a locomotive works called Hinkley and

Drury or Hinkley and Williams at different times. By the mid-1850s Hinkley's works had become the largest locomotive manufacturers in New England, and was one of the major producers in the United States. His locomotives were conventional in design, retaining features such as inside connections long after they had fallen out of favor with most railroads. The factory was closed in 1889.

Huntington, Collis Porter (1821–1900). A railroad financier and magnate and one of the CENTRAL PACIFIC 'Big Four,' Huntington was born in Harwinton, Connecticut, the son of William and Elizabeth Vincent Huntington. In 1836, he started working as a peddler in New York and in the South, accumulating enough cash to set up a store in Oneonta, New York, with one of his brothers. In 1849, he traveled to California to join the Gold

C. P. Huntington

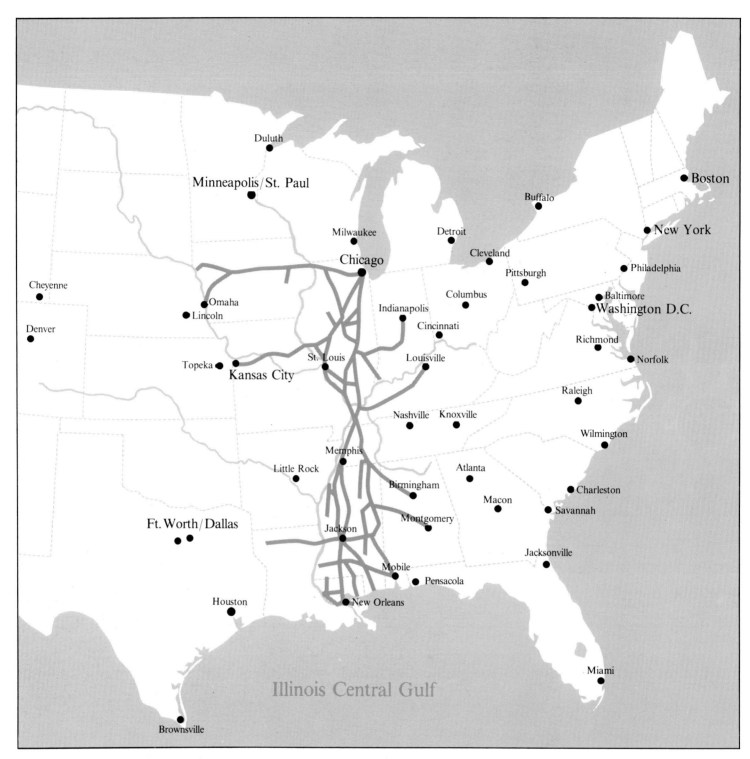

Illinois Central Gulf

Illinois Central
Gulf, Mobile & Ohio
Alton

Illinois Central Gulf

through arrangements with the New Orleans, Jackson and Great Northern Railroad and the Mississippi Central. Full control of these lines was assumed by IC in 1874. Some 550 miles of track from Cairo to New Orleans that had been laid in 5-foot gauge were converted to standard gauge in a single day on 29 July 1881. Through the 1880s and 1890s, rails were laid to Sioux Falls, South Dakota; Madison, Wisconsin; St Louis and Omaha.

In 1906 the IC came under the control of E H HARRIMAN. Electrification of a suburban line along the Chicago lakefront occurred in 1926. Illinois Central Gulf was formed in

1972 through merger with the Gulf, Mobile, and Ohio.

ICG is one of the leading grain carriers in North America, primarily because it is able to offer direct access to ports on the Gulf of Mexico. ICG is also an important coal carrier, utilizing unit trains for more than 90 percent of its coal traffic. ICG has a 20-year contract for delivering coal to a power plant in Marom, Indiana. This

is the longest-term contract ever entered into by a US railroad. Chemicals provide much of the traffic in Louisiana and Mississippi, generating some 20 percent of ICG's freight revenue. At the northern end of the system, steel, automobiles and automobile parts provide much of ICG's freight traffic. Automobiles are shipped in enclosed trilevel cars. ICG operates commuter rail service be-

An E6 Illinois Central passenger locomotive (*above*) and pioneer sleeping car (*right*).

tween Chicago and southern suburbs for the Chicago South Suburban Mass Transit District on its electrified track.

Locomotives: 1100
Freight cars: 39,200
Passenger cars: 175
Miles operated: 7100
(as of January 1983)

Indiana Harbor Belt Railroad. The Indiana Harbor Belt Railroad's main line runs between the industrial area at the southern end of Lake Michigan

An Illinois Central Gulf freight train pulls out of Chicago heavily loaded with plastic-covered industrial machinery and a long string of boxcars.

and Franklin Park, Illinois, forming a belt around Chicago. The major service provided by the IHB is connections outside the congested areas of Chicago. Incorporated in 1896 as the East Chicago Belt, the present name was assumed in 1907, when it took over rights on portions of the Chicago Junction Railway previously run by the Michigan Central.

Locomotives: 106
Freight cars: 33
Miles operated: 114
(as of January 1984)

Iowa Railroad Company. Running east-west across Iowa between Omaha and Bureau, Illinois, the Iowa Railroad Company operates as a grain carrier on former tracks of the Chicago, Rock Island and Pacific main line. Incorporated in 1981, service was extended east to Bureau through an interesting track-sharing arrangement with the CHICAGO, MILWAUKEE, ST PAUL AND PACIFIC (Milwaukee Road). The Milwaukee Road uses the track from 8:00 A.M. to 8:00 P.M. and the Iowa Railroad takes over from 8:00 P.M. to 8:00 A.M.

Locomotives: 12
Freight cars: 296
Miles operated: 456
(as of January 1984)

James, William T (1786–1865). An inventor and locomotive builder, James was probably born in Rhode Island. From about 1820 to 1839 he manufactured stoves in New York City. There is some evidence that he built four steam road carriages and three steam locomotives during that time. These machines were reportedly ahead of their time in that they had two-cylinder compound engines. In 1829 he built an unsuccessful engine for the BALTIMORE AND OHIO RAILROAD. A second effort resulted in an engine called the American, which was probably fitted with a new link motion of his design. This engine was also used by the New York and Harlem Railroad.

Jervis, John B. See Matthew, David; Mohawk and Hudson Railroad; Winans, Ross.

The John Bull. Also called the *Stevens*, this locomotive was built in 1831 at the Stephenson works at Newcastle upon Tyne, England, for the CAMDEN AND AMBOY RAILROAD. It was delivered

The *John Bull* (*above and below*) was constructed in 1931 and operated on Robert L Stevens' historic Camden and Amboy Railroad in New Jersey, which later became a part of the Pennsylvania Railroad system. It was renamed *Stevens* but is rarely referred to as such. The train was modified several times over the years and ceased operation in 1893.

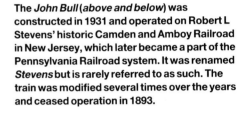

in a disassembled state, a circumstance that presented a serious problem to the railroad, since no one knew how to put it together. ISAAC DRIPPS, a young apprentice mechanic ROBERT STEVENS had lured away from a shipwright, assembled the engine. Dripps had never seen a locomotive in his life, and the Stephenson works had provided no plans, drawings or assembly instructions. Dripps also constructed a four-wheeled tender. Water was supplied from a whiskey cask mounted on the platform of the tender via a leather pipe made by a local cobbler.

The four-wheeled *John Bull* had a horizontal boiler and weighed some 10 tons. The 11-inch diameter cylinders had a 20-inch stroke. The drivers were 54 inches in diameter.

Members of the New Jersey legislature and Joseph Bonaparte (eldest brother of Napoleon and ex-king of Spain) were among the passengers in the trial run made on 12 November 1831. The *John Bull* did not go into regular service until 1833. The engine was modified several times during its more than 30 years of service. In 1833, Dripps, at Steven's suggestion, added a two-wheeled pilot to guide the locomotive around the Camden and Amboy's many sharp curves. Constructed of oak beams, the pilot was attached to extensions of the forward axle. A coil spring transferred part of

the weight to the wheels at the head of the contrivance. The number of drivers had to be reduced from four to two to accommodate the pilot. The device, which effectively prevented derailments, is widely believed to have been the first 'cow-catcher.' A tapering sleeve Dripps devised for the stack was one of the first spark arresters. A high, fully enclosed fuel car built by Dripps gave the engine the appearance of a shack on wheels. Other modifications included replacement of the wooden spoked wheels with new ones made of cast iron, and the addition of refinements such as whistles, bells and headlights.

The *John Bull*, on display at the Smithsonian Institution, is the oldest existing locomotive in the United States.

Judah, Theodore D (4 March 1826–2 November 1863). An American engineer and railroad builder, Judah was born in Bridgeport, Connecticut, the son of a clergyman. After completing studies at Rensselaer Polytechnic Institute, he worked for the New Haven, Hartford and Springfield Railroad and the Connecticut River Railroad, among others. In 1854, he went to California to become the chief engineer of the Sacramento Valley Rail Road, which ran east from Sacramento to Folsom, California. At

this time he became interested in the idea of constructing a railroad across the Sierra Nevada mountains that would eventually connect with railroads from the East to become a transcontinental railroad. He lobbied for his idea in the California legislature and the United States Congress, published pamphlets, made speeches and was active in the Pacific Railroad Convention of 1859. In 1860, he announced that he had found a route across the mountains. He convinced COLLIS P HUNTINGTON and others to invest in the venture, which was organized as the CENTRAL PACIFIC RAILROAD COMPANY. Construction began with the passage of the Pacific Railroad Act of 1862. Judah became disillusioned with the financial schemings of the Huntington group and traveled to New York to seek other financial support. He contracted typhoid fever while crossing the Isthmus of Panama, and died shortly after his arrival in New York.

Kansas City Southern Railway. The main line of the Kansas City Southern Railway runs between Kansas City and the Gulf Coast ports of

Right: Working for the CP, Theodore Judah devised the trans-Sierra route for the transcontinental railroad.
Below: The *John Bull* in passenger service.

New Orleans and Lake Charles, Louisiana, and Port Arthur, Texas. A line runs westward to Dallas from Shreveport, Louisiana. The earliest predecessor of the KCS was the Kansas City, Pittsburgh and Gulf started by Arthur Stilwell in 1890. The railroad built southward from Kansas City and Port Arthur was reached in 1897. The road went into receivership two years later and reorganized as the Kansas City Southern. The opening of oil fields in Louisiana and Texas dramatically increased freight traffic. Access to Dallas and Shreveport was obtained in 1939 when KCR merged with the Louisiana and Arkansas Railroad. In the 1970s, cooperative arrangements were worked out with the BURLINGTON

NORTHERN for operating unit coal trains from Wyoming's Powder River Basin to power plants in Arkansas, Louisiana and Texas. The KCR is a major carrier of chemicals produced by Louisiana and Texas factories.
Locomotives: 300
Freight cars: 7130
Miles operated: 1663

Lake Erie, Franklin and Clarion Railroad. The Lake Erie, Franklin and Clarion Railroad was created in 1913 from the merger of three small lines, the Pennsylvania Northern, the Pennsylvania Southern and the Pittsburgh, Clarion and Franklin. Primarily a carrier of coal, it also transports raw materials and finished glass for a glass factory.

Locomotives: 6
Freight cars: 1120
Miles operated: 15

Lake Superior and Ishpeming Railroad. Owned by the Cleveland Cliffs Iron Company, the Lake Superior and Ishpeming carries iron ore from mines in Michigan's Upper Peninsula to ports on Lake Superior. Opened in 1896, the road was merged with several other Cleveland Cliffs railroads in succeeding years.
Locomotives: 23
Freight cars: 2175
Miles operated: 60

Lamoille Valley Railroad. Operating between St Johnsbury and Swanton in northern Vermont, the Lamoille

Lehigh Valley No. 2006 was a Baldwin 4-6-2 camel-back locomotive. These powerful engines were capable of pulling heavy loads up steep grades.

Valley Railroad has had a checkered history filled with many misfortunes, bankruptcies and reorganizations since it was started in 1869 as the Vermont Division of the Portland and Ogdensburg Railroad. Originally intended as a bridge route to connect Portland, Maine, with the Great Lakes, it went into receivership in 1877 before it managed to reach Lake Champlain. Reorganized as the St Johnsbury and Lake Champlain, the lake was reached in 1880, and an extension to a junction with the Ogdensburg and Lake Champlain was completed in 1888. In the interim, however, the CENTRAL VERMONT RAILWAY gained control of the Ogdensburg and Lake Champlain. The CV refused to exchange traffic with the St Johnsbury and Lake Champlain, rendering the newly completed extension a useless but expensive appendage. Control of the St Johnsbury and Lake Champlain passed to the BOSTON AND MAINE in 1895, which ran the road until 1925. Local management resumed in 1925, but B&M retained ownership. Another bankruptcy followed in 1944. Reorganized as the St Johnsbury and Lamoille County Railroad in 1948, the B&M sold the line to local operators. The line was sold again in 1956 and 1967 to independent operators who had little financial success with the line. The state of Vermont bought the road in 1973, awarded an operating contract first to an individual, then to the Vermont Northern Railroad. Dissatisfied with its operation in both instances, the state then put the road's operation out for bids. A local group that included the line's major customers formed the Northern Vermont Corporation which bought the line and incorporated it as the Lamoille Valley Railroad in 1978. Primarily a carrier of talc, paper and grain, the line was still in operation in the mid-1980s.

Locomotives: 4
Freight cars: 50
Miles operated: 50
(as of January 1984)

Lehigh Valley Railroad. The earliest predecessor of the Lehigh Valley Railroad was the Delaware, Lehigh, Schuylkill and Susquehanna, chartered in 1846 to carry anthracite coal

from Mauch Chunk to Easton, Pennsylvania. The name Lehigh Valley was assumed in 1853 and the line opened two years later. The road expanded through building and acquisitions through the 1860s and 1870s, reaching Buffalo in 1876 when it financed the Erie Railroad's conversion from 6-foot to standard gauge. LV's own line was layed to Buffalo in 1892. By the 1920s, the PENNSYLVANIA RAILROAD had obtained substantial interests in LV. Virtually complete control by the Pennsylvania was a reality by the mid-1960s. In 1961, LV discontinued passenger service. LV was absorbed into CONRAIL in 1976.

Little Rock and Western Railway.
One of a number of small railroads created from trackage of the bankrupt and abandoned Chicago, Rock Island and Pacific, the Little Rock and Western operates between Perry and Pulaski, Arkansas. Owned by the Green Bay Packaging Company, it carries paper for the Arkansas Kraft Paper Mill.
Locomotives: 2
Freight cars: 350
Miles operated 54
(as of January 1984)

The *Penryn* (*top*) is a 4-4-0 American-type locomotive; (*above*) is a Baldwin 4-6-2 Pacific and the *Matt H Shay* (*below*) is a 2-8-8-8-2 Triplex configuration.

Locomotive wheel arrangements.
Locomotives are classified into general types on the basis of wheel arrangements. Until the turn of the century, a locomotive was referred to as a 'four-wheel locomotive,' 'six-wheel locomotive' and so on. Such designations told very little about the machine. An 'eight-wheel locomotive,' for example, could be one with eight driving wheels, or one with a four-wheel leading truck and four driving wheels, or one with a two-wheel leading truck, four driving wheels and a two-wheel trailing truck. Each of these is a different machine suitable for certain kinds of work.

A more specific system of wheel notation was devised by Fredric M Whyte of the NEW YORK CENTRAL RAILROAD. Whyte wrote an article on his system in the December 1900 issue of the *American Engineer and Railroad Journal*. In 1903 the system was adopted by the American Locomotive Company. Within a few years it became the wheel notation system in general use in North America for the classification of steam locomotives.

In the Whyte system, the number of wheels in the leading truck, number

Steam Locomotive
Wheel Arrangements

Type	Wheel diagram	Name(s)	Type	Wheel	Name(s)
0-2-2	Oo		4-4-4	ooOOoo	
0-4-0	OO		4-6-0	ooOOO	Ten-wheeler
0-4-2	OOo		4-6-2	ooOOOo	Pacific
0-4-4	OOoo	Forney 4-coupled	4-6-4	ooOOOoo	Baltic, Hudson
0-4-6	OOooo		4-8-0	ooOOOO	Mastodon
0-6-0	OOO		4-8-2	ooOOOOo	Mountain
0-6-2	OOOo		4-8-4	ooOOOOoo	Northern,
0-6-4	OOOoo	Forney 6-coupled			Greenbrier, Dixie
0-6-6	OOOooo		4-10-0	ooOOOOO	
0-8-0	OOOO		4-10-2	ooOOOOOo	Overland,
0-8-2	OOOOo				Southern Pacific
2-2-0	oO		4-12-2	ooOOOOOOo	Union Pacific
2-2-2	oOo				
2-4-0	oOO			*Articulated Locomotives*	
2-4-2	oOOo	Columbia	0-2-2-0	OO	
2-6-0	oOOO	Mogul	0-4-4-0	OO OO	
2-6-2	oOOOo	Prairie	0-6-6-0	OOO OOO	
2-8-0	oOOOO	Consolidation	0-8-8-0	OOOO OOOO	
2-8-2	oOOOOo	Mikado	2-6-6-0	oOOO OOO	
2-8-4	oOOOOoo	Berkshire, Kanawha	2-6-6-4	oOOO OOOoo	
			2-6-6-6	oOOO OOOooo	Allegheny
2-10-0	oOOOOO	Decapod	2-8-8-0	oOOOO OOOO	
2-10-2	oOOOOOo	Santa Fe	2-8-8-2	oOOOO OOOOo	Chesapeake
2-10-4	oOOOOOoo	Texas	2-10-10-2	oOOOOO OOOOOo	
4-2-0	ooO	Six-wheeler	4-4-6-2	ooOO OOOo	
4-2-2	ooOo	Bicycle	4-6-6-4	ooOOO OOOoo	Challenger
4-2-4	ooOoo		4-8-8-4	ooOOOO OOOOoo	Big Boy
4-4-0	ooOO	American	2-8-8-8-2	oOOOO OOOO OOOOo	Triplex
4-4-2	ooOOo	Atlantic	2-8-8-8-4	oOOOO OOOO OOOOoo	Triplex

A selection of wheel arrangements showing possible configurations including (*from top*): a 4-4-0; the 2-2-4 pioneer locomotive of Los Angeles; an A J Stevens valve motion engine; CP No. 82 with a four-wheel 'dinky' caboose; 2-4-0 Stella (*above right*); and a high-speed 4-6-6-4 Challenger (*right*).

of driving wheels and the number of wheels in the trailing truck are designated. Thus, a 4-6-2 has a four-wheel leading truck, six driving wheels and a two-wheel trailing truck.

Some wheel arrangements have come to be associated with a name. The 4-4-0 locomotive for example, is often referred to as the AMERICAN TYPE because it became the most widely used locomotive in North America during the nineteenth century. The BALDWIN LOCOMOTIVE WORKS named a 2-8-2 locomotive MIKADO because it was made for export to Japan. The first 4-4-2 was sold to the ATLANTIC COAST LINE; thus 4-4-2s came to be called 'Atlantics.'

This Canadian Pacific diesel locomotive with a C-C wheel arrangement has two sets of three driven axles.

Below: Of all railroads, Union Pacific made the greatest use of gas turbine engines like this Baldwin B-B-B-B, which was among the most powerful locomotives ever built. *Bottom:* A Santa Fe diesel transfer locomotive with a Co-Co wheel arrangement.

1961 General Motors diesel locomotive, one of many that the company built from 1945 on.

DIESEL AND ELECTRIC LOCOMOTIVE WHEEL ARRANGEMENTS

The general classification of diesel and electric locomotives is usually based on the number of axles. The number of driven axles is designated by a letter:

A = 1
B = 2
C = 3
D = 4

and so on

An 'o' after the letter indicates the axle is independently powered, while no 'o' designates connection of the axles by rods or gearing. The number of carrying wheels is indicated by a numeral.

A plus sign (+) indicates a locomotive with trucks in which the transmission of traction stresses is through an articulated member connecting the trucks rather than through the frame.

In North America there are virtually no modern diesel and electric locomotives with rod or gear-coupled axles. Thus the 'o' has fallen into disuse. However, it is generally retained in descriptions of historic locomotives, and in books dealing with locomotives in all parts of the world.

Typical diesel and electric wheel arrangements:

Bo-Bo
B-B
Co-Co
C-C
2-Co+Co-2
1-C-1
Do-Do

Long, Stephen H (1784–1864). An engineer and early locomotive builder, Long was born in New Hampshire. One of the few early American locomotive builders with a higher education, Long was graduated from Dartmouth College in 1809. Long served as an officer in United States Army Corps of Engineers, and taught at the United States Military Academy at West Point for a number of years. Long became interested in railroad engineering in the 1820s, advocating coal-burning engines years before they came into general use. His first locomotive patent, obtained in 1826, was for a coal-burning engine. From 1827 to 1830 Long and several other Army engineers were involved in planning and building the BALTIMORE AND OHIO RAILROAD. During this time he wrote *Railroad Manual*, the first book on railroads published in the United States. In 1832 he formed the American Steam Carriage Company in collaboration with William Norris and several others. Due mainly to his insistence on designing coal-burners, the venture was not successful. He obtained patents for eccentric valve gears in 1833.

Louisville and Nashville Railroad. The Louisville and Nashville was chartered in 1850 and began operations between these two cities in 1859. Over the next 40 years it expanded southward through acquisitions of smaller lines, including the Lexington and Ohio, which was the first railroad west of the Alleghenies. The L&N came under the control of the ATLANTIC COAST LINE in the 1900s. However, it continued to operate independently. L&N absorbed the Nashville, Chattanooga, and St Louis in 1957 and the Chicago, Indianapolis, and Louisville (Monon) in 1971. L&N became one of the 'Family Lines' after the merger of ACL and the SEABOARD COAST LINE in 1968. L&N continued to operate independently until 1982, when it merged with Seaboard Coast Line to form SEABOARD SYSTEM RAILROAD.

Maine Central Railroad. The Maine Central operates in southern Maine, northern New Hampshire and Vermont. The main line, running northward from Portland, serves Lewiston, Waterville and Bangor, where it diverges into a northern branch serving Mattawamkeag and Vanceboro, and a southern branch to Calais. Another line runs from Portland to St Johnsbury, Vermont. Incorporated in 1862, the Maine Central was created from the consolidation of two roads, the Androscoggin and Kennebec and the Penobscot and Kennebec, forming a 5ft 6in gauge line between Portland and Bangor. Other lines were soon absorbed, and the lines were converted to standard gauge. In 1911 and 1912, the Maine Central took over two 2-foot gauge lines, the Sandy River and Rangeley Lake, and the Bridgeton and Saco River. These railroads were held until the early 1920s. From 1933 to 1955 the Maine Central entered into cooperative management arrangements with the BOSTON AND MAINE.

Maine Central was sold to US Filter Corporation in 1980, which was absorbed by Ashland Oil shortly afterward. In 1981, the Maine Central was bought by Guilford Transportation Industries, which also owns the Boston and Maine, and the DELAWARE AND HUDSON. The Maine Central is primarily a carrier of paper products.

Locomotives: 65
Freight cars: 4377
Miles operated: 819
(as of January 1984)

Marinette, Tomahawk, and Western Railway. The Marinette, Tomahawk, and Western transports paper and coal for its parent company, Owens-Illinois Inc, between Bradley and Wausau, Wisconsin. Incorporated in 1894, the present name was assumed in 1912.

Locomotives: 3
Freight cars: 595
Miles operated: 13

Maryland and Delaware Railroad. The Maryland and Delaware was formed in 1977 by Rail Services Associates to operate on sections of track in the Delmarva Peninsula that had been part of the long defunct New York, Philadelphia, and Norfolk. That line was incorporated in 1884 as a subsidiary of the PENNSYLVANIA RAILROAD to operate down the peninsula from Wilmington to Cape Charles, and thence to Norfolk by ferry. The line fell into disrepair during the fading years of the Pennsylvania and the brief reign of the PENN CENTRAL. The line southward to Pockomoke was taken over by CONRAIL in 1976. The branch line, classified as light density by the United States Railway Association, were run by CONRAIL with a federal subsidy until Rail Services Associates took over. Three branches are run by RSA: Townsend to Chestertown and Centerville, Seaford to Preston and Cambridge, and Frankford to Snow Hill. The Maryland and Delaware is primarily a carrier of paper products, fertilizer and foodstuffs.

Locomotives: 4
Freight cars: 135
Miles operated: 148

Maryland Department of Transportation. The Maryland Department of Transportation subsidizes commuter rail service to Washington from Baltimore and Maryland suburbs to the northwest. Service includes trains to Brunswick, Maryland on the CHESSIE SYSTEM (BALTIMORE AND OHIO), a service to Baltimore, also on the Chessie System and two trains daily between Washington and Baltimore operated by AMTRAK. The Amtrak operation is run with cars leased from NEW JERSEY TRANSIT. An unsubsidized passenger service is operated between Brunswick and Martinburg, West Virginia. (See photo pg 116–17.)

Locomotives: 5
Passenger cars: 22
Self-propelled cars: 10
Miles operated: 151
(as of June 1983)

Maryland and Pennsylvania Railroad ('Ma and Pa'). The Maryland and Pennsylvania runs between Hanover and York, Pennsylvania. Its earliest predecessor, the 3-foot gauge Maryland Central Railroad, was incorporated in 1867. Over the next 35 years, it went through a long and complicated series of bankruptcies, reorganizations, acquisitions and mergers before emerging as the MARYLAND AND DELAWARE in 1901, shortly after being converted to standard gauge. The Maryland and Pennsylvania remained independent until 1971

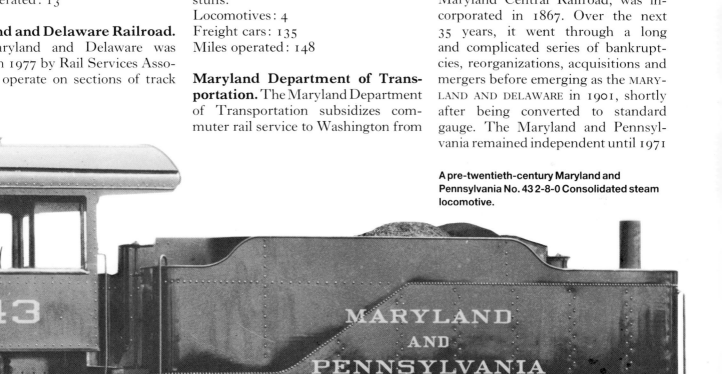

A pre-twentieth-century Maryland and Pennsylvania No. 43 2-8-0 Consolidated steam locomotive.

Above left: The Section A line subway station, the most advanced on the line, being built by the Maryland Department of Transport. *Above:* A new MBTA Blue Line car. *Left:* The recently completed MBTA Haymarket Station.

when it was bought by Emons Industries. Additional sections of old PENNSYLVANIA RAILROAD track were obtained when CONRAIL was formed. The Maryland and Pennsylvania carries paper products, furniture and foodstuffs. Emons Industries also leases freight cars, produced in a shop constructed at York in 1977.

Locomotives: 6
Freight cars: 2190
Miles operated: 66

Massachusetts Bay Transportation Authority. The Massachusetts Bay Transportation Authority operates the Boston area rapid transit system, commuter rail service, and suburban bus service. Its predecessor, Metropolitan Transit Authority of Massachusetts, assumed control of the Boston Elevated Railway in 1947. This system included subways, elevated trains, streetcars, buses and trackless trolleys (trolley buses) operating in Boston and 13 surrounding towns. The Massachusetts Bay Transportation Authority, which succeeded the MTA in 1964, had jurisdiction over 79 towns and cities in eastern Massachusetts. By the mid-1960s, three railroads, BOSTON AND MAINE; NEW YORK, NEW HAVEN AND HARTFORD and the NEW YORK CENTRAL (Boston and Albany) operated commuter trains to Boston. MBTA made its first subsidy payment to the Boston and Maine in 1965. Other subsidies and purchases of line and equipment followed. Former New Haven railroad lines to Attleboro, Stoughton and Franklin were bought in 1973. In that same year, a former New York Central line running westward from Riverside to Framingham was also purchased. Two years later, locomotives, cars and physical plants were purchased from B&M, which continued to operate the commuter service under contract to MBTA. PENN CENTRAL, which had run commuter service from Boston's South Station, was succeeded by CONRAIL on 1 April 1976. The large subsidy increase requested by Conrail induced MBTA to look elsewhere, and B&M was awarded the contract to operate the commuter lines to the south of Boston.

Locomotives: 37
Passenger cars: 92
Self-propelled passenger cars: 92
Miles operated: 244 (not including subways, streetcars, buses)

The MBTA Rapid Transit System is a multitime system serving Boston and surrounding suburbs. The Blue Line serves the northern suburbs, the Orange Line extends southward to Quincy, the Red Line serves the Cam-

bridge areas and the Green Line serves the western suburbs. Extensions are planned for the Red, Blue, and Orange lines. The $283 million Southwest Corridor project, which involves relocating the Orange Line from downtown Boston, is the largest single transit project ever undertaken in the Boston area.

Electrification system:
    Blue Line (rapid transit) 600V
      DC, third rail/catenary
    Green Line (light-rail trolley cars)
      600V DC, catenary
    Orange Line (rapid transit) 600V
      DC, third rail
    Red Line (rapid transit) 600V
      DC, third rail/catenary
Gauge: 4ft 8in
No. of stations: 83
Rolling stock: 354 rapid transit cars, 125 light rail, 100 trolley cars
Route mileage:
  Blue: 6
  Green: 19.5
  Orange: 11
  Red: 23.4

Matthew, David (1810?–1890?). A mechanic of obscure origins, Matthew was associated with many aspects of early American locomotive building. Apprenticed to the West Point Foundry in the mid-1820s, Matthew was involved in constructing many of the earliest American locomotives, including the DEWITT CLINTON, for which he was specifically hired by John B Jervis. He was named locomotive superintendent of the Utica and Schenectady Railroad in 1836. Matthew pioneered a number of railroad innovations. He claimed a number of firsts, including the roundhouse, snow plow, locomotive cab, geared turntable, spark arrester and a device for prewarming water in the tender with steam. Matthew left railroad work in 1842 to manage an iron foundry, but sued MATTHIAS BALDWIN for infringement of a smokestack patent in 1860.

McCloud River Railroad. The McCloud River Railroad operates in Northern California between Mt Shasta and Lookout, California, and to Burney on a branch line. Connection is made with SOUTHERN PACIFIC at Mt Shasta and with BURLINGTON NORTHERN at Lookout. Incorporated in

A snowplow locomotive of the McCloud River Railroad clears the line.

1897, the McCloud was owned for many years by the McCloud Lumber Company and later by US Plywood. It is now owned by ITEL Corporation. McCloud River has been a lumber-carrying railroad since its inception. Running through rugged, beautiful mountain country, it has a single switchback east of the Signal Butte Summit, which is about 1000 feet higher than McCloud, some five miles to the east. Because of the switchback, eastbound trains leaving McCloud come into McCloud in reverse. In 1982 the line was extensively rehabilitated through a grant from the Federal Railroad Administration. From time to time excursion trains operate on the line.

Locomotives: 4
Freight cars: 247
Miles operated: 96
(as of January 1984)

Meridian and Bigbee Railroad. Incorporated in 1917 as the Meridian and Bigbee River Railway, it did not begin operations until 1928. Until 1935 it operated between Meridian, Mississippi, and Cromwell, Alabama. The line east from Cromwell to Myrtlewood, Alabama, was completed in that year. The present name was assumed after a 1952 reorganization. In 1982, the line was purchased by James River Corporation from the American Can Company, which had

Above: A McCloud River Baldwin AS-616 diesel, serving the California mountain country, loaded with lumber in 1952. *Right:* Michigan Central locomotive No. 181, c1880, ready for departure, and Engine 245 in Delhi, Michigan, in 1889 (*below right*).

owned the road since 1955. The Meridian and Bigbee is primarily a carrier of chemicals, pulp and paper products.

Locomotives: 5
Freight cars: 475
Miles operated: 51

Metroliner. See Electric locomotives.

Metro-North Commuter Railroad Company. Metro-North operates commuter trains from New York City to Connecticut and areas of Upstate New York east of the Hudson River. The service is operated on former PENN CENTRAL track that had been inherited from the NEW YORK CENTRAL and the NEW YORK, NEW HAVEN AND HARTFORD. Until the end of 1982, this service had been operated by CONRAIL. At that time, Conrail divested itself of the service in accordance with provisions of the Northeast Rail Service Act of 1981. Metro-North, which was established by the Metropolitan Transit Authority of the state of New York, then took over operation of the trains (1 January 1983). Three divisions are operated: the Hudson (New York–Poughkeepsie), the Harlem (New York–Dover Plains) and the New

Haven (New York–New Haven, with branches to New Canaan, Danbury and Waterbury). The Hudson and Harlem divisions run on former New York Central track, the New Haven on former NY, NH & H track. Service within the state of New York is subsidized entirely by MTA, while the New Haven division is subsidized jointly by MTA and the Connecticut Department of Transportation.

Locomotives: 50
Passenger cars: 155
Self-propelled passenger cars:
    electric: 526
    diesel: 28

Metropolitan Atlanta Rapid Transit Authority (MARTA). MARTA was built with local sales-tax funding and a federal grant. Planned as a north-south, east-west two-line system, the first sections were completed

in 1979. The north-south line was extended in 1982 and 1984. Federal funding was made available in 1983 to extend the north-south line to Harts-field International Airport, and north-ward to the city's affluent suburbs. Additional plans call for extension of the east-west line and the construction of several branches.

MARTA trains operate automatic-ally with no motormen.

Electrification system: 750V DC, third rail

Gauge: 4ft 8in

No. of stations: 20

No. of cars: 120

Route mileage: 16

Michigan Interstate Railway. The Michigan Interstate Railway operates between Ann Arbor, Michigan and Toledo, Ohio. Its earliest predecessor was the Ann Arbor Railroad, which

was the product of two companies chartered in 1869 and 1872 to build a line between Ann Arbor and Toledo. Some 20 years and at least 12 re-organizations were required for the road's completion to Lake Michigan at Frankfurt, Michigan. The Wabash Railroad bought the Ann Arbor in 1925, holding it until 1963, when it was sold to the Detroit, Toledo, and Ironton. When the Ann Arbor entered into reorganization proceedings in 1973, it was bought by the state of Michigan and operated by the Michigan Interstate Railway Company. Disputes over money matters led to splitting the line among three railroads, including Michigan Interstate which operates the line between Ann Arbor and Toledo. The line is principally a carrier of automobiles, automobile parts and cement.
Locomotives: 3
Freight cars: 520
Miles operated: 49
(as of January 1984)

Michigan Northern Railway. The Michigan Northern operates between Grand Rapids and Mackinaw City, Michigan. Service to Alma, Frankfort and Charlevoix is also provided. The Michigan Northern was organized in 1975 to operate on a former PENNSYL-VANIA Railroad line between Grand Rapids and Mackinaw City not included in CONRAIL. Purchased by the Michigan State Highway Commission to maintain rail service in the area, it began operations in 1976. The line from Petosky to Charlevoix was purchased from the Chesapeake and Ohio in 1983. In that same year, MN took over operation of a state-owned line between Alma and Frankfort. The MN is primarily a carrier of lumber, sand, foodstuffs and LP gas. Seasonal passenger service to resort areas is also provided.
Locomotives: 7
Freight cars: 42
Passenger cars: 2
Miles operated: 430
(as of January 1984)

Mikado-type locomotive. First built by the BALDWIN LOCOMOTIVE WORKS, these 2-8-2 locomotives were named Mikado because the first units were built for export to Japan. These engines were among the most widely used freight locomotives in North America during the first quarter of the twentieth century. The Mikados were

The Canadian National 2-8-2 Mikado built by the Baldwin Locomotive Works was similar to the Santa Fe Baldwin Class Q 2-10-2.

The Baldwin-built California and Western 2-8-2 Mikado at Fort Bragg is a tourist attraction and a source of fascination for these young boys, intent on watching it prepare for departure.

widely exported and came to be regarded as typically American as the 4-4-0. They were considered to be very dependable and were able to take rough treatment in the most difficult running conditions.

Millholland, James (1812–1875). An American mechanic and locomotive builder, Millholland was born in Baltimore. As an apprentice in George W Johnson's machine shop, he assisted in the construction of the TOM THUMB. After this experience, he worked for a marine engine firm in New York City. Appointed master mechanic of the Baltimore and Susquehanna Railroad in 1838, he constructed two heavy 4-4-0 engines and rebuilt a number of older locomotives. Among his other innovations were a cast-iron crank axle for inside-connected locomotives and a six-wheel freight car. He also supervised the construction of an iron plate bridge in 1847. In that same year

he was hired by the Philadelphia and Reading Railroad, where he concentrated on developing a firebox for burning anthracite coal. His design was successful, and by 1855 the Philadelphia and Reading was one of the first all coal-burning railroads in North America. Millholland pioneered the use of innovations such as steel tires, superheaters and feed-water heaters. He designed a number of locomotives including a powerful 0-12-0 in 1863.

Milwaukee Road. See Chicago, Milwaukee, St Paul and Pacific Railroad Company.

Missouri-Kansas-Texas Railroad ('Katy'). The Missouri–Kansas–Texas Railroad operates between the Gulf Coast at Galveston and Omaha/ Council Bluffs. Service is provided to many important Texas and Midwest market areas, including Houston, San Antonio, Dallas, Fort Worth, Okla-

homa City, Tulsa, Wichita, Salina, Topeka, Kansas City and St Louis. The line between Salina, Kansas and Dallas is run by a subsidiary, the Oklahoma, Kansas, and Texas on former Rock Island track. MKT started in 1865 as Union Pacific Railway, Southern Branch (no corporate connection with the UNION PACIFIC RAILROAD). The intent was to build south toward New Orleans from Junction City, Kansas. With the help of a land grant, construction started in 1869. Building quickly, the line reached the southern Kansas border ahead of two competing roads, thereby earning the right to continue construction southward through present-day Oklahoma. In that same year, the Tebo and Neosho, a small railroad running between Sedalia, Missouri, and Parsons, Kansas, was absorbed, and the name Missouri, Kansas, and Texas Railroad was assumed. MKT continued to expand through the 1870s, reaching

A Northern Pacific Class W-5 2-8-2 was well suited for the rugged terrain it encountered in the northwestern United States.

Denison, Texas, in 1872, and fighting the Atlantic and Pacific over rights to a crossing at Vinita, Oklahoma. In 1873, MKT came under the control of JAY GOULD. Dallas and Fort Worth were reached in 1881, and in 1882 the International and Great Northern was bought. A year later MKT bought the Galveston, Houston, and Henderson. Gould, always scheming, then leased the Galveston, Houston, and Henderson to the International and Great Northern. By this time Gould's rail empire had grown to include the St Louis and Iron Mountain, MISSOURI PACIFIC, Texas and Pacific, Wabash and the central branch of the UNION

PACIFIC, which had become the Missouri Pacific's running westward from Atchison, Kansas. MKT and several other Gould railroads went into receivership in 1888 and 1889. Gould was thrown out of the MKT organization in 1888. A Texas-based holding company, the Missouri, Kansas and Texas of Texas was formed in 1886 to hold the road's Texas trackage, in compliance with a Texas law requiring railroads operating in Texas to maintain their offices in that state. MKT came out of receivership in that same year and went into another period of expansion lasting into the 1910s. By 1904 MKT had extended to serve

Houston, St Louis, Shreveport, San Antonio, Tulsa and Oklahoma City. The Texas Central was acquired in 1910, and two more lines, the Wichita Falls and Northwestern, and the Witchita Falls and Southern, were acquired a year later. The present name, Missouri–Kansas–Texas was assumed in 1923 after a reorganization. The MKT declined in the 1950s, but a program of rebuilding and diversification in the late 1960s restored the road to profitability by the early 1970s. The Texas City Terminal is owned jointly with the Missouri Pacific and the ATCHISON, TOPEKA AND SANTA FE.

The MKT is primarily a carrier of

coal and grain, which it carries in unit trains. Lumber, steel products, chemicals and automobiles also account for much of MKT's traffic. In the early 1980s, MKT was investigating the possibility of electrifying the main line from Fort Worth to Houston.

Locomotives: 203
Freight cars: 5464
Miles operated: 2175
(as of January 1983)

Missouri Pacific System (Mo-Pac). The states served by the Missouri Pacific Corporation comprise more than one-third of the land area of the United States. Its rail lines extend from Chicago to the Gulf Coast of Louisiana and Texas, serving the central tier of states from Louisiana and Texas to Kansas, Missouri and Nebraska. Points in Colorado, Tennessee and Mississippi are also served. In 1982, the Missouri Pacific Corporation and the UNION PACIFIC CORPORATION merged to form Pacific Rail Systems Inc, a holding and managing company for Missouri Pacific, Union Pacific and Western Pacific. While each of the three railroads maintains its separate identity, the Western Pacific is operated as a Union Pacific subsidiary. The traffic departments of all three railroads have been merged to provide a common operating and pricing policy. Pacific Rail Systems Inc operates as a wholly owned subsidiary of Union Pacific Corporation.

The earliest predecessor of the Missouri Pacific was the Pacific Railroad, which was chartered in 1851 to build westward from St Louis to the Pacific Coast. The Southwest Branch of the Pacific Railroad eventually became the St Louis and San Francisco (Frisco). By 1865 the Pacific Railroad had reached Kansas City, and in 1876 it was reorganized as the Missouri Pacific Railway. JAY GOULD obtained control of Missouri Pacific in 1879. He soon built an empire of western railroads which included the St Louis and Iron Mountain; International and Great Northern; MISSOURI, KANSAS AND TEXAS; Texas and Pacific; Wabash; Galveston, Houston, and Henderson; and Central Branch, Union Pacific, which later became Missouri Pacific's line extending westward from Atchison, Kansas. During Gould's reign, the Missouri Pacific was extended northward to Omaha and westward to Pueblo. Other roads in this group were also expanded.

Starting in 1884, a number of the Gould roads went into receivership. The Missouri Pacific emerged relatively unscathed from the financial chaos with the International and Great Northern and the Texas and Pacific added to it. The name Missouri Pacific Railroad was assumed in 1917, after a reorganization which included absorption of the bankrupt Iron Mountain Line. When Gulf Coast Lines was obtained in 1924, the name of the system was changed to Missouri Pacific Lines. Additional lines were absorbed in the 1960s and 1970s. An interest was acquired in the Chicago and Eastern Illinois in 1961. Full control and a merger followed in 1967 and 1976, respectively. The latter year also saw merger with the Texas and Pacific, and sale of part of the C&EI to the LOUISVILLE AND NASHVILLE. A half interest in the Chicago and Alton was bought in 1968. Several other small subsidiary lines were absorbed in 1977 when Missouri Pacific became a wholly owned subsidiary of the Missouri–Pacific Corporation.

Often called the 'North American rail link,' Missouri Pacific connects with almost all United States railroads and with the National Railways of Mexico. Mo-Pac is the largest carrier of chemicals in the United States. Other major commodities carried include automobiles and automobile parts, coal, foodstuffs and metal products.

Locomotives: 1600
Freight cars: 50,000
Miles operated: 1843
(as of January 1983)

Mitchell, Alexander (1832–1908). A machinist and locomotive builder, Mitchell was born in Nova Scotia. His first railroad experience was with the CAMDEN AND AMBOY RAILROAD as a machinist. From 1859 to 1861 he was assistant superintendent of the Trenton Locomotive Works, after which he went to the LEHIGH VALLEY RAILROAD, where he remained for the rest of his career. A 2-8-0 locomotive he designed and built in 1866 was the prototype of one of the most significant and successful classes of freight locomotives in North America. At about the same time, he assisted in the development of the first 2-10-0 built in the United States. Two of these engines were built by the Lancaster Locomotive Works. One, rebuilt as a 2-8-2 and called the *Bee*,

was the first engine of this wheel plan to be used in the United States.

Mohawk and Hudson Railroad. One of the earliest American railroads, the Mohawk and Hudson was chartered by the New York legislature in 1826. Its founder was George Featherstonaugh. A parent company of the NEW YORK CENTRAL RAILROAD, the line ran some 15 miles from Albany to Schenectady between the Hudson and Mohawk Rivers. The actual building of the line was supervised by John B Jervis. As was the case with most early American railroads, the Mohawk and Hudson was originally intended to be a horse-drawn line. However, the directors of the Hudson and Mohawk ruled quickly in favor of steam power, and its first locomotive, the DEWITT CLINTON, was ready in 1831. The *DeWitt Clinton*'s first run on the Hudson and Mohawk was made on 9 August 1831. Providing an important link between Schenectady and the Erie Canal, the Mohawk and Hudson prospered through the 1830s and early 1840s. By the late 1840s, the line began to have financial problems. Later called the Albany and Schenectady Railroad, it was incorporated into the New York Central in 1853.

Monongahela Railway. The Monongahela Railway is a coal-carrying railroad that operates between Brownsville and Blacksville, Pennsylvania, on one branch and between Brownsville and Keyport, West Virginia, on another. Incorporated in 1915, with the merger of the Monongahela Railroad and the Buckhannon and Northern Railroad, it expanded in the 1920s and 1930s through the absorption of several smaller lines. It is jointly owned by the BALTIMORE AND OHIO component of the CHESSIE SYSTEM, CONRAIL and the PITTSBURGH AND LAKE ERIE.

Locomotives: 11
Freight cars: 10
Miles operated: 136
(as of January 1984)

The Monster. Designed by ISAAC DRIPPS and ROBERT STEVENS, the *Monster* was built by the CAMDEN AND AMBOY RAILROAD in the early 1830s; the exact date is not known. The appropriately named 30-ton *Monster* may have been the first eight-wheel connected engine in the United States. Although the wheel arrangement was

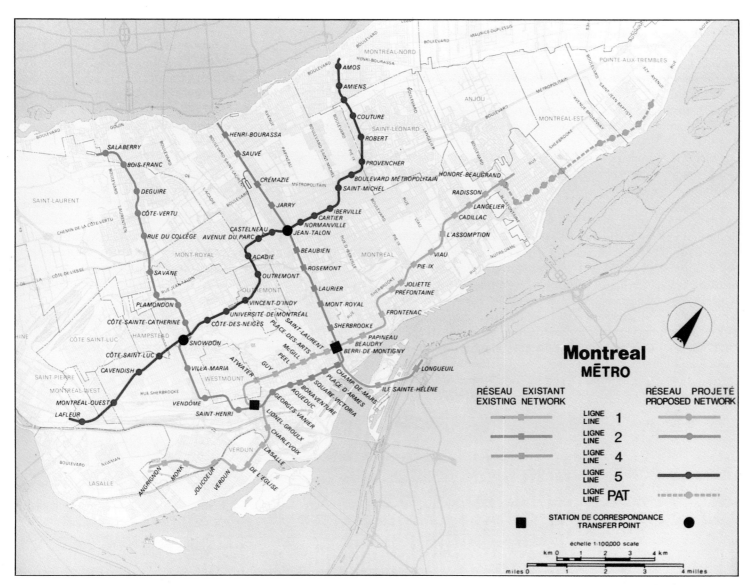

Right: A train in a Montréal Transit station.

0-8-0, it was not a true 0-8-0 since spur gears rather than connecting rods were used to couple the second and third driving axles. Built without a frame, the axle-box box pedestals were riveted directly to the boiler. The 18-inch diameter cylinders were mounted at about a 30-degree angle. The 30-inch stroke pistons operated forward, and were connected to oscillating beams called 'horse's necks,' which moved in a pendulum-like manner. The 'horse's necks' were connected by main rods to the third pair of driving wheels. The overall effect was one of a very busy, overly complicated mechanism. Four locomotives based on the *Monster* design were built in 1852 and 1854 by the Trenton Locomotive Works, of which Dripps was a partner, for the Camden and Amboy Railroad.

Montréal Urban Community Transportation Commission (Commission de Transport de la Communauté Urbaine de Montréal). The Montreal Urban Community Transportation Commission contracts the operation of commuter trains to and from Montreal. It also operates the rapid transit and bus systems in the city. The management and funding of CANADIAN NATIONAL's service, including electrified lines between Montréal and Deux Montagnes, was assumed on 1 July 1982. CANADIAN PACIFIC commuter routes to Vandreuil and Rigaud were assumed on 1 November 1982. Regarded as one of the quietest transit systems in North America, the track has security rails flanked by concrete running tracks and lateral guide bars. A new cross-city line with 12 stations is expected to be completed in 1987. A 2-mile extension from Plamondon to Du College opened in January 1984.

Electrification system: 750V DC, third rail
Gauge: 4ft 8in
No. of stations: 54
Rolling stock: 759
Route mileage: 324
Locomotives: 16
Passenger cars: 70

National Railroad Passenger Corporation (Amtrak). Amtrak was created by the Rail Passenger Service Act, passed by Congress in 1970. According to the provisions of the act, railroads could discontinue their passenger service, turning over passenger equipment to Amtrak. Most American railroads, suffering disastrous losses from passenger service, quickly agreed. Notable exceptions were the DENVER AND RIO GRANDE WESTERN, Rock Island and Southern Railway. Beginning in 1971, Amtrak began operating the first nationwide passenger service in the United States. The D&RGW discontinued its last passenger service in 1983, agreeing to an assumption of passenger service on its Denver–Salt Lake City route by Amtrak. The Rock Island went bankrupt in 1980 and the Southern turned over operation of its last passenger train to Amtrak in that same year.

The only track owned and operated by Amtrak is the Boston–New York–Washington Northeast Corridor. All other track, with the exception of a former New York Central section between Porter, Indiana, and Kalamazoo, Michigan, is owned and operated by freight-hauling railroads, a circumstance which has limited Amtrak's efforts to increase the speed and frequency of service on its routes other than the Northeast Corridor.

The Northeast Corridor Improvement Project (NECIP), started in the 1970s, was nearing completion in

Below: A well-lit and spacious Montreal Transit station, one of 54 in the system.

Above: Amtrak's *Empire Builder* makes the run from Chicago to Seattle with bilevel Superliner cars, the first train to be equipped with them. Amtrak reinstated the passenger service through the northwest when it took over Burlington Northern's routes. *Below:* Amtrak's *San Diegan* heads south from Los Angeles, hugging the Pacific coast.

Above and top: Amtrak has been replacing and updating old equipment. The Superliner bilevel passenger cars shown here are used on long-distance runs west of Chicago. The popular *California Zephyr* (*right*) service was discontinued in 1970.

1984. With the track improvement, the Federal Railroad Administration authorized a top speed of 120 miles per hour on a few sections between New York and Washington, and a 100 miles per hour maximum is possible north of New York. Three hour and fifty-minute METROLINER service between Boston and New York was made possible by the track improvement. These trains are hauled by diesel locomotive from Boston to New Haven, and by electric locomotive from New Haven to New York. The original Metroliner electric multiple-unit trainsets (emus) used on the New York–Washington route have been transferred to the Harrisburg–Philadelphia–New York service.

Commuter services are operated on the Northeast Corridor by several state and regional agencies under the

Above and top: Amtrak's Superliner diners are on the upper level of the bilevel cars. *Right:* The *Empire State Express* turboliner on its daily run between New York City and Niagara Falls.

provisions of Clause 403(b) of the act that created Amtrak:

* MARYLAND DEPARTMENT OF TRANSPORTATION
   Baltimore–Washington
* MASSACHUSETTS BAY TRANSIT AUTHORITY (MBTA)
   Boston to Attleboro
* Metropolitan Transportation Authority
   service to Long Island on the Long Island Railroad from Pennsylvania Station, New York City
* Metropolitan Transportation Authority and Connecticut Department of Transportation
   portion of METRO NORTH commuter service from New Rochelle, New York, to Grand Central Terminal, New York City
* New Jersey Department of Transportation
   commuter service between

Amtrak's *Coast Starlight* fast service between
San Francisco and Los Angeles was once the
Daylight when it was run by Southern Pacific.

Amtrak's *Empire* (*top*) service runs along the Hudson River in New York. *Above:* Amtrak assumed operation of the Metroliner service in 1971 and it now serves the Harrisburg-Philadelphia-New York route. *Right:* Amtrak's Heritage Fleet cafeteria/lounge car.

Trenton, New Jersey, and Pennsylvania Station
* SOUTHEASTERN PENNSYLVANIA TRANSPORTATION AUTHORITY (SEPTA)
commuter service between Wilmington and Philadelphia; commuter service from Trenton to Philadelphia (in conjunction with the New Jersey Department of Transportation)

Amtrak also owns and operates the Washington Terminal Company, with facilities adjacent to Washington's Union Station. Commuter cars from other railroads are serviced and overhauled at Amtrak's Beech Grove facility near Indianapolis.

The locomotives and cars inherited from the original participating railroads are referred to as the 'Heritage Fleet.' New locomotives and rolling stock, including diners and sleepers, have been added over the years, and many of the older pieces of equipment have been rebuilt. Bilevel 'Superliner' cars are used on many of Amtrak's long-distance runs west of Chicago. Gas-turbine trainsets, imported from France and manufac-

Above: The Northeast Corridor is the only track owned and operated by Amtrak. *Above right:* The AEM-7 locomotives replaced Metroliners on the New York-Washington route. *Below and right:* Amtrak's *San Francisco Zephyr.*

tured under license in the United States by Rohr, are used on service between New York and Buffalo.

By the end of 1982, Amtrak was operating 220 diesel locomotives, 62 electric locomotives, 14 gas-turbine cars, 109 emu cars, 14 diesel railcars, and 1390 cars on some 23,400 miles of track.

New Jersey Transit. New Jersey Transit operates commuter rail services to New York City from points in New Jersey. Service is also provided from Spring Valley and Port Jervis, New York. The Port Jervis service is operated for the Metropolitan Transportation Authority of New York. In 1983, New Jersey Transit took over commuter service formerly operated by CONRAIL. State involvement in New Jersey commuter rail service began in 1968 when the New Jersey Department of Transportation bought some

diesel locomotives for the Central of New Jersey. Two years later, diesel locomotives were bought for the ERIE LACKAWANNA, and used locomotives and coaches were bought for the New York and Long Beach Railroad, which supplied service for points along the shore from Bay Head northward. When CONRAIL was formed, it took over New Jersey commuter services, which were run on track formerly owned by the Erie Lackawanna, PENNSYLVANIA, Central of New Jersey and the New York and Long Branch. New Jersey Transit, formed in April 1982 to operate the service, took over from Conrail on 1 January 1983. New Jersey Transit owns all the track except the line between Trenton and New York, which is former Pennsylvania Railroad track now owned by AMTRAK.

Locomotives: 110
Passenger cars: 490
Self-propelled passenger cars:
   diesel: 22
   electric: 13

New Orleans, Opelousas and Great Western. See Southern Pacific Company.

New Orleans Public Belt Railroad. The New Orleans Public Belt Railroad provides switching service in the New Orleans port area. Opened by the city of New Orleans in 1900, the line is built along the Mississippi River and the Industrial Canal. The Huey P Long Bridge, the longest railroad bridge in North America, is owned by the New Orleans Public Belt. It is almost 4.5 miles long, including the approach trestles. The main span over the Mississippi River is 3524ft long.

Locomotives: 10
Freight cars: 1250
Miles operated: 47
(as of January 1984)

New York Central. The earliest predecessor of the New York Central was the MOHAWK AND HUDSON, one of the first railroads in the United States. The New York Central was formed in 1853 when the Mohawk and Hudson Railroad and nine other small New York railroads merged. NYC was closely associated with the Vanderbilt family. CORNELIUS VANDERBILT, the family patriarch, began to buy into the road in the 1860s. In 1869, Vanderbilt's Hudson River Railroad was merged with the New York Central to form the New York Central and Hudson Railroad. The name New York Central was reassumed in 1914.

Through acquisitions and control of other railroads, the New York Central became one of the most extensive rail empires in the United States. Its Grand Central Terminal in New York City was widely regarded as the greatest in the world. The New York Central and its subsidiaries extended as far north as Montréal, east to Boston, west to St Louis and south to Charleston, West Virginia. Included among its larger subsidiaries were the Boston and Albany; Michigan Central; PITTSBURGH AND LAKE ERIE and the Cleveland, Cincinnati and St Louis (Big Four). New York Central's New York–Buffalo main line followed the Hudson and Mohawk river valleys. Hence the road advertised that it followed the 'Water Level Route.' The *Twentieth Century Limited* New York–Chicago train was widely regarded as the ultimate in passenger travel in the United States. After World War II the road declined, and it merged with the PENNSYLVANIA RAILROAD to form Penn Central in 1968. Penn Central declared bankruptcy in 1970 and was absorbed by CONRAIL in 1976.

New York City Transit Authority. One of the oldest rapid transit systems in the world, the NYCTA has had

serious equipment failure problems in recent years. In an attempt to overcome these problems, the NYCTA was authorized to undertake the most massive program of car replacement in the history of US transit. Orders included 1150 cars for the Interborough Rapid Transit Line (IRT) and 225 for the Independent/Brooklyn Manhattan Transit (IND/BMT) Line. IRT cars were ordered from Nissho–Iwai and Kawasaki of Japan and Bombradier of Canada.

Westinghouse–Amrail received the contract for the IND/BMT cars. Starting in 1981, a five-year plan of improvements was initiated for the completion of East 63rd Street line extension to 21st Street in Queens and several other improvements, including track, station and signaling renovations.

Electrification system: 600V DC, third rail
Gauge: 4ft 8in
No. of stations: 458
Rolling stock: 6267
Route mileage: 232

New York, New Haven and Hartford Railroad. At its peak, the New York, New Haven and Hartford provided service between New York and Boston, covering the states of Connecticut, Massachusetts, Rhode Island and eastern New York with an extensive rail network. The NYNH&H was incorporated in 1872 with the merger of the New York and New Haven Railroad and the Hartford and New Haven Railroad. Expansion through acquisition and leasing of other lines in southern New England followed rapidly. One of the first major electrification projects in the United States was carried out in 1907, when the NYNH&H electrified the four-track main line between New York and New Haven. The line declared bankruptcy in 1936, reorganized in 1947, but went into bankruptcy again in 1961. Poor management and competition from the Connecticut Turnpike, which runs parallel to the New York–New Haven main line, were contributing factors in the road's demise. The New Haven was absorbed into Penn Central shortly after the formation of that company by the merger of the NEW YORK CENTRAL and the PENNSYLVANIA.

Niagara Frontier Transportation Authority, (Buffalo). Work on the Buffalo system started in 1979. In 1981 construction was started on eight underground stations. Most of the 12-mile surface section is planned for a transit pedestrian mall free of vehicles. This section features a free fare.

Electrification system: 650V DC, overhead wire
Gauge: 4ft 8in
No. of stations: 8 planned
Rolling stock: 27
Route mileage: 6.4

Norfolk and Portsmouth Belt Line Railroad. The Norfolk and Portsmouth Belt Line Railroad provides switching service in the Norolk, Virginia area. It was incorporated as the Southeastern and Atlantic Railroad in 1896, and received its present name two years later. It is owned jointly by the CHESSIE SYSTEM, NORFOLK AND WESTERN, SEABOARD SYSTEM and SOUTHERN RAILWAY.

Locomotives: 15
Miles operated: 30

Norfolk Southern Corporation. The Norfolk Southern Corporation is a holding company formed in 1982 to coordinate the merger and operations

One of New Haven Railroad's streamlined 4-6-4 Hudson locomotives. New York Central ran several types of Hudsons in the 1930s on its New York-Chicago express service.

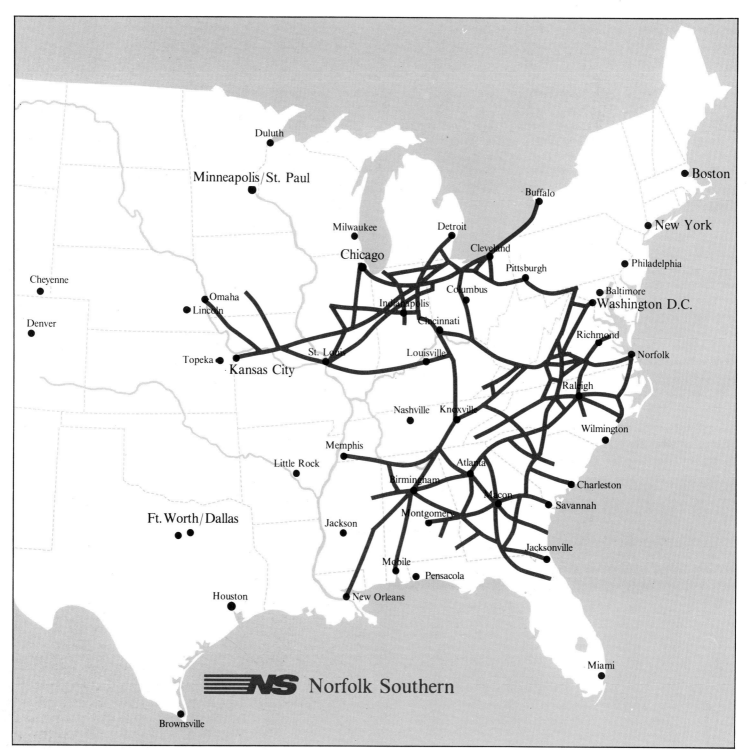

NS Norfolk Southern

of the NORFOLK AND WESTERN and SOUTHERN RAILWAYS. Although each line continues to operate independently, several terminal operations have been consolidated. The combined Norfolk and Western and Southern Railway System provide coordinated rail service from northern Florida and the Gulf Coast northward to the industrial belt between Buffalo and Chicago, and westward to Kansas City, Omaha, St Louis and Memphis. In 1982 the Norfolk Southern Corporation was the most profitable railroad operation in the United States, earning more than $411 million dollars, a figure which represents about a third of the total income of all Class I railroads.

Norfolk and Western Railway. Operating in 14 states and one Canadian province, the Norfolk and Western operates between Norfolk, Virginia, and Buffalo, New York, in the east, and westward to Kansas City, St Louis and Omaha. The industrial areas of Pittsburgh, Cleveland, Cincinnati, Indianapolis and Detroit are served, as well as the coal fields of West Virginia, eastern Kentucky and southern Ohio. The earliest predecessor of the Norfolk and Western was the Norfolk and Petersburg, which

was chartered in 1850 to build a line between these two Virginia cities. Petersburg was reached in 1858; part of the track crossing the Dismal Swamp was laid on a mat of trees and logs. The Norfolk and Petersburg consolidated with the Southside Railroad (Petersburg to Lynchburg) and the Virginia and Tennessee (Lynchburg to Bristol, Tennessee) in 1867; the three roads merged completely in 1870, to become the Atlantic, Mississippi, and Ohio. In 1881, the AM&O was sold to the Clark banking interests of Philadelphia, who renamed it Norfolk and Western. Expansion in the 1890s and 1900s exten-

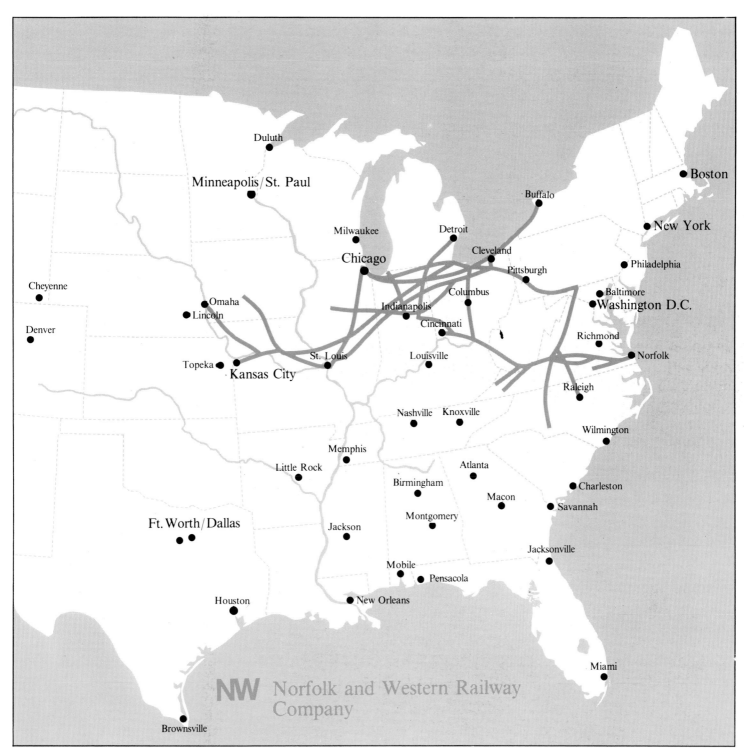

Duluth

Minneapolis/St. Paul

Buffalo

Boston

Milwaukee Detroit

New York

Cleveland

Chicago Pittsburgh

Philadelphia

Cheyenne

Columbus

Baltimore

Omaha Indianapolis Washington D.C.

Lincoln Cincinnati

Denver Richmond

St. Louis Louisville Norfolk

Topeka

Kansas City Raleigh

Nashville Knoxville

Wilmington

Memphis

Atlanta

Little Rock

Birmingham Charleston

Macon Savannah

Montgomery

Ft. Worth/Dallas Jackson Jacksonville

Mobile

Pensacola

Houston New Orleans

NW Norfolk and Western Railway
Company

Miami

Brownsville

ded the N&W to Columbus and Cincinnati, Ohio, and to North Carolina. A coal-hauling railroad, the N&W resisted dieselization until the 1960s. The Norfolk and Western merged with the Virginian Railway in 1959, in the first of a series of mergers and acquisitions that resulted in the Norfolk and Western of today. The Atlantic and Danville was bought in 1962. The big merger year was 1964 when the Wabash; the Akron, Canton, and Youngstown; and the New York, Chicago and St Louis (Nickel Plate Road) were absorbed. The Wheeling and Lake Erie had previously been merged with the Nickel Plate. In 1982

the Norfolk Southern Corporation was formed as a holding company to effect the merger of the Norfolk and Western with the SOUTHERN RAILWAY SYSTEM. Although each railroad remains autonomous, many operations are coordinated. Approval to purchase CONRAIL was granted in 1984.

The Norfolk and Western remains primarily a coal carrier. Other major commodities carried include agricultural products. The road also operates commuter service between Chicago and Highland Park, Illinois, for the Regional Transportation Authority.
Locomotives: 1320
Freight cars: 85,900

Passenger cars: 23
Miles operated: 8000

North Louisiana and Gulf Railroad. The North Louisiana and Gulf Railroad operates between Gibsland and Hodge, Louisiana. A sister line, the Central Louisiana and Gulf, operates between Hodge and Alexandria, Louisiana. Both are owned by the Continental Group, the parent company of the Continental Can Company, and serve to carry pulpwood, wood chips and finished paper products to and from a Continental Can factory in Hodge. The North Louisiana and Gulf was incorporated in 1906. The

A 4-6-4 shiny new Hudson-type New Haven locomotive had a greater capacity than the 4-4-0s.

North Louisiana and Gulf was formed in 1980 when Continental Group bought the Rock Island's former trackage between Hodge and Winnfield, and Winnfield to Alexandria. The Rock Island had obtained trackage rights on the latter route from the Louisiana and Arkansas, a subsidiary of the KANSAS CITY SOUTHERN RAILWAY.
Locomotives: 5
Freight cars: 990
Miles operated: 40
(as of June 1983)

Northern Pacific Railway. See Burlington Northern.

The Octoraro Railway. The Octoraro Railway operates in the mushroom-growing country of southeastern Pennsylvania and the northern tip of Delaware. The Maryland town of Colora is also served. Much of the trackage of the Octoraro Railway is that of the Penn Central's Octoraro branch which ran from Media, southwest of Philadelphia, to Colorado, Maryland. In 1971, a washout stopped service on this line. The line was purchased by the SOUTHEASTERN PENNSYLVANIA TRANSPORTATION AUTHORITY for possible use as a commuter line. However, Rail Development Incorporated leased the line for a freight operation. Interchange with other railroads, nonexistent since the washout, was obtained through building a connection to the Wilmington and Northern branch of the Reading Railroad at Chadds Ford Junction. The connection was completed in 1977. The Octoraro is a somewhat X-shaped system, with the arms of the 'X' crossing at Chadds Ford Junction. The line·runs between Wawa and Colora, Pennsylvania, on one arm, and between Modena, Pennsylvania, and Wilmington, Delaware, on the other. In addition, there is service from Wilmington to Hockessin, Delaware, on former BALTIMORE AND OHIO track. This section is owned by Historic Red Valley Inc, which operates excursion trains as the Wilmington and Western Railroad.
Locomotives: 4
Freight cars: 142
Miles operated: 68
(as of January 1984)

Old Ironsides. The first locomotive sold by MATTHIAS BALDWIN, *Old Ironsides*, was built for the Philadelphia, Germantown and Norristown Rail-

Norfolk & Western
Virginian
Wabash
Akron, Canton & Youngstown
New York, Chicago & St. Louis (Nickel Plate)
Wheeling & Lake Erie
Southern
Central of Georgia
Cincinatti, New Orleans & Texas
Alabama Great Southern

Norfolk Southern

Old Ironsides, the first railroad train in Pennsylvania and the first built in the United States, is shown (*right*) leaving the old depot at Ninth and Green streets, Philadelphia, Pennsylvania. Regular passenger service began on 26 November 1832, when the locomotive with six cars filled with passengers left Philadelphia on its way to Germantown. *Old Ironsides* was the first locomotive to be built by Matthias Baldwin.

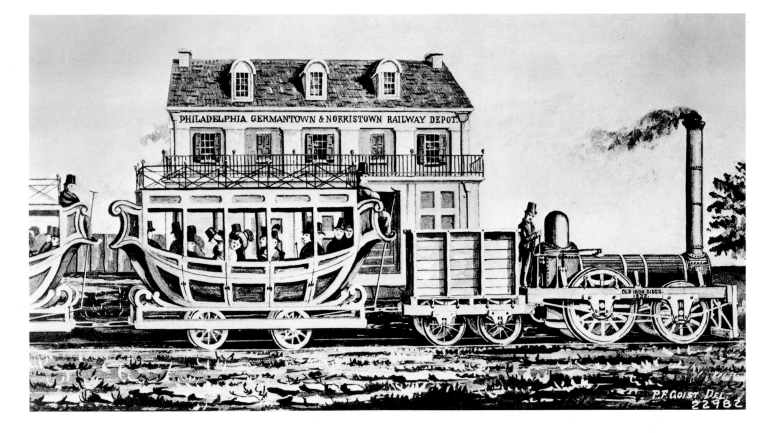

The range of Ontario Northland working stock
includes diesel locomotive No. 1517 road unit for
main-line passenger service, No. 1605 for
hauling freight, and a freshly painted caboose.

road in 1832. The influence of the *John Bull* on Baldwin was quite obvious in the design of *Old Ironsides*. Like the *John Bull*, *Old Ironsides* was an 0-4-0 locomotive with a horizontal boiler. Both the *John Bull* and *Old Ironsides* were similar to the Planet class of locomotive then quite popular in Britain. The 5.5-ton *Old Ironsides* had 9.5-inch-diameter cylinders with an 18-inch stroke. The drivers were 54 inches in diameter while the front wheels were 45 inches in diameter.

Baldwin experienced great difficulty in constructing the engine because of a dearth of skilled mechanics and proper tools and machinery. Although the trials were successful, some minor problems were noted. The minor imperfections caused a delay in payment to Baldwin, and a reduction in price from the originally agreed $4000 to $3500. The locomotive was put into regular service on 26 November 1832, three days after its trial.

Ontario Northland Railway. The Ontario Northland Railway operates between North Bay and Moosonee, Ontario, on James Bay. There are branches to Elk Lake, Timmins, Iroquois Falls and from Swastika to Noranda, Québec. The Ontario and Northland began in 1902 with an act of the Ontario Legislative Assembly authorizing the construction of the Temiskaming and Northern Ontario Railway. The legislative action was in response to the need for transportation in the rapidly growing northeastern

Ontario Northland diesel road locomotive No. 1735 was built with a lowered nose for good visibility. The narrow nose design of freight locomotives No. 1802, No. 1306 and No. 1400 allows for improved visibility during operations. The boxcar is one of a large stock of freight cars on this line.

part of the province and connection with Toronto. Construction started at North Bay, which was on the Canadian Pacific line to Montréal and the terminus of a Grand Trunk line from Toronto. By 1909 the railroad had reached Cochrane, some 225 miles north of North Bay. Traffic was dramatically increased after the discovery of silver near Cobalt, and gold in the Timmins area and in the Noranda region of Québec. The gold discoveries encouraged the building of branch lines to these areas. The line was completed to Moosonee in 1931. The present name was assumed in 1946. Minerals and forest products make up more than 84 percent of Ontario Northern's carload freight movements. Newsprint is a major source of freight revenue. Passenger operations include the Northlander service between Toronto and Timmins, and service to Moosonee. Trainsets were leased in 1977 from Trans-Europe Express for use on the Northlander route. In 1969, the power cars of these four-car sets were replaced with FP7 diesel locomotives. Ontario Northland is operated by the Ontario Northland Transportation Commis-

An Oregon Pacific and Eastern Railway freight
locomotive on tracks which parallel Interstate
Highway 5 near the Oregon town of Eugene.

sion, which also has interests in trucking, shipping, aviation, buses and telecommunications.

Locomotives: 39
Freight cars: 930
Passenger cars: 45
Miles operated: 574
(as of September 1984)

Oregon, California and Eastern Railway. The Oregon, California and Eastern Railway is a log-carrying railroad operating between Klamath Falls and Bly, Oregon. Construction was started in 1917 by Robert E Strahorn with the aid of a Klamath Falls municipal bond issue. The present terminus of Bly was reached in 1928. SOUTHERN PACIFIC purchased the line in 1927, and sold a half interest to GREAT NORTHERN a year later. The two roads worked out an arrangement where each operated the road alternately for five-year periods. In 1975, it was purchased by the Weyerhauser Company.

Locomotives: 11
Freight cars: 150
Miles operated: 66
(as of January 1984)

Oregon Northwestern Railroad. The Oregon and Northwestern Railroad operates between Seneca and Hines, Oregon, carrying lumber to connect with a branch of the UNION PACIFIC at Burns. Incorporated in 1904, the road is owned by the Edward Hines Lumber Co.

Locomotives: 4
Freight cars: 440
Miles operated: 51
(as of January 1984)

Palmer, William Jackson (18 September 1836–13 March 1909). An

American railroad entrepeneur, Palmer was born in Kent County, Delaware, the son of John and Matilda Jackson Palmer. Educated in Quaker and public schools in Philadelphia, he started in railroading at age 18 when he went to work for an engineering firm surveying for the Hempfield Railroad in Washington County, Pennsylvania. Palmer studied railroad and mine management in England. In 1857 he became private secretary to John Edgar Thomson, president of the PENNSYLVANIA RAILROAD. Palmer served with distinction in the Civil War, advancing from captain to brigadier general. After the war he was put in charge of construction on the Kansas Pacific Railroad. Under his management, the last 150 miles of this road were completed in 150 days. He was also in charge of construction for the Denver Pacific Railroad from Denver to Cheyenne, Wyoming. While surveying the route for this road, he

decided to build a railroad from Colorado to the Mexican border. He organized the DENVER AND RIO GRANDE Company in 1870 with a capitalization of $10 million. Building with no federal assistance, construction of the narrow gauge Denver and Rio Grande proceeded rapidly. Battles, legal and physical, were fought with the SANTA FE for the control of important mountain passes, including the Royal Gorge of the Arkansas River, which the Denver and Rio Grande won. He left the presidency of the Denver and Rio Grande to become president of the Rio Grande Western which he had organized previously. In 1901, the Rio Grande Western was sold to the Denver and Rio Grande.

Passenger trains—The Great Ones. The success of Pullman cars convinced railroad management that money could be made by offering luxury and the aura of prestige to

those who could afford to pay for it. By the turn of the century many railroads were actively competing to offer the finest in luxury train travel, and railway sales managers soon discovered that giving a train a name made it something much more special than just a way to get from one place to another. One of the first railroad officials to come to this conclusion was George Daniels, the NEW YORK CENTRAL's passenger agent in the 1890s and early twentieth century. In 1891, Daniels started a fast New York–Buffalo service called the *Empire State Express*, which set a new speed record between these points. He followed with the *Exposition Flyer*, a New York–Chicago train assembled for the Chicago World's Fair of 1893. On its initial run, pulled by locomotive 999, it reportedly set a new record of 112.5 mph. Daniels continued this service, renaming it the *Twentieth Century Limited* to evoke the idea of

Union Pacific's *City of Portland* articulated streamliner went into service in the late 1930s.

SP's *Coast Daylight*, one of the early luxury streamliners, served San Francisco and Los Angeles.

continued progress for the NEW YORK CENTRAL in the new century.

The *Twentieth Century Limited* became the most famous of all the name trains. Its name became synonymous with luxury and prestige. The New York Central's claim that the *Century* was a 'national institution' was never seriously disputed. At its peak, the *Century* was an all-Pullman train featuring dining cars, barber and beautician service, observation and lounge cars, a library, stenographic and telephone service. Passengers walked on a red carpet rolled out on the platform to board the train. In 1958, coaches were added to the *Century*, tarnishing its image of luxury. The last *Century* was run in 1967.

The PENNSYLVANIA RAILROAD ran a rival New York–Chicago service called the *Broadway Limited*, which offered comparable luxury and speed.

The SANTA FE's *Super Chief* was as well known as the *Century*. This Chicago–Los Angeles service was the first diesel-hauled, all-Pullman

streamliner in the United States. Introduced in 1937, it made the Chicago–Los Angeles run in 39.5 hours, some 14 hours better than its predecessor, the *Chief*. Known for the excellence of its food and the luxury of its facilities, the *Super Chief* attracted the rich and the famous, including many film stars. Economies came in the 1960s with the combining of the *Super Chief* with the all-coach *El Capitan*. AMTRAK took over Santa Fe's passenger service in 1970, changing the service to the *South–West Limited* in 1973.

The various Zephyrs started in 1935 with the *Pioneer Zephyr*, a three-car articulated train which ran at an average speed of 77.5 mph on its inaugural Denver–Chicago run. The *California Zephyr* was the first to be equipped with Vistadome cars. Routes were arranged to go through the most scenic areas. The *California Zephyr* was discontinued in 1970.

UNION PACIFIC started its own group of articulated train sets with the *City of Salina* in 1935. A similar train called the *City of Portland* quickly followed. The *City of Los Angeles* was an 11-car articulated train jointly owned with the Chicago and North Western Railway.

Southern Pacific ran a popular 'Daylight' service between San Fran-cisco and Los Angeles. Orange and silver streamlined cars were built for these trains, which featured fast time and superb service. SP's Los Angeles–New Orleans *Sunset Limited*, which was started in 1894, was an exceptionally luxurious train. A service called the *Sunset Limited* is still run by AMTRAK. This train includes a section from Chicago which connects with the New Orleans section at San Antonio.

In Canada, the CANADIAN PACIFIC and CANADIAN NATIONAL ran two rival transcontinental services, the *Canadian* and the *Super Continental*, respectively. The *Canadian* supplanted a previous train called the *Dominion*. Both featured superb service and spectacular scenery. Since VIA RAIL has taken over passenger service in Canada, the *Super Continental* has been discontinued.

Among the more famous coast-to-coast trains that followed a northerly route in the United States were the *Empire Builder* (GREAT NORTHERN), *North Coast Limited* (NORTHERN PACIFIC) and the *Olympian Hiawatha* (CHICAGO, MILWAUKEE, ST PAUL AND PACIFIC). When it started in 1900, the *North Coast Limited* ran from St Paul to Seattle. In 1911, its eastern terminus was changed to Chicago. The *Empire Builder*, in direct competition with the *North Coast Limited*, was started in 1929 by JAMES J HILL, who was often referred to by that title. The *Olympian Hiawatha* was the best-known of a number of Hiawathas. It started as a streamlined service in 1947.

On the East Coast, the *Orange Blossom Special* offered luxury for Florida-bound passengers, and the *Merchant's Limited* provided parlor car comfort for businessmen making a run between Boston and New York.

Amtrak runs more than 50 name trains. However, with the uncertainty of Amtrak's future, the number and quality of these trains changes constantly. Some of these names are old, familiar ones such as the *Broadway Limited, Silver Meteor, Crescent* and the *Sunset Limited*, while others such as *The Potomac, Eagle* and the *Baystate* are the products of Amtrak publicists.

Penn Central. See Conrail.

The Pennsylvania. This engine, built by JAMES MILLHOLLAND in 1863 for the Philadelphia and Reading Railroad, was the first North American engine with six pairs of driving wheels. A powerful machine, it was used

Above: Amtrak's Superliner-equipped *Empire Builder* service used to belong to Great Northern. *Right:* Santa Fe's *Super Chief* winds across New Mexico.

mostly for pusher service in hauling coal trains over the hilly country between the Delaware and Schuylkill Rivers. Similar in appearance to the CAMEL LOCOMOTIVE, the original design did not specify a tender. Water and fuel were carried on the engine. The 50-ton locomotive had 20-inch-diameter cylinders with a 26-inch stroke and 43-inch-diameter driving wheels.

Pennsylvania Railroad. At its peak, the Pennsylvania Railroad was the largest railroad in the United States in terms of revenue and tonnage. Its management felt more than justified in calling the Pennsylvania 'The Standard Railroad of the World.' Incorporated in 1846, it opened between Harrisburg and Altoona in 1850. Expansion followed rapidly through building and acquisition of other roads. Among the acquired railroads were some of the oldest in the nation and their descendents, including the CAMDEN AND AMBOY, the Philadelphia and Columbia, and the Philadelphia, Germantown and Norristown. The Pennsylvania eventually expanded

The 4-4-0 engine was the widely used, American type, common throughout the nineteenth century. *Above:* A Pennsylvania Railroad locomotive, suitably adorned, was used for Abraham Lincoln's funeral in 1865. When the Pullman sleeping cars, on the tracks behind the locomotive, were included in the funeral train, the track and platforms had to be reconstructed to accommodate them. At this time, the Pennsylvania had been operating for 15 years and was on its way to becoming the largest railroad in the United States. *Right:* A group of the Pennsylvania's large fleet of imposing steam locomotives line up amid clouds of billowing steam. *Below:* The first high-speed electric traction to be used on any steam railroad in the United States was on the Burlington and Mount Holly branch line of the Amboy Division of the Pennsylvania Railroad, photographed in 1895. This photograph shows the first experimental trip made by motor coach No. 1 and trailer passenger coach No. 281 on 3 June 1895. Regular service was inaugurated on 22 July 1895.

A Pennsylvania Railroad 4-6-2 Pacific (*above*) and 2-8-2 Mikado (*below*), which both became the standard freight locomotives in the United States.

westward to Chicago and St Louis, northwestward to New York and southward to Washington DC. Operating in much the same area as the NEW YORK CENTRAL, the Pennsylvania competed vigorously. It built tunnels under the Hudson River which gained access to New York, where it erected Pennsylvania Station, a response to NYC's Grand Central. The Pennsylvania offered its own crack New York–Chicago train, the *Broadway Limited* to compete with NYC's *Twentieth Century Limited*. The Hell Gate bridge enabled the Pennsylvania to provide through service from the South to Boston. One of the best known engineering projects undertaken on the Pennsylvania was the Horseshoe Curve near Altoona, Pennsylvania. In the 1920s and 1930s, the main lines between Washington DC and New York, and Philadelphia and Harrisburg were electrified. Among the

Above: A shark-nosed 'A' unit locomotive under construction, in the process of being engined.
Above right and right: Two Pennsylvania Railroad electric GG1 locomotives, designed for the main lines, first went into service in 1934.

railroads controlled by the Pennsylvania were the NORFOLK AND WESTERN, the Wabash; the Long Island; the Detroit, Toledo and Ironton; and the TOLEDO, PEORIA AND WESTERN, which was owned jointly with the SANTA FE. Pennsylvania merged with New York Central in 1968 to form PENN CENTRAL, which went into bankruptcy in 1970.

Perkins, Charles Elliot (24 November 1840–8 November 1907). A railroad builder and executive, Perkins was born in Cinncinati, Ohio, of parents who were related to the great Forbes family of Boston. Perkins was taken from his Ohio public school to the famous Milton (Massachusetts) Academy to complete his education,

The Baldwin Locomotive Works supplied the Pennsylvania Railroad with 50 of these massive Class T-1 4-4-4-4 engines. Duplex engines such as these incorporated a pair of two-cylinder steam engines in one nonarticulated frame and were put into use in the 1930s. They were capable of reaching high speeds and carrying heavy loads, but consumed large amounts of fuel. By the beginning of the 1950s they were being replaced with diesels.

and was subsequently encouraged by one of his Forbes cousins to enter railroading. His first position was as clerk for the Burlington and Missouri River Railroad, a line in Iowa that was slated to join the CHICAGO, BURLINGTON AND QUINCY to give access from Chicago to Omaha. Perkins' rise through the managerial ranks to general superintendent was to prove a valuable training-ground for future responsibility as the westward push of railroads made opportunities available.

When the Burlington and Missouri was charted in Nebraska to complete the Omaha connection, Perkins was in a position of great responsibility. He used this to complete construction and eventually to run the operation of the entire system as president of the Chicago, Burlington and Quincy with efficiency and great financial acumen. He saw the agricultural and marketing needs of the area as a vital link to the nation's economy and growth. Of his railroad, which had achieved intercontinental status when it formed a junction with the UNION PACIFIC in 1873, it was described as, '... the Broadway of this continent ... the chief commercial thoroughfare between Chicago and San Francisco.'

Under Perkins' leadership, the road acquired lines in Wyoming, the Big Horn Southern and the Chicago, Burlington and Northern Railroad. This combined strength gave the Chicago, Burlington and Quincy almost 8000 miles of track.

Even after his retirement from the presidency, Perkins worked as a director, mostly interested in the railroad's finances. Unlike the 'robber barons,' his interest in railroading was apparently concentrated only with the economically sound development of transportation in America.

Pittsburgh and Lake Erie Railroad.

The Pittsburgh and Lake Erie Railroad operates between Ashtabula, Ohio, on Lake Erie and Brownsville Junction and Connellsville south of Pittsburgh. The raw materials for making steel—iron ore, coal, coke and limestone—are carried to Pittsburgh-area steel mills, and steel products are carried away. The line was chartered in 1875 under its present name. In 1879 it was open for business between Youngstown, Ohio, and Pittsburgh. CORNELIUS VANDERBILT of the NEW YORK CENTRAL subscribed to Pitts-

burgh and Lake Erie stock from the outset to compete with the PENNSYLVANIA RAILROAD in this rich coal and steel area. The New York Central achieved outright control of the Pittsburgh and Lake Erie in 1889. The two railroads jointly owned the Pittsburgh, McKeesport and Youghiogheny, a line incorporated in 1881 to operate from Pittsburgh southward through McKeesport. Pittsburgh and Lake Erie bought NEW YORK CENTRAL's half share in 1956, and it was soon absorbed into the Pittsburgh and Lake Erie. When PENN CENTRAL went bankrupt in 1970, the Pittsburgh and Lake Erie chose to remain independent rather than become part of CONRAIL, and largely due to lobbying efforts on the part of Pittsburgh and Lake Erie management, the Regional Rail Reorganization Act of 1973 was amended to allow solvent subsidiaries of Penn Central to stay out of Conrail. The independence of the line was effected when Penn Central sold it to an entity called the Pittsburgh and Lake Erie Company. Pittsburgh and Lake Erie has a number of subsidiary lines, including the wholly owned Montour Railroad, which owns the Youngstown and Southern Railroad. The MONONGAHELA RAILWAY is owned jointly with Conrail and the BALTIMORE AND OHIO component of the CHESSIE SYSTEM. The Pittsburgh, Chartiers and Youghiogheny Railroad and the Lake Erie and Eastern are owned jointly with Conrail. Commuter service to Pittsburgh is run by the Baltimore and Ohio for the PORT AUTHORITY OF ALLEGHENY COUNTY on Pittsburgh and Lake Erie tracks. Trackage rights had been granted to the Baltimore and Ohio as early as 1934. Pittsburgh and Lake Erie operates a state-subsidized commuter service between College, Pennsylvania, and Pittsburgh.

Locomotives: 95
Freight cars: 17,380
Passenger cars: 5
Miles operated: 273

Pittsburgh and Shawmut Railroad.

The Pittsburgh and Shawmut is a coal-carrying railroad operating in western Pennsylvania between Brockway and Freeport Junction, northeast of Pittsburgh. The earliest predecessor was the Brookville and Mahoning, started by Edward Searles with the financial help of his wife who had been previously married to Mark Hopkins, one of the 'Big Four' who

built the CENTRAL PACIFIC. From 1908 to 1916 the line was leased to the Pittsburgh, Shawmut and Northern. The present name was assumed in 1910. The road is now controlled by the Dumaine family, which once had large interests in the NEW YORK, NEW HAVEN, AND HARTFORD RAILROAD and other New England railroads.

Locomotives: 12
Freight cars: 1290
Miles operated: 96
(as of January 1984)

Port Authority of Allegheny County.

The Port Authority of Allegheny county operates commuter rail service between Pittsburgh and Versailles, as well as bus and streetcar service in Pittsburgh. The supervision of the commuter service was assumed in 1975. The BALTIMORE AND OHIO had offered commuter rail service in the area since the 1930s, largely on PITTSBURGH AND LAKE ERIE track. Use of Pittsburgh and Lake Erie trackage avoided the need to go through downtown McKeesport.

Locomotives: 2
Passenger cars: 9
Miles operated: 19

Port Authority Transit Corporation (PATCO). PATCO provides service between Philadelphia and Camden, New Jersey. It is owned by the Delaware River Port Authority. Extensions to Mt Laurel and Glassboro, New Jersey, are in the study phase.

Electrification system: 600V DC, third rail
Gauge: 4ft 8in
No. of stations: 13
Rolling stock: 121
Route mileage: 14.6

Prairie Central Railway. The Prairie Central Railway operates in a roughly L-shaped route between Decatur and Mt Carmel, Illinois. The section between Paris and Decatur is a former PENNSYLVANIA RAILROAD line that had been taken over by the Wabash Railroad in 1978. The line was bought by Trans-Action Lines Ltd and incorporated as the Prairie Central Railway after Wabash gave up operation when the state of Illinois withdrew its subsidy. In 1982, a segment of former NEW YORK CENTRAL line between Paris and Lawrenceville was leased. Application to obtain the Lawrenceville–Mt Carmel section was filed in the same year. The Prairie Central is mostly a carrier of grain and fertilizer.

Locomotives: 7
Freight cars: 160
Miles operated: 165
(as of January 1984)

Prairie Trunk Railway. The Prairie Trunk Railway operates between Springfield and Shawneetown, Illinois. Owned by Trans-Action Lines Ltd, the Prairie Trunk is run on former BALTIMORE AND OHIO track purchased in 1977. The last five miles into Shawneetown is former LOUISVILLE AND NASHVILLE track owned jointly with the SEABOARD SYSTEM. The Prairie Trunk is primarily a carrier of grain and fertilizer.

Locomotives: 4
Freight cars: 30
Miles operated: 130
(as of June 1984)

Providence and Worcester Railroad. The Providence and Worcester operates in southeastern New England, serving the areas of Gardner, Worcester, Fall River and Newport, Massachusetts; Providence, Rhode Island; and the Connecticut points of Willimantic, New London, and Old Saybrook. The original Providence and Worcester was chartered in 1844 to provide service between these two cities. It eventually became part of the NEW YORK, NEW HAVEN, AND HARTFORD through leasing to the New York, Providence and Boston, which in turn, was leased to the New Haven. The Providence and Worcester was reincorporated in 1968, and a 1970 request for independence from PENN CENTRAL was granted in 1973. Modest expansion occurred in the early 1980s with the purchase of small lines in Rhode Island, former New Haven lines and acquisition of freight rights on AMTRAK trackage between Westbrook, Connecticut, and Attleboro, Massachusetts. A variety of commodities are carried, including chemicals and newsprint. Weekend excursion trains are run between Worcester and Uxbridge, Massachusetts.

Locomotives: 12
Freight cars: 1070
Miles operated: 370

PATCO's original fleet is being supplemented in the 1980s with new cars of the same basic design built by Canadian Vickers under license to the original builder, the Budd Company.

Pullman, George Mortimer (3 March 1831–19 October 1897).

Pullman, an inventor and industrialist, was the man whose name was most synonymous with luxury in railroad travel. Born and educated in Chautauqua County, New York, of a father who worked as a general mechanic, Pullman's early employment was in small-town merchandising and cabinet-making. In his 20s, he moved to Chicago where his carpentry contracting for the city earned him some renown.

As a freelance contractor, he did a certain amount of train traveling, enduring the primitive hard-built sleeping accommodations on the country's trains. In an effort to try out an improvement, Pullman convinced the Chicago and Alton Railroad to allow him to remodel two coaches into sleeping cars. Into these, he put two ranks of berths—the upper hinged to the car's side. In 1859 the C&A gave him a third car to convert, and in this he raised the upper berth by pulleys to lie flush with the ceiling during nonsleeping hours. These cars were enormously popular with the public, but railroad companies were loath to expend large sums for conversion.

In 1864, with his partner, Ben Field, Pullman constructed his own railroad car, the *Pioneer*, which incorporated the earlier hinged upper berth feature and an additional system of convertible folding cushions for the lower berth. Both of these devices were patented. However, the *Pioneer* was too wide for most station platforms. When the car was included in President Lincoln's funeral train, platforms had to be changed to accommodate it. Public demand soon forced other railroads to alter their tracks and station platforms to accommodate sleeping car.

So great was the demand that Pullman and Field organized the Pullman Palace Car Company in 1867, a corporation which eventually developed into a leader of American industry. Pullman was now able to design variations and additions to the sleeping car—the 'hotel car' (with small kitchen) in 1867, a dining car in 1868.

George M Pullman (*above left*) converted coach No. 9 of the Alton Railroad into a sleeping car (*right*) in 1859, the first Pullman sleeping car. The Silver Palace sleeping car (*left*) was trimmed in carved wood and bright paint. Pullman's main competitor was Webster Wagner, from whom the New York Central bought its sleeping cars.

3661, Car 9

AAR-49

BARBER SHOP
"THE OLYMPIAN"

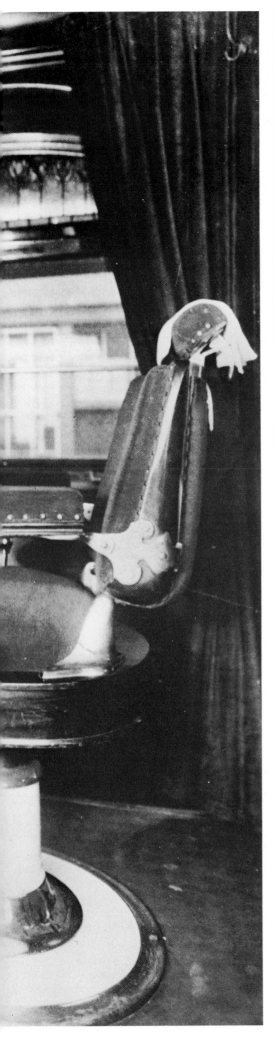

The Pullman Palace Car Co designed and built the *Maritana* for Maine Central Railroad in 1875 (*above*), as well as the barbershop for the *Olympian* (*left*).

Later, coaches, smoking cars, card rooms, libraries and even barber shops were added to the line.

As the years went on, Pullman cars were to become so luxurious and comfortable as to warrant the appelation 'hotels on wheels.' The *Pioneer*, for example, had elegant wood finishes, chandeliers, linen on the berths, marble washtands and provision for an attendant separate from regular train personnel. Subsequent Pullman cars, under Pullman's direction, were designed and decorated with elegant cabinetry, such as rare-wood panel-ling, carvings, inlays and semi-precious metal finishing. Private cars could be decorated as lavishly as the patron's taste and purse allowed.

Even Pullman's many manufacturing plants could not always keep up with the demand for these cars. Before his huge Chicago plant was opened in 1881, Pullman had to buy cars from his competitors and refinish them to his standards.

Pullman's business acumen was excellent, but his personality was apparently choleric and abrasive. His financial interest in a New York railroad company stemmed from his desire for revenge against the NEW YORK CENTRAL, which had bought WEBSTER WAGNER's sleeping cars. His desire to control all aspects of his empire led to the founding of the plant town of Pullman, Illinois, a community alternately called a model of industrial health and safety, and, conversely, a shockingly feudal 'company town.' Pullman's struggles with the emerging American Railroad Union in 1893 stemmed from his cutback of wages while retaining the mandatory costs of the workers/tenants in Pullman, Illinois. The resulting strike-breaking actions of President Cleveland, who sent federal troops into the area, is an important chapter in the history of the American labor movement.

Although Pullman is often characterized adversely—'an improver, not an inventor,' and 'an autocrat'—he did succeed in making railroad travel for the middle as well as the upper classes more comfortable and more acceptable as a standard means of travel.

Québec North Shore and Labrador Railway. The Québec North Shore and Labrador Railway transports iron ore from the Ungava tract along the Newfoundland–Québec border to port facilities on the St Lawrence River. From Arnaud Junction to Pointe-Noire on the St Lawrence, the ore is carried by the Arnaud Railway. There are no connections with the main North American railway system. The Québec and North Shore began with the formation of the Iron Ore Company of Canada in 1949. A railroad to bring the ore out was a prime necessity, and construction started in 1951. The route was surveyed by helicopter, and one of the largest civilian airlifts in history was used to bring in supplies during construction, which was completed in 1954. The northern terminus is in Schefferville, Québec, just north of the Newfoundland border and 207 miles north of the southern terminus at Sept-Iles. As a recently constructed railway, it is equipped with state-of-the-art technology, including centralized traffic control, welded rail and radio-control of mid-train helper locomotives. A branch from Ross Bay Junction (224 miles north of Sept-Iles) to Labrador City and Wabush Lake was completed in 1960. This branch, which serves the mining area near Carol Lake, is jointly owned by the Iron Ore Company of Canada and the Wabush Lake Railway Company. It is an automated

The Chicago and Alton Railroad timetable dated October 1881 boasted superb Pullman sleeping cars.

electric railway, requiring no personnel on its 6-mile loop. Unit trains are constantly in motion on this line. The Québec North Shore and Labrador operates some of the heaviest and longest trains in the world. Trains are usually more than 1.5 miles long and weigh more than 28,000 tons. The railroad also operates biweekly passenger trains, which are the only land transportation available in this area. There are no through roads north of Sept-Iles.

Locomotives: 76
Freight cars: 4235
Miles operated: 397

Reading Railroad. See Conrail.

Regional Transportation Authority (Chicago). The Regional Transportation Authority is the coordinating agency for commuter rail service in the Chicago area. Railroads operating subsidized service include the BURLINGTON NORTHERN, the CHICAGO AND NORTH WESTERN, the ILLINOIS CENTRAL GULF, the NORFOLK AND WESTERN and the CHICAGO, SOUTH SHORE AND SOUTH BEND. The latter is operated jointly with the Northern Indiana Commuter Transportation District. The Northeast Illinois Railroad Corporation, a subsidiary of the Regional Transportation Authority, uses its own crews to operate commuter trains on the MILWAUKEE ROAD and former Rock Island track to Joliet. Some of the rolling stock and stations used in Chicago commuter rail service are owned by local transit districts.

Locomotives: 130
Passenger cars: 690
Electric multiple-unit cars: 210

Miles operated: 429
(as of January 1984)

Richmond, Fredericksburg and Potomac Railroad. The Richmond, Fredericksburg and Potomac operates between Washington DC and Richmond, Virginia. It is a unit of CSX CORPORATION, serving primarily as a bridge road between the CHESSIE SYSTEM at Washington, and the SEABOARD SYSTEM at Richmond, the other rail units of CSX. Chartered in 1834, it provided service from Richmond to the Potomac River, where passengers could continue their journey to Washington by steamboat. All-rail service between Washington and Richmond was not provided until 1872. At that time the Alexandria and Fredericksburg, a subsidiary of the PENNSYLVANIA RAILROAD, completed a line to connect with the RF&P at Quantico. The northern leg of the journey to Washington was on the Alexandria and Washington, also a Pennsylvania Railroad subsidiary. These two lines were combined to become the Washington Southern in 1890. The Richmond–Washington Company was formed in 1901 to coordinate the operation of the Washington Southern and the RF&P. Washington Southern was fully absorbed into RF&P in 1920. A large volume of TOFC traffic runs on the RF&P. Paper products, foodstuffs and chemicals are among the chief commodities carried.

Locomotives: 41
Freight cars: 1620
Miles operated: 1620

Roberval and Saguenay Railroad. Owned by the Aluminium Company of America, the Roberval and Saguenay carries bauxite from Port Alfred on Québec's Saguenay River to the company's plant at Arvida, Québec. Incorporated in 1911 as the Ha! Ha! Bay Railway, the original line ran some 20 miles from Bagotville to a Saguenay River inlet near Arvida. The name was quickly changed to Roberval–Saguenay, and to Roberval and Saguenay in the 1920s. The Alma and Jonquiere Railroad was bought in 1968. Operating between Alma and Saguenay Power Junction, it does not connect directly with the Roberval and Saguenay. A CANADIAN NATIONAL line runs between Saguenay Power Junction and Arvida. It was merged with the parent road in 1974.

Locomotives: 14

Freight cars: 290
Miles operated: 55

Rogers, Thomas (16 March 1792–19 April 1856). An American locomotive manufacturer, Rogers was born in Groton, Connecticut, a direct descendant of Thomas Rogers of the Mayflower. At age 16 he was apprenticed to a carpenter. After military service in the War of 1812, he went into the building construction business in Patterson, New Jersey. In 1819, he formed a company for the manufacture of looms and other textile machinery. He engaged both in manufacturing the machinery and in spinning cotton. In 1830, HORATIO ALLEN ordered 100 sets of wheels and axles from Rogers for the South Carolina Railroad. This was the beginning of Roger's locomotive building. His first locomotive, the *Sandusky*, was completed the following year.

Rogers was responsible for several innovations in locomotive design, few of which he bothered to patent. Con-

In 1917 overnight freight service on RF&P between points 400 to 500 miles apart was commonplace.

sequently, he was one of the most widely copied locomotive builders in the world. He placed an inverted cone in the smokestacks of his locomotives to scatter the sparks. Among his other innovations were an arrangement for forcing connecting rods in and out of gear with V-hooks placed at the ends of the rods in communication with the reversing lever and shaft, and the use of hollow spokes and rims. The Rogers Works was one of the leading producers of 4-4-0 or AMERICAN TYPE ENGINES. Rogers' 4-4-0s tended to be longer than most others. The Rogers Works also introduced the 'wagon-top' boiler, which sloped downward from the cab toward the front of the locomotive, and it produced a widely used 2-6-0 engine.

Sacramento Valley Rail Road. See Judah, Theodore; Southern Pacific Company.

St Louis Southwestern. See Southern Pacific Company.

St Maries River Railroad. The St Maries River Railroad operates between Plummer Junction and Bovill, Idaho. It was started in 1980 with the purchase of a section of former MILWAUKEE ROAD mainline between Plummer and Avery, and a section of branch line from St Maries to Bovill by the Potlach Corporation, which was concerned about continuation of rail service at its facilities in the area. The St Maries River Railroad operates on the former main line from Plummer to St Maries, and on the former branch line from St Maries to Bovill. It is operated by Kyle Railways through a subsidiary, Idaho Western Inc. The section of main line from Avery to St Maries is operated by the Potlatch Corporation as a logging railroad. The St Maries Railroad is primarily a carrier of logs, plywood and wood chips.

Locomotives: 5

A Southern Pacific freight train pulls out of the tunnel at Tehachapi Loop, built to allow trains to gain altitude to climb the Tehachapi Mountains north of Los Angeles. The Santa Fe locomotives are pulling out of the loop to begin the ascent. In 1983 these two companies announced their intention to merge as Santa Fe Southern Pacific Corporation.

Freight cars: 515
Miles operated: 71
(as of January 1984)

San Diego and Arizona Eastern Transportation Company. The San Diego and Arizona Eastern Transportation Company was organized by Kyle Railways to be operated by that company under contract to the Metropolitan Transit Board of San Diego. The earliest predecessor of this operation was the San Diego and Arizona which was started in 1907 with financial backing from John D Spreckels and E H HARRIMAN. The plan was to bring Southern Pacific into San Diego, challenging the dominance of the SANTA FE in that area. The route went south from San Diego, into Mexico at Tijuana, reentering the United States at Tecate. The line was completed in 1919 to a junction with SOUTHERN PACIFIC at El Centro. The route could not compete with the Santa Fe's much faster San Diegan service via Los Angeles. In 1951, passenger service on this line, then called the San Diego and Arizona Eastern Railway, was ended. The section of the line in Mexico (Tijuana and Tecate Railway) was sold to the Mexican Government in 1970, with trackage rights retained by Southern Pacific. A 40-mile section between El Centro and Plaster City was abandoned in 1976 after it was damaged by a hurricane. The Metropolitan Transit Development Board purchased three sections of the line in 1979; Plaster City to the Mexican border, San Diego south to Tijuana, San Diego east to El Cajon. A 16-mile trolley line was constructed from San Diego to San Ysidro. This 'Tijuana Trolley' shares track with freight trains. Principal commodities carried include copper concentrates and grain.
Locomotives: 9
Miles operated: 60

Santa Fe Railroad. See Atchison, Topeka and Santa Fe Railway Company.

Santa Fe Southern Pacific Corporation. The Santa Fe Southern Pacific Corporation was formed on 23 December 1983 from the combination of Santa Fe Industries Inc and the Pacific Company, parent companies of the ATCHISON, TOPEKA AND SANTA FE RAILWAY and the SOUTHERN PACIFIC COMPANY, respectively. Santa Fe Southern Pacific Corporation almost

immediately applied for full merger of the two railway systems. Pending approval, the two roads continue to operate independently. The ICC must make a final decision by October 1986. Several railroads, including the DENVER AND RIO GRANDE WESTERN and the MISSOURI–KANSAS–TEXAS expressed opposition to the merger or were willing to accept it only if they were granted extensive trackage rights over Santa Fe and Southern Pacific lines. (See pp 178–9, 254–5.)

Seaboard Air Line. The earliest predecessor of the Seaboard Air Line was the Portsmouth and Roanoke, organized in 1832 to build a railroad from Portsmouth, Virginia, to the Roanoke River port of Weldon, North Carolina. By 1900, a group of railroads forming a route from Portsmouth to Atlanta, Georgia, had come to be called the Seaboard Air Line Railway. The name became official in 1900, and expansion to Florida was obtained with acquisition of the Florida Central and Peninsular Railroad. Further expansion into Florida was undertaken during the 1920s land boom, but with the collapse of the boom, the line went into receivership. Emerging from receivership in 1945, SAL bought two small lines in Georgia, in 1958 and 1959, by which time merger talks with the ATLANTIC COAST LINE were under way. The merger, which included the LOUISVILLE AND NASHVILLE, was effected in 1967 and the companies became the SEABOARD COAST LINE. The Louisville and Nashville was merged with the SEABOARD COAST LINE in 1982, two years after the SEABOARD AND CHESSIE SYSTEM merged to become CSX CORPORATION. (See chart, p 57.)

Seaboard Coast Line. The Seaboard Coast Line was formed in 1968 with the merger of the ATLANTIC COAST LINE and the SEABOARD AIR LINE. The Piedmont and Northern was obtained in 1969, and the Durham and Southern Railroad was bought in 1976. After these acquisitions, the area of operation was much the same as that of the SEABOARD SYSTEM RAILROAD. In the company's advertising, the railroad was referred to as the 'Family Lines,'

and the various railroads in the 'family' were listed. In 1980, the Seaboard Coast Line (including the LOUISVILLE AND NASHVILLE) and the CHESSIE SYSTEM were merged to form the CSX CORPORATION. L&N continued to operate independently until 1982, when it was completely merged with the Seaboard System. (See chart, p 57.)

Seaboard System Railroad. The Seaboard System Railroad is one of the rail units of the CSX CORPORATION. The others are the CHESSIE SYSTEM and the RICHMOND, FREDERICKSBURG AND POTOMAC in which CSX has a controlling interest. The Seaboard operates an extensive system throughout the southeastern United States, and extends through Kentucky to serve Cincinnati, Indianapolis, St Louis and Chicago. The Seaboard System is the result of a long series of mergers. In 1967 the SEABOARD AIR LINE RAILROAD merged with the ATLANTIC COAST LINE to form the SEABOARD COAST LINE. The LOUISVILLE AND NASHVILLE, which had been controlled by the Atlantic Coast Line since the turn of the century, was included in the merger. Also included was the Nashville, Chattanooga and St Louis Railroad and the Chicago, Indianapolis, and Louisville (Monon) which the Louisville and Nashville had absorbed in 1959 and 1971, respectively. The system also included the Clinchfield Railroad and the Georgia Railroad, both of which had been jointly leased by the ACL and the L&N. These merged companies were incorporated as Seaboard Coast Line Industries. However, in its advertising the company referred to itself as the 'Family Lines.' In November 1980 Seaboard Coast Line merged with Chessie System to form CSX Corporation.

Seaboard serves more ocean ports than any other railroad in the United States. Serving a large area, Seaboard carries a wide variety of commodities. Coal represented 22.5 percent of Seaboard's total freight revenues in 1983. Almost 75 percent of the coal is moved on unit trains. Seaboard is one of the leading transporters of fresh fruits and vegetables from central Florida to the Northeast. Much

Atchison, Topeka & Santa Fe
Southern Pacific
St. Louis Southwestern (Cotton Belt) ——→ **Santa Fe Southern Pacific**

of this produce is moved on the *Orange Blossom Special*, a fully-integrated road-rail-road service. This train operates on a record-setting 22-hour schedule. In 1983 it earned $11.2 million and the Golden Freight Car, the industry's most prestigious award. Other commodities carried include chemicals, phosphate rock, wood and paper products. (See map and chart, p 57.)
Locomotives: 2365
Freight cars: 116,500
Miles operated: 15,400

Seattle and North Coast Railroad.

The Seattle and North Coast Railroad operates between Port Angeles and Port Townsend, Washington, along the coast of the Strait of Juan de Fuca. Car barges operate in Admiralty Inlet between Port Townsend and Seattle. The Seattle and North Coast operates on a former section of MILWAUKEE ROAD track. This line had been built in 1915 as the Seattle, Port Angeles and Western Railroad in 1915. It was taken over by the Milwaukee Road three years later. The line was bought by North Coast Lines shortly before the Milwaukee Road closed, and operations began on 21 March 1980. The S&NC carries paper products and supplies to and from several paper mills.
Locomotives: 7
Freight cars: 300

Sierra Railroad.

The Sierra Railroad operates between Standard and Oakdale, California. It was incorporated as the Sierra Railway in 1890 to serve an area east of Stockton. Almost exclusively a carrier of lumber and wood products, the Sierra also operates seasonal passenger excursion trains. The Sierra Railroad has been used for on-location filming in the production of a number of movies and television productions such as *High Noon* and *Petticoat Junction*. The line was re-incorporated as the Sierra Railroad in 1935, acquiring the property of the Sierra Railway in 1937.
Locomotives: 3
Freight cars: 250
Miles operated: 50

Sierra Railroad locomotive No. 28 on the turntable at the old roundhouse in Jamestown, California, surrounded by vintage rolling stock. The railroad was built to connect the mines and lumber mills in Tuolumne County with other parts of the state.

Soo Line. The Soo Line operates northwestward from Chicago through the north-central states of Wisconsin, Michigan (Upper Peninsula), Minnesota, North Dakota and extreme eastern Montana. The earliest predecessor of the Soo Line was the Sault Ste Marie and Atlantic, incorporated in 1883 by a group of Minneapolis businessmen to run from Minneapolis/St Paul to Sault Ste Marie, where it connected with the CANADIAN PACIFIC. A year later the same promoters incorporated the Minneapolis and Pacific to serve the wheat-growing areas of Minnesota and North Dakota. In 1888, these two roads and two smaller lines were merged to form the Minneapolis, St Paul and Sault Ste Marie. CANADIAN PACIFIC soon gained control of the line to prevent its being used by the GRAND TRUNK RAILWAY as a competing line to western Canada. The line expanded in the 1890s and 1900s by building and leasing lines in North Dakota, Wisconsin and Minnesota. The name Soo Line, which had long been a nickname, became the official name after a 1961 reorganization. In that year, the Minneapolis, St Paul and Sault Ste Marie; the Wisconsin Central (a subsidiary) and the Duluth, South Shore and Atlantic were merged to form the Soo Line. The Minneapolis, Northfield and Southern Railway was acquired in 1982. The Soo Line carries a variety of commodities including grain, lumber, steel, potash and sulfur. More than 55 percent of Soo Line stock is owned by Canadian Pacific.
Locomotives: 250
Freight cars: 12,500
Miles operated: 4507
(as of January 1983)

South Central Tennessee Railroad. The South Central Tennessee operates on a section of track between Colesburg and Hohenwald, Tennessee, abandoned by the LOUISVILLE AND NASHVILLE in 1978. Run as a subsidiary of Kyle Railways, the South Central Tennessee is primarily a carrier of wood chips and carbon black.
Locomotives: 3
Freight cars: 95
Miles operated: 50
(as of January 1984)

Southeastern Michigan Transportation Authority. The Southeastern

The Sierra Railroad is a tourist attraction.

Michigan Transportation Authority operates commuter service between Detroit and Pontiac, Michigan. The Authority was created in 1967, and in 1974 SEMTA entered into an agreement with the GRAND TRUNK WESTERN RAILROAD to operate the commuter service GTW had operated previously at a loss. SEMTA now owns the locomotives, cars and stations. The trains are operated by GTW crews.

Locomotives: 5
Passenger cars: 30
Miles operated: 28
(as of January 1984)

Southeastern Pennsylvania Transportation Authority (SEPTA). Established in 1963 by the Pennsylvania legislature, the Southeastern Pennsylvania Transportation Authority operates commuter services in the Philadelphia area. In 1968 SEPTA acquired the Philadelphia Transportation Company, which operated trolley cars, buses and subways in Philadelphia. Two years later, the Philadelphia Suburban Transportation Company (Red Arrow Lines), which operated a 5ft 2in gauge trolley line to Media and Sharon and a standard gauge line (former Philadelphia and Western) to Norristown, was acquired. Several bus routes were also acquired in that year. Rolling stock for PENN CENTRAL and READING was purchased in 1974. The commuter rail system operated by SEPTA is called the SEPTA Regional High Speed Lines. Trains operate from both the former Reading Station and the Penn Center Suburban Stations, a former Pennsylvania Railroad station. SEPTA operates the former PENNSYLVANIA RAILROAD 'main line' to Chestnut Hill and Paoli, and to Trenton, New Jersey. Service to West Trenton, New Jersey and to Chestnut Hill, Doylestown, Newtown, Norristown and Warminster, Pennsylvania, is run on ex-Reading lines. Two major construction projects were in progress in the mid-1980s: a line from 30th Street Station in Philadelphia to Philadelphia International Airport, and a tunnel connecting Suburban Station with the Reading Terminal. These projects should increase traffic significantly.

Locomotives: 3
Passenger cars: 6
Self-propelled passenger cars:
    343 electric
    16 diesel
(as of January 1984)

In Philadelphia, SEPTA operates full subway/elevated rapid transit trains and light rail vehicles.
Full Metro System
Electrified system: 600V DC
    (bottom contact on Market Street–Frankford; top contact on Broad Street)
Gauge:
    Broad Street: 4ft 8in
    Market Street–Frankford: 5ft 2in
    No. of stations: 53

SP No. 2076 was built by Rogers in 1881.

Rolling stock: 384
Route mileage: 24.2
Red Arrow Division (light rail)
Norristown line
Electrified system: 600V DC top-contact third rail
Gauge: 4ft 8in
No. of stations: 22
Rolling stock: 17
Route mileage: 13.7
Media–Sharon Hills Line
Electrification system: 600V DC overhead wire
Gauge: 5ft 2in
No. of stations: 51

Rolling stock: 46
Route mileage: 12

Southern Pacific Company. One of the largest railroads in North America, the Southern Pacific and its subsidiaries, the Northwestern Pacific Railroad and the St Louis Southwestern Railway (the Cotton Belt), operate more than 13,000 miles of track. Operating in the midwestern and southwestern United States, Southern Pacific lines run north from San Francisco to Portland, Oregon, west to Ogden, Utah, and southward to Los Angeles. Lines run east from Los Angeles to Tucson and El Paso, connecting with lines that run northeastward to Kansas City and St Louis. The so-called Sunset Route extends westward from Houston to New Orleans and northwest to Memphis and St Louis. In 1983 Santa Fe Industries and Southern Pacific Company merged to form the SANTA FE SOUTHERN PACIFIC CORPORATION, and immediately filed for permission to merge Southern Pacific and the ATCHISON, TOPEKA AND SANTA FE. Pending approval of the merger, both railroads continued to operate as independent railroads.

The Southern Pacific has a long and complex history that can be traced to the Sacramento Valley Rail Road, which was started in the early 1850s, soon after California was admitted to the Union. In 1852, the Sacramento Valley hired THEODORE D JUDAH to plan a line eastward from Sacramento to Folsom and Placerville. This work was completed in 1856, but Judah's main interest was building a line over the Sierra Nevada, a line that would eventually become part of a trans-

continental railroad. Judah surveyed the route, incorporated a company he called the California Central Railroad and obtained financial support from four, Sacramento merchants, CHARLES CROCKER, Mark Hopkins, COLLIS P HUNTINGTON and LELAND STANFORD. The pacific Railroad Act of 1862 called for the formation of two companies, the UNION PACIFIC, which was to build westward from the Mississippi River and the CENTRAL PACIFIC, chartered to build eastward from California. The two lines met at Promontory, Utah, in 1869, forming the first transcontinental railroad. Expansion and intricate financial manipulations continued

Previous page: The *C P Huntington* began service in 1864 and was Central Pacific's third locomotive. It later became Southern Pacific's No. 1 (*below*). The photograph taken in the San Francisco Yard during the 1920s of it alongside the mighty 2-10-2 emphasizes the difference in size. *Left:* The SP station at Townsend and Third in San Francisco in 1952.

No. 4449 in Daylight livery rounds a bend in the Siskiyous under a full head of steam. The train was refurbished and donated to the city of Portland, Oregon, in 1958. It is the only Daylight left in existence.

at a rapid pace following the completion of the transcontinental line. Central Pacific expanded eastward to San
Francisco through the building of a
line called the Westward Pacific (not
the same entity as the Westward
Pacific that was absorbed by Union
Pacific in 1983) and acquisition of the
California Pacific Railroad running
from Sacramento to Vallejo. The
Southern Pacific Railroad, which had
been organized in the 1860s, was
acquired by the Central Pacific in
1868. The SP had previously absorbed
the San Francisco and San Jose
Railroad, which operated along the

Southern Pacific No. 4159 (*left*) and No. 4034 (*right*), a 2-8-8-2 Mallet, were both examples of early cab-aheads. With the tender in the rear, the ventilation problem encountered in the snowsheds and tunnels of the Sierra was remedied. Southern Pacific was the first and only major user of cab-aheads. *Below left:* A Southern Pacific 2-8-4 locomotive hauls a Santa Fe coal car, Pacific Fruit Express reefer and Union Pacific boxcar through New Mexico.

San Francisco Peninsula. Expansion northward to Oregon and southward to Los Angeles continued through additional absorption of smaller lines, including the California and Oregon, and construction. By the mid-1870s, the line was operating under the charter granted to the Southern Pacific. Los Angeles was reached in 1876, and the Colorado River at Needles, California, was reached a year later. EDWARD H HARRIMAN, who bought out the Huntington estate in 1900, improved the San Francisco–Los Angeles route through the construction of the Bayshore cutoff. This construction allowed a water level route to replace a steeply graded inland route. El Paso was reached in 1881 through the construction of a line called the Galveston, Harrisburg and San Antonio. Expansion east of El Paso was achieved through building a number of lines, including Buffalo Bayou, Brazos and Colorado and the New Orleans, Opelousas and Great Western. The BBB&C later became the Galveston, Harrisburg and San Antonio. The NOO&GW was sold to a steamship entrepreneur, Charles Morgan, who

Southern Pacific locomotives hauling a long line of boxcars (*far right*) and trailer trucks (*right*), which are lighter and cheaper to transport.

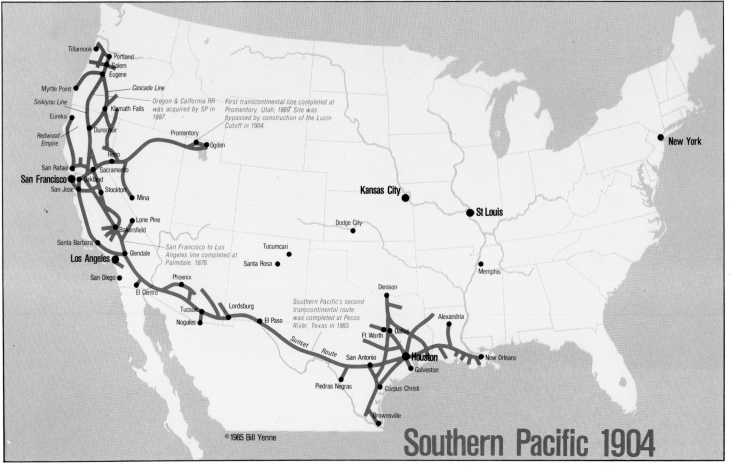

Tillamook
Portland
Salem
Eugene
Myrtle Point
Cascade Line
Siskiyou Line
Klamath Falls
Eureka
Oregon & California RR was acquired by SP in 1887.
Dunsmuir
Promentory
First transcontinental line completed at Promentory, Utah, 1869. Site was bypassed by construction of the Lucin Cutoff in 1904.
Redwood Empire
Reno
Ogden
San Rafael
Sacramento
San Francisco
Oakland
San Jose
Stockton
Mina
Lone Pine
Bakersfield
Kansas City
St Louis
Santa Barbara
Dodge City
Glendale
Los Angeles
San Francisco to Los Angeles line completed at Palmdale, 1876.
Tucumcari
Santa Rosa
Memphis
San Diego
Phoenix
El Centro
Denison
Tucson
Lordsburg
Southern Pacific's second transcontinental route was completed at Pecos River, Texas in 1883.
Nogales
El Paso
Alexandria
Ft Worth
Dallas
Sunset Route
San Antonio
Houston
New Orleans
Piedras Negras
Galveston
Corpus Christi
Brownsville
New York

©1985 Bill Yenne

Southern Pacific 1904

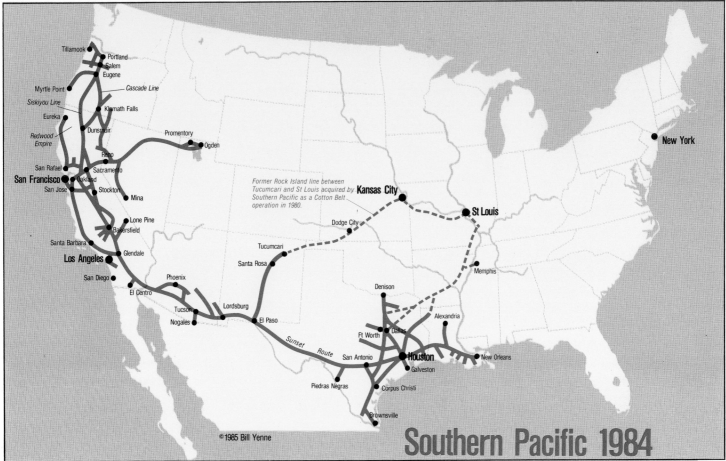

Tillamook

Portland
Salem
Eugene

Myrtle Point

Cascade Line

Siskiyou Line

Klamath Falls

Eureka

Dunsmuir

Promentory

Redwood Empire

Reno

Ogden

San Rafael

Sacramento

New York

San Francisco
Oakland

Stockton

San Jose

Mina

Former Rock Island line between
Tucumcari and St Louis acquired by
Southern Pacific as a Cotton Belt
operation in 1980.

Kansas City

St Louis

Lone Pine

Dodge City

Bakersfield

Santa Barbara

Tucumcari

Los Angeles

Glendale

Santa Rosa

Memphis

San Diego

Phoenix

Denison

El Centro

Tucson

Lordsburg

El Paso

Nogales

Alexandria

Dallas

Sunset Route

Ft Worth

San Antonio

Houston

New Orleans

Galveston

Piedras Negras

Corpus Christi

Brownsville

©1985 Bill Yenne

Southern Pacific 1984

Above: A Pacific Fruit Express train passes through Arizona in 1938. PFE was formed jointly by SP and UP in 1906 to carry fresh fruits and vegetables from the Pacific states across the country in refrigerator cars. *Below:* The 4-10-2 wheel configuration of No. 5000 was typical of Southern Pacific's 1930s vintage locomotives. *Overleaf:* A Southern Pacific Cotton Belt train loaded with coal.

SOUTHERN PACIFIC LINES

5000

reorganized it as the Louisiana and Texas Railroad.

The Shasta Route was opened through the extension of the California and Oregon and the acquisition of the Oregon and California, which gained access to Portland, Oregon. Further construction in Oregon was pushed through in the late 1920s with the building of the Natron cutoff between Eugene, Oregon, and Black Butte, California, via Klamath Falls, Oregon. Called the Cascade Line, this route had fewer curves and steep grades than the older route through Ashland.

The El Paso and Southwestern system was bought in 1924. This line extended into additional areas in Arizona and New Mexico. The St Louis Southwestern, obtained in 1934, is operated as a subsidiary of the Southern Pacific Transportation Company.

In the 1930s SP introduced the 'cab-in-front' steam locomotive. These were 4-8-8-2 oil-fired, articulated steam locomotives with the cab placed in front of the boiler and the tender trailing behind the smokebox. This arrangement improved visibility, and tended to put the smoke and fumes behind the crew in the many tunnels and snow sheds on SP lines. Southern Pacific was one of the first railroads to switch to diesel locomotives, starting in the mid-1930s. Dieselization was encouraged by the difficulty of maintaining sufficient supplies of water along SPs long desert routes.

Left: In 1946 the Electro-Motive Division of General Motors supplied Southern Pacific with 20 diesel locomotives of 6000hp each, the first of a large fleet for freight service, the 6000 series of engines. The first main-line diesel freight locomotives were put into service the following year. They were 4 (B-B) class with a cab at each end so the locomotive could be operated in either direction without being turned. *Below:* The Southern Pacific baggage car for American Railway Express was powered by a combination of gas and electricity.

SP switch engines at work in a Beaumont, Texas chemical plant (*above*), and in a busy freight yard (*right*).

Southern Pacific owned several electric street railway and interurban lines, including the Portland, Eugene and Eastern, the Interurban Electric Railway, which served the San Francisco area, and Pacific Electric. The latter, which operated in and around Los Angeles, was the largest interurban line in the United States. SP operates a commuter service between San Francisco and San Jose under supervision of the state of California.

Locomotives: 2621
Freight cars: 67,933
Passenger cars: 92
Miles operated: 10,110
(as of January 1984)
St Louis Southwestern Railway Company (Cotton Belt)
Locomotives: 319
Freight cars: 18,961
Miles operated: 2180

Southern Railway System. The Southern Railway system operates in 13 states, primarily in the Southeast. Service is also provided to Cincinnati, St Louis and Louisville. The Southern Railway is merged with the NORFOLK AND WESTERN under the corporate control of the NORFOLK SOUTHERN CORPORATION. The earliest precursor of the Southern Railway was the South Carolina Canal and Rail Road Company, which was chartered in 1828 to

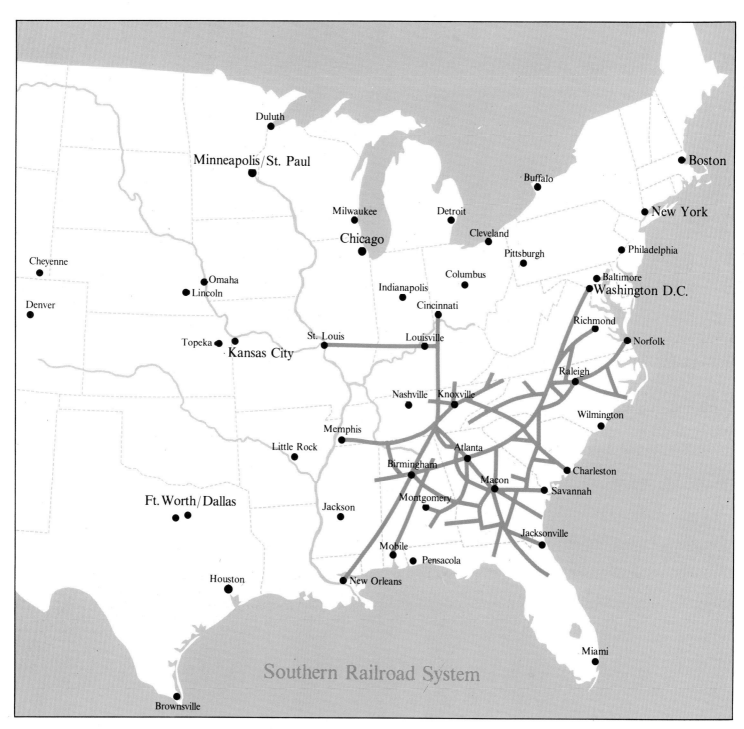

Southern Railroad System

build along the Savannah River between Charleston and Hamburg, South Carolina. When this 136-mile line opened, it was the longest in the world. The Richmond and Danville was among the larger roads which eventually became part of the SRS. Several other lines joined the R&D in a loose association which included what is now the SRS main line between Washington and Atlanta. Another major component was the East Tennessee, Virginia and Georgia. The Southern Railway came into corporate existence in 1894 with the combining of the R&D and the ETV&G. The SRS continued to grow, mainly through acquisition of other railroads. A notable addition to

the SRS was the Central of Georgia, which was acquired in 1963. The Norfolk Southern was purchased in 1974. In 1982, names were changed so that Norfolk Southern could be used to designate the merged Southern and Norfolk and Western systems. The SRS refused to join AMTRAK when it was formed, continuing to its own passenger service, notably the *Silver Crescent* service from Washington to New Orleans, for a number of years. With the purchase of CONRAIL by Norfolk Southern in 1985, SRS became part of the largest railroad system in the United States.

Locomotives: 1,459

Freight cars: 75,359

Miles operated: 10,119

Stanford, Leland. See Southern Pacific Company; Transcontinental railroad (United States).

Stevens, John (1749–1838). An engineer, inventor and transportation pioneer, Stevens was born in New York City, the son of John and Elizabeth Alexander Stevens. The elder Stevens, who came to America at age 16 as an indentured law clerk, prospered as a ship owner and merchant, acquired land and became important in New Jersey politics. He was able to provide tutors for his son and to send him to King's College (now Columbia University). During the Revolutionary War, he was commissioned as a captain, serving as a county loan com-

missioner collecting money for the Continental Army. He also served as treasurer of New Jersey and as surveyor-general of that state.

In the late 1780s, Stevens became interested in steamboats. He started to draft plans for steam engines, and in 1789 petitioned the New York legislature for an exclusive license to build steamboats, but was refused. He then worked with Congress in formulating the nation's first patent laws, which were adopted in 1790. Patents he received a year later for an improved vertical steam boiler and a Savery-type steam engine were among the first to be awarded under the new law. With the help of the master mechanic Nicholas Roosevelt and several recently arrived English workmen, he was able to start actual construction of steamboats in the late 1790s, and succeeded in obtaining an exclusive right for the operation of steamboats in New York waters in 1798. By 1804, a small steamboat called *Little Juliana* had been completed and taken on several successful trial trips across the Hudson River. Powered by a multitubular boiler of Stevens' design, the little boat was propelled by twin screw propellers. In 1806 he began construction of a 100-foot steamboat, the *Phoenix*. Before he could finish this vessel, Robert Fulton made his successful trip up

Robert Stevens (*right*), son of John Stevens (*above right*), failed in his attempt to make an American Crampton (*above*).

the Hudson in the *Clermont*, and the monopoly for operating steamboats in New York waters was awarded to Fulton and Robert Livingston, Stevens' brother-in-law. Stevens turned down an invitation to join Fulton and Livingston. Forbidden to operate in New York waters, he sent the *Phoenix* around Cape May to the Delaware River in 1809, making this vessel the first ocean-going steamboat. The *Phoenix* was used in a Philadelphia–Trenton service, while the *Little Juliana* was operated on Long Island Sound from Connecticut.

Leaving steamboat operations to his sons, Stevens turned his attention to developing steam power for railways. He sent letters to politicians urging them to support railways rather than canals. In 1812 he published *Documents Tending to Prove the Superior Advantages of Rail-Ways and Steam-carriages over Canal Navigation*, which was a detailed account of his views of all phases of railways. He approached several state legislatures, succeeding in 1815 when the New Jersey Legislature authorized the forming of a company 'to erect a rail road from the River Delaware near Trenton to the River Raritan at or

near New Brunswick.' This legislation was the first railroad act in the United States. The Pennsylvania legislature passed an act in 1823 granting Stevens a charter for building a railroad from Philadelphia to Columbia, Pennsylvania. Although the act expired before Stevens could raise the necessary capital, the legislature passed another act in 1828 appropriating $2,000,000 for the building of the Philadelphia and Columbia Railroad, which was later incorporated into the PENNSYLVANIA RAILROAD. In 1830 the New Jersey Legislature granted a charter for the CAMDEN AND AMBOY RAILROAD. Stevens' sons Robert and Edwin were named president and treasurer, respectively. Always an avid proponent of steam power, Stevens designed and built a small steam locomotive in 1825. He ran this engine on a circular track

The *Stourbridge Lion* took to the rails in the hills of northern Pennsylvania in 1829. The engine was brought over from England by Horatio Allen, the first American engineer for the Delaware and Hudson Canal Company. The train had a horizontal boiler, vertical cylinders and walking beams connecting two pairs of drivers. The reconstructed *Stourbridge Lion* (*left*) now resides in the Arts and Industries Building of the Smithsonian Institution in Washington DC.

erected on his Hoboken, New Jersey, estate. It was the first steam locomotive constructed in America. However, it was never used in regular service.

Stevens, Robert L (1787–1856) An inventor and engineer, Stevens was born in Hoboken, New Jersey, the son of John and Rachel Cox Stevens. He learned mechanics by assisting his father, JOHN STEVENS, in his various projects, such as the design, construction and operation of the steamboat *Little Juliana*. In 1809, when John Stevens was denied a charter to operate steamboats in New York waters, he sent the steamboat *Phoenix* around Cape May to Philadelphia. Robert Stevens was the master of the *Phoenix* on this first ocean voyage of a steamboat. The *Phoenix* was used in a Philadelphia–Trenton service which Robert Stevens managed.

Recognized as a pioneer in naval architecture, Stevens designed some 20 steamboats, many of which incorporated his inventions. His inventions include a 'cam-board' cutoff for steam engines, improved poppet valves and walking beams, a split paddle wheel, a force-draft firing system for boilers and boilers improved to the point where they could carry pressures of 50 pounds per square inch.

In 1830 he became president and chief engineer of the Camden and Amboy Railroad and traveled to England to buy locomotives and rails. During the four-week voyage he whittled a model of a new rail pattern from a pine block. Shaped like an inverted 'T,' the new rail required only offset-headed spikes for fasteners. The 'T' rail, as it came to be called, eventually became the most widely used type of rail in the world. With great difficulty Stevens found a mill in England that would roll the new rail, and in 1831 22 shiploads of 16-foot rail sections arrived in Philadelphia. Also delivered in 1831 was the engine *John Bull*, which Stevens had purchased during his trip to England. The *John Bull*, shipped disassembled, was put together by ISAAC DRIPPS, a young mechanic recently hired by Stevens, without benefit of blueprints or instructions. Renamed the *Stevens*, but seldom referred to by that name, the *John Bull* was modified considerably over the years and used until 1893.

The new track was laid on rows of stone blocks to which rails were fastened by means of iron plates and spikes. When the shipments of stone blocks were slowed, Stevens resorted to the use of wooden crossties as a temporary measure. The wooden crossties proved to be more resilient and smooth running than the stone blocks; trains could run at higher speeds than they had on the stone. Stevens soon replaced all the stone blocks with wood crossties, a practice eventually adopted by all railroads. In the process of laying these rails, Stevens designed the 'hook-headed spike,' which was not much different in configuration from the spikes used today, the 'iron tongue,' (called the fish plate today) and various nuts and bolts used in track construction.

Stevens established a company locomotive shop near his home. Among other innovations, Stevens and Dripps devised a valve gear for reversing locomotives. In 1834, the Camden and Amboy shops turned out a large, 30-ton locomotive called the MONSTER, noted for the complexity of its drive mechanism. Attempts to build fast engines based on the Crampton design popular in Europe were not successful.

Stourbridge Lion. The *Stourbridge Lion* was the first steam locomotive to be operated on a North American railroad. Built by Foster, Rastrick and Company of Stourbridge, England, it was bought by HORATIO ALLEN for use on the Delaware and Hudson Canal Company, to operate on a 16-mile line between Carbondale, Pennsylvania, coal mines and the canal at Honesdale. The first run was made on 9 August 1829 with Allen at the controls. (Later he admitted to his trepidations about making the run alone.) The *Stourbridge Lion* proved to be too heavy for use on American tracks. It was put into use as a stationary engine. A replica of the *Stourbridge Lion* is on display in Honesdale, Pennsylvania.

Texas Mexican Railway ('Tex-Mex'). The Texas Mexican Railway operates between Flour Bluff on the Gulf of Mexico (near Corpus Christi) to Laredo, Texas. Its earliest predecessor was the San Diego and Rio Grande Narrow Gauge Railroad, chartered in 1875. The present name was assumed in 1881 when it came under the control of the National Railways of Mexico. However, NRM's interest was held by the Manufacturers Hanover Trust Company of New York until 1982, when the line was sold to private investors in Mexico. Most freight carried by TMR is interchanged with NRM at Laredo. Principal commodities carried include chemicals, grain, gravel and scrap iron.

Locomotives: 16
Freight cars: 1121
Miles operated: 157

Toledo, Peoria and Western Railroad. The Toledo, Peoria and Western operates between Logansport, Indiana, and Keokuk, Iowa. Chartered in 1863 as the Toledo, Peoria and Warsaw, the road was opened in 1868 between Warsaw, Indiana, and the Illinois–Indiana state line. The line's turbulent history includes several bankruptcies, reorganizations, sales and leases. The name Toledo, Peoria and Western was first assumed in 1880 when it was leased to the Wabash, St Louis and Pacific. The lease, which was supposed to be for 49.5 years, lasted only four years. The TP&W was bought in 1927 at a foreclosure sale by George P McNear Jr. In 1941, when McNear refused to go along with an industry-wide pay increase, a bitter and violent strike ensued. The government operated the TP&W during World War II. In 1947 McNear was murdered. Reorganized again in 1952 under the same name, the line was purchased in 1960 by the SANTA FE, which sold a half interest to the PENNSYLVANIA RAILROAD. A portion of Pennsylvania line was bought in 1976, extending the line to Logansport, Indiana. As a subsidiary of Penn Central the Pennsylvania Company had come to own a half share of TP&W, and in 1979 it sold its share to Santa Fe. Full merger with Santa Fe is expected before the end of the 1980s.

Locomotives: 29
Freight cars: 382
Miles operated: 472
(as of January 1984)

The Tom Thumb. This was an experimental locomotive built in 1830 by PETER COOPER. Consisting of nothing more than a small donkey engine on a wheeled platform, the locomotive was built as a demonstration to convince BALTIMORE AND OHIO RAILROAD stockholders of the advantages of steam power over horses. The engine had one cylinder, 13 inches long and three inches in diameter. The tubes in the vertical boiler were made from musket barrels. A fan driven by the

engine via a belt improved the draft. In the 1830 race between the *Tom Thumb* and a horse, both pulling similar loads on parallel tracks, the *Tom Thumb* was ahead until the fan mechanism failed. Nevertheless, the demonstration was convincing, and the Baltimore and Ohio was all steam-powered by 1835.

Toronto, Hamilton and Buffalo Railway. The Toronto, Hamilton and Buffalo Railway operates in the southern Ontario peninsula between Port Colborne and Waterford, via Hamilton. Incorporated in 1884, the line opened in 1895 and was bought by the CANADIAN PACIFIC, the NEW YORK CENTRAL and its Michigan Central and Canada Southern satellites in that same year. In 1977 the interest that had passed to the PENN CENTRAL with the New York Central–Pennsylvania merger, and the Canada Southern interests were bought by Canadian Pacific. The road is now wholly owned by Canadian Pacific. Major commodities carried include fertilizer, chemicals, iron and steel.

Locomotives: 17
Freight cars: 1120
Miles operated: 111

Toronto Transit Commission. The new Scarborough Line, scheduled for opening in 1985, will feature inter-

The *Tom Thumb* (*above right*), the first locomotive built in America, raced with a horse-drawn car on 25 August 1830 (*above*). *Right*: Excavation on the Toronto Transit system.

mediate capacity transit system (ICTS) cars. These cars are relatively light-weight vehicles operating on standard gauge, continuously welded track. The 5-station system will operate on a 600V DC system with a wayside power distribution.

Electrification system: 570V DC, third rail
Gauge: 4ft 11in
No. of stations: 59
Rolling stock: 632
Route mileage: 35.5

Transcontinental railway (Canada). The first steps toward the building of a Canadian transcontinental railway came in 1857 with the establishment of an Imperial Commission to investigate its feasibility. The Commission sent out a survey team which returned with a discouraging report. The barriers of the Rockies and the Selkirk Mountains seemed insurmountable to the surveyors. They did, however, discover Kicking Horse Pass through the Rockies, a gap in the mountains through which the line to the Pacific would eventually run. Another team sent out some eight years later by the government of British Columbia issued

a more favorable report. However, the Canadian Government took no action until British Columbia threatened to withdraw from the Confederation because of its isolation from the rest of Canada. When British Columbia was admitted to the Dominion in 1871, a clause in the Articles of Union specified that a railroad was to be built connecting the coast of British Columbia with the rest of the country. Construction did not begin until 1875.

Two companies, the Canada Pacific Railway Company and the Inter Oceanic Railway, were formed to build the line. Political scandal in connection with these companies led to the downfall of a Canadian Government. The Conservative government of John A McDonald pressured the companies to combine into one, under the leadership of Hugh Allen, who had been the head of the Canada Pacific Company. When it was revealed that Allen had been a heavy contributor to the Conservative Party, McDonald was forced to resign. McDonald was returned to office, and in 1880 he arranged with George

Above left: A Canadian Pacific Railroad crew in front of their construction camp north of Lake Superior. *Left:* This timber trestle near Lake of the Woods was typical of the flimsy, nonstandard construction that was tolerated on government contracts. When Canadian Pacific took over the Lakehead–Winnipeg section between 1881 and 1883, such structures were replaced with earth fills. *Right:* With the era of mechanization still far in the future, ties are carried forward from the supply train on the shoulders of the tracklayers, 1883.

Stephen, the president of the Bank of Montréal, to form a syndicate for relaunching the project. The Stephen syndicate and the Canadian Government signed an agreement in 1881 which led to the incorporation of the CANADIAN PACIFIC RAILWAY COMPANY. The Canadian Pacific received a $25 million subsidy, 25 million acres of land and two railroads (the Port Arthur–Selkirk–Winnipeg–Emerson and the Port Moody–Savona). With the receipt of these inducements, construction began in earnest.

The North side of Lake Superior proved to be as much an obstacle as the mountains. Newly laid track sank in the spruce swamps or muskegs. The American railroad magnate JAMES J HILL, was a member of the syndicate. He had a personal interest in giving up attempts to lay track in the muskegs of southern Ontario. He proposed to stop the line at a point on the Lake Superior shore, and then use steamers to connect with his own railroad in the United States—the St Paul, Minneapolis and Manitoba—reconnecting with the Canadian Pacific in Manitoba. However, most people involved with the project were determined to keep the Canadian Pacific an all-Canadian railway, and Hill's plan was rejected.

It was largely through the efforts of another American, WILLIAM CORNELIUS VAN HORNE, that the Canadian Pacific

Above: A CPR crew extending a timber retaining wall near Eleven Shed in Rogers Pass. This was the era before specially designed work clothes. Hats were worn to prevent sunstroke. *Left:* In 1885 Donald A Smith drove the iron spike that completed the CPR transcontinental main line.

was built entirely on Canadian soil. Taken on as general manager by the Canadian Pacific, van Horne pushed the project through with unflagging determination. More than 12,000 worked on the project, draining swamps, diverting rivers and blasting away rocky obstructions. Spikes had to be heated to keep them from cracking in the 40 and 50 degrees-below-zero cold. By the spring of 1884, the Rockies had been crossed via Kicking Horse Pass. By 1885, the syndicate was in serious financial difficulty. Stephen and his cousin, Sir Donald Smith, had invested their personal fortunes, mortgaged everything they owned, and were having no success persuading the government to advance more money. Smith sent a telegram to Stephen bearing the one word, 'Craigellachie,' a reference to the war cry of Clan Grant in his native Scotland, 'Stand fast Craigellachie!'

When the project seemed to be doomed to failure, help came from an unexpected source. Louis Riel,

Above: A Central Pacific work train at the rail head in the Sierra Nevada in 1865. *Left:* Chinese coolies carve their way through the Sierra Nevada with pick and shovel, one-horse dump carts and black powder.

had raised an army and was threatening the northwest regions. Van Horne offered the completed sections of the railroad to the Canadian Army, a massive troop movement was undertaken and the rebellion was put down. The incident gave McDonald the strong argument he needed to convince Parliament that a transcontinental railway was needed for the country's security, and more money was appropriated, albeit reluctantly. The line was completed on 7 November 1885 with the driving of a golden spike in the Gold Range Mountains of British Columbia, at a place named Craigellachie in honor of the occasion.

Transcontinental railroad (United States).

Talk of building a railroad westward to the Pacific started almost as soon as the earliest US railroads were in operation. In 1832, a Dr Hartwell Carver of Rochester, New York, wrote articles in -which he proposed building a railroad westward from Lake Michigan to the Oregon Country. At the time, the area west of the Mississippi River was a wilderness, much of which was devoid of water and wood necessary to keep trains running. It seemed impossible.

In 1844, Asa Whitney, a New Yorker in the China trade, proposed to Congress that the government sell him 77,952,000 acres of land at 16 cents an acre. The idea was to sell the land, use the profits to build a railroad westward, selling more as needed to complete a railroad from Lake Michigan to the Columbia River. He envisioned the transcontinental railroad

Union Pacific construction crews gather outside the paymasters car at Blue Creek station. The average pay was $3 a day. Crew numbers grew from 250 in 1865 to 10,000 by the completion of the transcontinental railroad in 1869. Many of them were Irish and most were Civil War veterans.

as an important link in trade between the West and the Orient.

Whitney traveled extensively, promoting his scheme, and won votes of approval from 17 state legislatures, a circumstance he hoped would make a strong case with Congress. However, he did not have the approval of Missouri because Senator Thomas Hart Benton of that state has his own ideas about a transcontinental railroad. His conception of such a railroad was one owned by the government and that had St Louis as its eastern terminus. The Benton forces prevailed, and Congress tabled the Whitney proposal, which had also been attacked by railroad experts as impractical. An attempt by Whitney to persuade the British to build a railroad across Canada was also unsuccessful.

Positive results of the failed Whitney proposal included increased interest in the idea of a western railroad and the realization of the need for accurate surveys. Benton arranged for a survey westward from St Louis, to be carried out by his son-in-law, John C Frémont, already known as the 'Pathfinder' for his many westward treks. Frémont started out in 1848, along a route that roughly followed the 38th parallel from St Louis to San Francisco. The expedition was a disaster, resulting in the deaths of ten of his men. Although the expedition yielded no definitive data on the topography, Benton used it as the basis of his proposal to the Senate for setting aside a 100-mile-wide strip of land straddling the 38th parallel for a government-owned 'central national highway.' In the meantime, several other routes had been suggested, including the Southern Trail, favored by the Army as a way to move troops quickly from Texas to California and the well-known Emigrant Trail through the Platte Valley, over the Continental Divide at South Pass, and on to Oregon or California.

In March of 1853, Congress authorized a survey of the major possible routes for a western railway. Secretary of War Jefferson Davis was instructed to determine which of the routes was most feasible. Davis, of course, favored a southern route, but attempted to conceal his obvious preference by not including the southern route in the surveys, hoping that all the others would be inconclusive, leaving the southern route as the only alternative. Under pressure from skeptics, the

Southern Trail was later included and five surveys were done:

- Great Lakes to Puget Sound between the 49th and 47th parallels; Isaac S Stevens (Northern Trail)
- Omaha westward, through the Platte Valley; GRENVILLE M DODGE (Emigrant Trail)
- Westward from St Louis along the 38th parallel; John W Gunnison (Benton's Buffalo Trail)
- Westward from Fort Smith, Arkansas, along the 35th parallel to Albuquerque, through the Mojave Desert to California; Amiel Whipple
- El Paso westward, along the Mexican border and through an area south of the Gila River; John Pope and J G Parke (Southern Trail)

Congress specified a ten-month deadline for the surveys, thus practically assuring sketchy data. Nevertheless, Davis had data from all the expeditions in time for his 'impartial evaluation.' As expected, Davis chose the southern route, even though much of it passed through Mexican territory. James Gadsden, an emissary to Mexico, was then authorized by Congress to purchase enough land from Mexico to accommodate the proposed route. The Gadsden Purchase passed, despite opposition from Benton. Secession and the outbreak of the CIVIL WAR before a final decision could be made effectively ended all further consideration of the Southern Trail route.

Much of the route that was eventually to become the transcontinental railroad west of the Rockies was determined by THEODORE JUDAH, who had been hired to do surveying for the Sacramento Valley Railroad in 1854. Judah had convinced himself that the 22 miles he was surveying between Sacramento and the western slope of the Sierra Nevada would eventually become the first leg of a transcontinental railroad. He published a pamphlet, *A Practical Plan for Building the Pacific Railroad* in which he severely criticized previous surveys. He achieved some success in several lobbying trips to Washington, but the lawmakers were more concerned with the impending outbreak of the Civil War than with railroads. He spent the early 1860s making a thorough survey of possible routes in the Sierra Nevada, discovering a number of negotiable slopes with the help of Daniel (Doc) Strong, a pharmacist from the Sierra foothills town of Dutch Flat. He and Strong optimistically drew up maps

A construction camp of the Central Pacific Railroad in Utah in April 1869. The construction crew included tracklayers, graders, teamsters, herdsmen, cooks, bakers, blacksmiths, bridgebuilders, carpenters, masons and clerks.

Temporary and permanent bridges under construction along Central Pacific lines of the transcontinental railroad. Citadel Rock is in the background.

and articles of association for a Pacific railroad, and tried to find investors. The major investors, or 'Big Four,' were the Sacramento merchants COLLIS P HUNTINGTON, Leland Stanford, Mark Hopkins and Charles Crocker.

The route that was to be chosen eastward from the Mississippi River had been surveyed by GRENVILLE M DODGE, both in the employ of Thomas Durant of the Rock Island, and on his own. This route was basically the old Emigrant Trail. Once the Civil War had started and Jefferson Davis had departed, there were no longer any serious obstacles to choosing this route, which was clearly the most logical. Durant and the Big Four out in Sacramento were anxious to get going, but needed government help for so massive a project.

The help came with the passage of the Pacific Railroad Act of 1862. The Act authorized that two roads, the CENTRAL PACIFIC and the UNION PACIFIC, would build the transcontinental railroad. The Central Pacific, which was to build from California eastward, was awarded plots of land ten miles wide in alternate sections along the right of way for each mile of track laid. For each mile of track on the plains, a loan of $16,000 was made. Loans of $32,000 and $48,000 were granted for each mile on the Great Basin, and mountains (Rockies and Sierra), respectively. The Union Pacific built westward from Omaha. Loans and land grants similar to those given the Central Pacific were granted.

Judah immediately ran into trouble with his backers, who wanted to build only as far as Nevada until there were more potential customers in the region. The frustrated Judah traveled east in an attempt to seek new backers to buy out the Big Four and their allies. During the trip he contracted a fever in Panama and died.

The Union Pacific began construction in December of 1864. The job of chief engineer was taken over by Grenville M Dodge upon his resignation from the Army. Dodge, too, had his difficulties with management, who wanted to make the line as long as they could in order to collect more mileage money from the government, while Dodge wanted to make the line as short, well-built and efficient as possible. The dispute was settled by Ulysses S Grant in Dodge's favor.

Both the UP and CP were in financial difficulty from the beginning.

The last rails of the Union Pacific and Central Pacific were joined at Promontory, Utah, on 10 May 1869. Union Pacific's No. 119 and Central Pacific's *Jupiter* halted within a few feet of each other. UP's Thomas Durant and CP's Leland Stanford drove the ceremonial silver and gold spikes that marked completion of the railrqad.

Few investors were willing to sink money into the uncertain enterprise of a Pacific railroad, particularly when there was so much fast money to be made from war-related enterprises. The CP Big Four paid for the groundbreaking with their own funds, and then induced the California legislature to grant $10,000 for every mile of track laid in California. Enough voters were bought to assure passage of a bond issue which gave an outright grant of $600,000 to the CP. Even that relatively small sum was tied up in litigation. The CP managed to get an extra $1 million in federal loans on the basis of dubious geological reports on just where the Sierra mountain range began.

The UP also had difficulty selling stock. The charter specified that $2 million worth of stock had to be sold before operations could begin. Durant solved the problem by putting up ten percent of the cost as a loan for any buyer.

Both Durant and Huntington of the CP and UP, respectively, traveled to Washington to persuade congressmen, by lobbying and bribing, to improve on the Railway Act of 1862. This was accomplished with the Railway Act of 1864. Land grants were doubled to 20 square miles in alternate sections for each mile of track laid. The 1862 act specified that the loans were to be deferred until track had actually been laid. The 1864 act allowed two-thirds of the funds to be released before track-laying began.

By June of 1864 CP had completed 31 miles of track. The UP, however, had not been able to get beyond the Omaha city limits. An exasperated Abraham Lincoln called on Oakes Ames, a millionaire Congressman from Massachusetts, to get things going. Ames invested about $1,000,000 and persuaded other wealthy Bostonians to invest. The money went not directly to UP, but to a company called Credit Mobilier. Organized by Durant and an eccentric financier and publicist named Charles Francis Train, the ostensible purpose of the Credit Mobilier was to carry out the actual building of the UP by selling stock and entering into the necessary contracts for supplies and labor. The real purpose was to provide a base for a few people to make millions from contracts, kickbacks and other schemes. The Credit Mobilier, as corrupt as it was, did provide an incentive for investment,

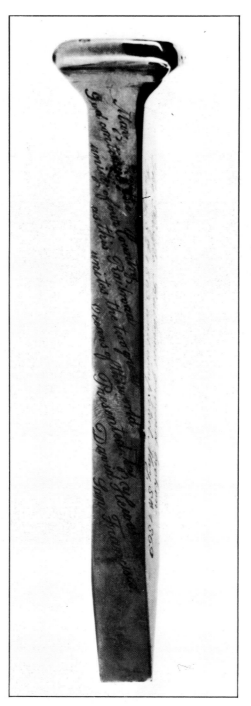

The golden spike driven at Promontory, Utah.

and the UP was soon pushing westward.

An operation similar to the Credit Mobilier, the Contract & Finance Company, was set up by the Big Four of the CP. It made these gentlemen and a few others in the inner circle of the CP extremely wealthy men. The work gangs were made up of Irish immigrants, Civil War veterans (North and South), released convicts and a few locals from the plains. The UP was plagued by bands of Indians who resisted the intrusion of the work gangs and the railroad into their hunting areas. Despite these difficulties, the UP made rapid progress, completing another 450 miles of track

by the end of 1868.

The CP faced formidable engineering challenges in laying track across the mountains. The scarcity of labor in the West led Crocker to bring in Chinese, who proved to be highly efficient and industrious. By 1867, some 6000 Chinese were working on the CP. The CP completed the mountain work by 1868, and was soon racing across the Nevada plain almost as fast as the UP was pushing westward across Nebraska. The rivalry goaded the two lines into extra efforts, and by 1869 they had actually constructed parallel lines. Representatives of the two lines competed vigorously to get as much mileage and the subsequent subsidies as possible at the expense of the other. On 10 April 1869, Congress designated the compromise meeting point as Promontory, Utah. As the lines approached, Crocker added a few Irish to his crews. He won a $10,000 bet from Union Pacific directors when his gangs laid 10 miles of track in one day.

Locomotives from the UP and CP met at Promontory on 10 May 1869. Using a silver sledge, Durant drove a golden spike into a polished wooden tie to symbolize the completion of the great work. The UP had laid 1038 miles and the CP 742 miles.

Tuscola and Saginaw Bay Railway. The Tuscola and Saginaw Bay operates in eastern Michigan between Ann Arbor, Alma and points in the Saginaw Bay area including Saginaw, Munger and Colling. The T&SB began operations in 1977 on former CONRAIL track that had been part of the NEW YORK CENTRAL's line between Detroit and Bay City, Michigan. In 1982, the T&S assumed operation of the small Ann Arbor Railroad which had been bought by the state of Michigan. Principal commodities carried include molasses, coal, grain and auto parts.

Locomotives: 6
Freight cars: 159
Miles operated: 208

Union Pacific Corporation. The Union Pacific Corporation was formed in 1969 as a holding company of which the UNION PACIFIC RAILROAD COMPANY is a corporate subsidiary. In addition to transportation, Union Pacific Corporation has interests in fossil fuels and land development. Application was filed in 1980 with the Interstate Commerce Commission seeking a merger of the Union Pacific and MISSOURI PACIFIC, and the acquisition of the Western Pacific by the Union Pacific. Efforts by a number of other railroads to block the mergers and acquisitions were rejected by the courts in 1982. The consolidation was approved with several conditions, including the granting of trackage rights to SOUTHERN PACIFIC, DENVER AND RIO GRANDE WESTERN and MISSOURI–KANSAS–TEXAS. Western Pacific is now operated as a district of Union Pacific. Union Pacific and Missouri Pacific are incorporated as Union Pacific System, but each continues to operate independently.

Union Pacific Railroad Company.

The Union Pacific operates an extensive system in 13 states from Kansas City and Council Bluffs, Iowa westward to Ogden/Salt Lake City. Lines extend southwestward from Salt Lake City to Los Angeles and northwestward to Portland and Seattle through Wyoming, Montana and Idaho.

Right: UP brakeman Edward McEntee in the early 1900s. *Below:* The UP photographer's car in Wyoming in 1868 recorded progress along the line.

Above: A UP poster announces the great event of 10 May 1869. *Right:* Union Pacific No. 4022 Big Boy steam engine hauls freight across Wyoming in 1957.

Union Pacific started with the Pacific Railroad Act of 1862, which granted the company a charter to build a railroad westward from Omaha toward the Pacific Coast. A similar charter was granted to the Central Pacific to build eastward from the Pacific. E H HARRIMAN gained control in 1897 and built a rail empire that included the ILLINOIS CENTRAL, SOUTHERN PACIFIC and the Chicago and Alton. Union Pacific had to divest itself of its Southern Pacific stock in 1913, but the two roads continued to cooperate in many aspects of their operations. Union Pacific was noted for the BIG BOY locomotive. First built in 1941, these 4-8-8-4 articulated locomotives weighed 1,104,200 pounds. They were intended for hauling heavy trains up up steep mountain grades.

In the 1980s Union Pacific con-

Union Pacific Nos. 2419, 2930, 2938 and 2903 3000hp GE diesels haul an eastbound coal train near Perkins, Wyoming.

Left: The UP westbound classification yard in North Platte. *Above:* A UP diesel coal train at the Carbon County Mine in Wyoming. *Below:* A UP railroad machinist in the Omaha shop.

Above: A UP coal train loading at Prospect Point Mine. *Left:* The Union Pacific Omaha shops are just outside the city.

tinued to work with the CHICAGO AND NORTH WESTERN TRANSPORTATION COMPANY in the Powder River Basin project. The project involved building new routes to transport coal from Wyoming's Powder River Basin, the largest coal-producing region in the United States. The major UP coal-for-export route is the 784-mile line from Salt Lake City to the Pacific Coast at Long Beach and Los Angeles.

The merger of the Union Pacific, MISSOURI PACIFIC and Western Pacific occurred on 22 December 1981. Western Pacific became a subsidiary of Union Pacific. Missouri Pacific and Union Pacific continued to operate independently. (See maps on pp 254–55.)

Locomotives: 1742
Freight cars: 67,778
Miles operated: 1432
(as of January 1984)

Urban Mass Transportation Assistance Act. Passed in 1974, the act provided for the Federal Government to fund up to 80 percent of the costs of new urban mass transit systems. Among the systems built with these funds are those in Washington DC, Atlanta and Baltimore. Under the Reagan administration, funding has been severely cut and new construction has slowed considerably.

US Military Railroad. See American Civil War railroads.

Utah Railway. The Utah Railway is a coal-carrying road operating between Provo and Mohrland in the coal-mining region of central Utah. Opened in 1914, it was run for three years by the DENVER AND RIO GRANDE before assuming its own operation in 1917. Much of its operation is on trackage rights obtained from the Denver and Rio Grande. The Utah Railway is owned by the Sharon Steel Corporation.

Locomotives: 8
Freight cars: 0
Miles operated: 95

Vanderbilt, Cornelius (27 May 1794–4 January 1877). An American financier, Vanderbilt was a railroad and steamship entrepreneur, born at Port Richmond, Staten Island, New York and descended from Dutch colonists who settled on Long Island in the seventeenth century. His first business venture, which he started at the age of 16, was a ferry service between Staten Island and New York that he operated with a small sailboat he bought for $100. During the War of 1812, he obtained contracts for provisioning forts in and around New York Harbor. With the profits gained from these contracts, he built several schooners that were used in Long Island Sound coastal trading, in Hudson River trade and along the Eastern Seaboard as far south as Charleston. In 1818, he sold his sailing vessels and went to work as a captain for Thomas Gibbons, who ran a ferry service between New Brunswick, New Jersey and New York City. Gibbons was engaged in fierce competition with Robert Fulton, who had been granted a monopoly for steam navigation in the state of New York. Fulton had brought suit against Gibbons for violating the monopoly, and their battles were violent physically as well as legally. Vanderbilt was very skillful at avoiding the sheriffs who were sent out to arrest any steamship captain entering New York waters in violation of the monopoly. In 1824, the Supreme Court ruled that the monopoly was unconstitutional.

With money made in Gibbon's employ and from a New Brunswick riverfront hotel run by his wife, he opened his own steamship business in 1829. Starting with a line on the Hudson River between New York City and Peekskill, he immediately demonstrated his intense competitiveness by

William H Vanderbilt, son of Cornelius.

cutting fares, triggering a rate war between the various lines on the river. When the fare between New York City and Peekskill had gone down to 12.5 cents, his chief competitor, Daniel Drew, sold out to him. Vanderbilt then extended his operations to Albany on the Hudson, to points along Long Island Sound, and on to Providence and Boston. His vessels, the best of which he named after himself, were generally regarded as fast, safe and elegant. Vanderbilt reaped great profits from the California Gold Rush traffic. Many Forty-Niners made the trip by ship to Panama, crossed the dangerous Panamanian jungle to the Pacific on mule back, and completed the journey to California by ship. Vanderbilt established a route through Nicaragua. The line was initially called the American Atlantic and Pacific Ship Canal Company, an allusion to some rather ambitious plans to construct a canal. He could not finance the canal venture. However, the route, which ran along rivers, Lake Nicaragua, and a 12-mile road he built, was faster and safer than the trek through the isthmus.

The new company, called the Accessory Transit Company, was so successful that at least eight new vessels had to be built to accommodate the demand for passage. In 1853, Vanderbilt, who by now was widely referred to as the 'Commodore,' his entire family (including grandchildren) and several friends went on a grand tour of Europe in a luxury yacht, the *North Star*, which Vanderbilt had built for the purpose. While he was gone, Charles Morgan and Cornelius Garrison, the managers of the Accessory Transit Company, succeeded in taking over the company through stock manipulation. Vanderbilt regained control through stock manipulation more clever than that of his rivals. Morgan and Garrison had allied themselves with William Walker, an American soldier of fortune, who had seized control of the Nicaraguan Government. Walker rescinded Vanderbilt's charter and handed over the Nicaraguan operation to Morgan and Garrison. Vanderbilt handled this situation by successfully plotting Walker's overthrow. Vanderbilt then entered into a deal that could be described as extortion. He informed the Pacific Mail Steamship Company and the United States Mail Steamship Company, the chief operators on the Panama route to California, that he would abandon his Nicaragua operation if they would buy the *North Star* for $400,000 and pay him $40,000 a month. The two companies had little choice but to agree to those terms and to the $56,000 a month he demanded a year later in 1858. From 1858 to 1860, he operated a trans-atlantic steamship company.

Vanderbilt started to buy into railroads when he was almost 70, purchasing stock in the New York and Harlem Railroad. He convinced the New York City Council to allow an extension of the line as street car tracks to the Battery, an action that caused the stock to increase in value. A plot by Daniel Drew to sell the stock short and get the city council to rescind the extension charter failed. Vanderbilt bought the stock as it was offered, keeping the price up. When it was discovered that some of the short sellers were offering more shares than actually existed, many of the speculators were ruined. Vanderbilt gained control and made his son William Henry Vanderbilt the vice-president. Vanderbilt then bought control of the Hudson River Railroad, and petitioned the legislature for permission to merge the two lines. Drew once again tried to sell stock short and to manipulate the legislature, a scenario that ended in almost exactly the same way as the attempt to sell New York and Harlem stock short. Vanderbilt then started to buy NEW YORK CENTRAL RAILROAD stock with the intention of gaining control of the line. Once again, Drew tried to thwart Vanderbilt. He offered his Hudson River Boat Line to the New York Central directors for transporting freight from Albany to New York City. However, the river froze, forcing Drew and his allies to use the Hudson River Railroad. Vanderbilt halted the trains on the east side of the river, New York Central stock plunged, and Vanderbilt bought practically every share put on the market. He secured control of the New York Central in 1867. His lines were merged in 1869 as the New York Central and Hudson Railroad. An attempt to gain control of the Erie Railroad in 1868 was thwarted by Drew, JAY GOULD, and JIM FISK, who controlled the Erie. In 1873 the Lake Shore and Michigan Central Railway was bought, and in 1875 the Michigan Central Railroad and the Canada Southern Railway were added. The New York Central was extended to Chicago, making it one of the great American railroads. In 1873 he started construction of Grand Central Terminal. When Vanderbilt died, his personal fortune was estimated to be more than $100,000,000.

A stylish William K Vanderbilt at the races in 1915. He removed himself from major executive responsibilities in the early 1900s.

Vanderbilt, William Kissam (12 December 1849–22 July 1920). A railroad financier, Vanderbilt was born in Staten Island, New York, the second son of William Henry Vanderbilt and the grandson of CORNELIUS VANDERBILT. At age 19, he was sent to work in the offices of the Hudson River Railroad, which had recently come under the control of his grandfather. In 1877, he was named vice-president of the New York Central and Hudson River Railroad, also controlled by Cornelius Vanderbilt. In 1883, after his father had retired, William K Vanderbilt was designated chairman of the Lake Shore and Michigan Southern Railroad, a subsidiary line of the NEW YORK CENTRAL. He also served as president and chairman of the board of the New York, Chicago, and St Louis Railroad.

After the death of his father in 1885, William H and his brother, Cornelius Vanderbilt II, assumed control of the various Vanderbilt interests, a task that fell completely to William H after Cornelius's disabling illness in 1896. Although he served well in his executive positions, he was never particularly fond of the work, and in the 1900s he transferred the major executive responsibilities to others while still retaining a seat on the boards of many Vanderbilt railroads.

van Horne, William Cornelius (3 February 1863–11 September 1915). A railroad builder and executive, van Horne was born in Will County, Illinois, the son of Cornelius C van Horne and his second wife, Mary Minier Richards van Horne. Starting at age 14, he worked as a telegraph operator for the ILLINOIS CENTRAL RAILROAD and the Michigan Central Railroad. He was one of the first telegraph operators in the country to receive by sound rather than use the recording tape. In 1862, van Horne worked for the Chicago and Alton Railroad as ticket agent and telegraph operator, advancing to train dispatcher in 1864, and to superintendent of telegraph and superintendent of transportation in 1868 and 0000 respectively. Van Horne's rapid advancement continued with his appointment as general superintendent of the St Louis, Kansas and Northern Railway, a subsidiary of the C&A, in 1874. Two years later, he became general manager of the Southern Minnesota Railroad, restoring this bankrupt road to profitability, and eventually becoming its president. After the SMR was sold, he served briefly as general superintendent of the C&A, before assuming a similar post for the CHICAGO, MILWAUKEE AND ST PAUL.

As superintendent of the CM&STP, he was in competition with JAMES J HILL'S GREAT NORTHERN. Hill, impressed with van Horne's abilities, recommended him to the CANADIAN PACIFIC RAILWAY for what was to be the crowning achievement of van Horne's career—the building of the Canadian transcontinental line. The line was completed in 1886.

Van Horne served in various executive positions for the CPR from 1881 to 1899, including the presidency from 1888 to 1899, when he resigned for reasons of health. However, he retained the title of chairman of the board in an inactive capacity until he severed all connection with the CPR in 1910.

A trip to Cuba in 1900 aroused his interest in building a railway in that country. He started the 350-mile line before Cuba gained its independence and could grant a charter. The charter was granted, and the road was ready for business on 1 December 1902. In 1903 he agreed to direct the completion of a railroad in Guatemala from Puerto Barrios to Guatemala City. This 65 miles of track, delayed by financial problems and insurrections, was not completed until 1908.

Samuel Vauclain (*left*) and Sir William Cornelius van Horne (*right*).

In addition to his activities in Cuba and Guatemala, he held executive positions in a number of companies including paper, concrete, and iron and steel firms in Canada, Brazil and Mexico.

Vauclain, Samuel M (18 May 1856–4 February 1940). An American inventor and locomotive manufacturer, Vauclain was born in Philadelphia, the son of Andrew and Mary Campbell Vauclain. He received his early education in Altoona, Pennsylvania, where his father worked in the PENNSYLVANIA RAILROAD machine shops. The younger Vauclain was an apprentice in these same shops and served for a short time as an inspector for the Pennsylvania Railroad. He became a foreman at the BALDWIN LOCOMOTIVE WORKS in 1883, and remained with this company for the rest of his career. In 1889 Vauclain designed and built the first compound locomotive. The compound design greatly improved economy and fuel efficiency. Vauclain's first compound, delivered to the BALTIMORE AND OHIO, was very successful, and these engines became widely used on North American railroads. Among his other railroad-related inventions were a wrought-iron center for locomotive truck and driving wheels and a rack and adhesion locomotive. Vauclain became general superintendent of the Baldwin works in 1909, vice president in 1911 and senior vice president until 1929, after which he was chairman of the board.

Vermont Railway. The Vermont Railway is the latter-day revival of the Rutland Railroad which was abandoned in 1963. The Rutland was incorporated in 1843 and survived many adversities, including bankruptcies, floods and labor troubles before being done in by a strike that started in 1961. To provide the state with rail service, the state of Vermont bought the line and engaged Jay Wulfson to operate it between White Creek, New York (near Bennington), and Burlington. Beginning operations in 1961, the line was soon receiving and shipping more tonnage than had all of the Rutland before its demise. The Clarendon and Pittsford was purchased from the Vermont Marble Company in 1972. The VR also operates a section of

track between Rutland and Bellows Falls, and between St Johnsbury and Stanton.

Locomotives: 7
Freight cars: 1260
Miles operated: 130
(as of January 1984)

VIA Rail Canada. VIA Rail Canada manages all former CANADIAN PACIFIC and CANADIAN NATIONAL passenger rail service in Canada except for commuter trains. VIA was established in 1977 as a subsidiary of Canadian National, and assumed responsibility for marketing rail passenger service in that same year. Canadian National's passenger equipment was taken over on 31 March 1978 and VIA became a Crown Corporation the next day. In September of 1978, Canadian Pacific's passenger equipment and service were acquired. Most CN and CP personnel involved in passenger services became employees of VIA. In September of 1978, the two major transcontinental trains in Canada, CN's *Super Continental* and CP's *Canadian*, were combined east of Winnipeg. More train combinations and discontinuations followed. A notable discontinuation was CN's *Montréal–Halifax Scotian*. It was replaced by an extension of CP's *Montréal–St Johns Atlantic Limited* to Halifax. The *Atlantic*'s route through northern Maine provided a faster route, which became much more popular and heavily patronized than the older CP route. However, the *Atlantic* was discontinued in 1981. In 1981 and 1982, VIA took delivery of the first group of Canadian-built LRC (Light, Rapid, Comfortable) locomotives and cars. LRC locomotives and the cars, equipped with automatic tilt mechanisms, are designed for operation at speeds up to 125 miles per hour. Various mechanical problems and track conditions have prevented utilization of this equipment at full speed. Most of VIA's routes operated at a loss in 1982. Rail improvement projects, which will allow LRC trains between major cities such as Montréal and Toronto to operate at close to maximum speed, were under way in the 1980s. The hope was that increased speed would attract more passengers. (See photo on pp 242–43.)

Locomotives: 148
Passenger cars: 940
Self-propelled (diesel) cars: 85
Miles operated: 11,560

VIA Rail's *Canadian* in the Rockies provides high-speed travel across Canada. VIA Rail still offers dining car service in the 1980s.

A Washington Metropolitan Area Transit commuter train from Silver Spring, Maryland, in the nation's capital in 1979.

Wagner, Webster, (2 October 1817–13 January 1882). A railroad sleeping-car magnate, Wagner was born in the New York town of Palatine Bridge, descended of German immigrants who had long been in the area. His boyhood was typical of the time—some formal education, farm-work and grounding in a trade, in Wagner's case, wagon-building and general carpentry. In 1843, after an unsuccessful business venture, Wagner joined the NEW YORK CENTRAL RAILROAD at Palatine Bridge as station master, later becoming freight agent as well.

Wagner's association with the New York Central was to prove fortunate. Under the patronage of CORNELIUS VANDERBILT, the Central's 'Commodore,' in 1858 Wagner designed and manufactured four sleeping cars with a tier of berths whose bedding was hidden away by day in a built-in closet. This arrangement met a growing need for overnight accommodation, and the Central soon was using such cars on all its branch lines. By 1865, Wagner had also devised a 'drawing room' car, complete with overstuffed chairs for more affluent passengers. Both of these innovations gave Wagner great personal success, and the New York Central Sleeping Car Company (at Palatine Bridge) soon became the Wagner Palace Car Company.

One of the great manufacturing rivalries of the nineteenth century was the feud between Wagner and the legendary GEORGE PULLMAN. In 1870, Wagner contracted with Pullman's company to use the Pullman-patented folding upper berth and lower berth seat cushion arrangement in his cars, with the stipulation that the patent release would be only for Wagner's affiliation with the NEW YORK CENTRAL. But when the Michigan Central Railroad failed to renew its contract for cars with Pullman in 1875, Wagner stepped into the breach, using the Pullman patent, and thereby violating his contract with Pullman. The legal battles raged for many years, and Wagner was dead when the case finally was settled. He died in one of his own sleeping cars in a railroad accident at Spuyten Duyvil, New York.

Washington Metropolitan Area Transit Authority (Washington DC). The first section of the Washington Metro was opened in March 1976, and construction is still in progress.

When present construction plans are completed, the system will have five lines running on 101.5 miles and 86 stations, 56 of which will be underground. Although the trains operate automatically, each train carries an operator who opens and closes doors, makes announcements and checks on passenger movements. The automatic train control (ATC) system has three subsystems: automatic train supervision (ATS), automatic train operation (ATO) and automatic train protection (ATP). The ATS system provides information so that the ATO can operate the trains at high-performance, on-time levels. However, the ATP system overides both the other systems to either stop or slow trains if necessary for safe operations.

Electrification system: 750V DC, third rail
Gauge: 4ft 8in
No. of stations: 51
Rolling stock: 298
Route mileage: 46.7

Westinghouse, George (6 October 1846–12 March 1914). An inventor and manufacturer, Westinghouse was born at Central Bridge, New York, the eighth child of George and Emeline Vedder Westinghouse. At age 15, Westinghouse ran away to join the Union Army, but was soon sent home. When he was 16, he enlisted in the Army with his parents' consent. After his honorable discharge in 1864, he joined the Navy for a short time, rising to the grade of acting third-assistant engineer before he was discharged in 1865.

After leaving the Navy, he attended Union College in Schenectady for a short time, but soon returned to his father's agricultural implement factory, where he started his inventing career. His first patent, for a rotary steam engine, was obtained on 31 October 1865. In that same year, he turned his attention to the needs of railroads, obtaining a patent for a device that replaced derailed cars on the tracks. In 1868 and 1869, he devised railroad frogs—devices enabling the crossing of tracks.

In the field of railroad inventions, Westinghouse is best known for his air-brakes. His first air-brake patent was issued on 13 April 1869, and in September of that year, he established the Westinghouse Air Brake Company. Westinghouse's air-brake was one of

Left: George Westinghouse opened many doors for industry as a result of his numerous inventions. *Right:* Many VIA Rail routes are still going strong even though some were discontinued in 1981 (*see entry, pg 238*).

the most significant inventions in the history of railroading. It made high-speed travel much safer by eliminating the need for tightening down the brakes on each car, a procedure that seldom brought the train to a safe stop in time to avoid collisions in emergency situations.

Westinghouse's first system, the 'straight air-brake,' consisted of a steam-driven pump, mounted on the locomotive, that forced compressed air into a reservoir. Opening of a valve in the reservoir allowed air to rush through a series of pipes and hoses to a cylinder in each car, where the air drove a piston which pushed brake shoes against the tires of the wheels. The first installation was on a Panhandle Railroad passenger train, where it was soon credited with preventing a collision with a horse-drawn wagon crossing the tracks.

Westinghouse spent the next few years improving his original design. The straight air-brake would not work if there was a rupture anywhere in the system, and the air was rather slow in reaching the rear cars. His 'automatic air-brake,' invented in 1871, failed safe. On each car there was a small auxilliary tank equipped with a triple-valve mechanism that opened and closed air passages as needed to bring the brake shoes against the tires.

Railroads were slow to adopt the air-brake because of the considerable expense. Many installed them only after public outcry following a wreck that forced them to do so. Eventually, use of air-brakes became mandatory.

Westinghouse turned his attention to railroad signals, forming the Union Switch and Signal Company in 1882. He devised systems of electrical control of switches, an enterprise that contributed to developing his interest in electricity.

In the ten-year period between 1880 and 1890, Westinghouse took out more than 125 patents. In his lifetime he took out almost 400 patents. His interests included railroad equipment, production, transmission, and utilization of electrical power and natural gas. He extended his operations to Europe, and soon had a worldwide empire employing more than 50,000 people. Westinghouse promoted the use of alternating current (AC) rather than the direct current (DC) favored by Thomas Edison. Although AC was attacked as dangerous by Edison and others, it eventually became the major form of commercial electricity. DC, however, was widely used for powering electric locomotives.

Wheel arrangements. See Locomotive wheel arrangements.

Whistler, George W (1800–1849). A civil engineer and locomotive designer, Whistler was a graduate of the United States Military Academy at West Point. Whistler was one of the few early railroad figures with a formal academic education. From 1834 to 1837, he was superintendent of the Locks and Canal Machine Shop, where he was involved in the design of some of the first locomotives in New England. In 1842 he went to Russia to supervise the construction of the Moscow to St Petersburg Railway, but died before its completion.

White Pass and Yukon Corporation Limited. The White Pass and Yukon is a 3-foot-gauge railroad operating between Skagway, Alaska, and Whitehorse, Yukon Territory. The White Pass and Yukon was started in 1898 to connect the Yukon gold-mining area with a tidewater port at Skagway. Crews began working northward from Skagway and southward from Whitehorse in 1898, meeting at Carcross,

The Crystal City Station of Washington's metro system in 1977 (*see entry on pg 242*).

Yukon, on 29 July 1900. WP&Y prospered for a few years when mining was at its peak, but went into reorganization when mining fell off. World War II and the building of the Alaska Highway brought new business to WP&Y. The increased traffic was more than WP&Y could handle, and the United States Army Military Railway Service took over operation, supplying several narrow gauge locomotives purchased from US lines. After the war, WP&Y resumed carrying ores. It also developed a tourist business, connecting with cruise ships at Skagway. WP&Y developed a container specifically designed for use on its narrow gauge cars. A ship designed to carry the narrow gauge containers was also designed. Put into service in 1954, the *Clifford J Rogers* carries containers between Vancouver and Skagway. In addition to rail services, the company operates an oil pipeline parallel to its track. WP&Y is still a carrier of ore concentrates. In 1983, there was a suspension of operations.

Locomotives: 19
Freight cars: 420
Miles operated: 420

Winans, Ross (17 October 1796–11 April 1877). An American inventor and mechanic, Winans was born in Sussex County, New Jersey, the seventh child of William and Mary Winans, descendants of Dutch settlers dating from the 1660s. Winans received only an elementary school education and was largely self-taught in mechanics. He became interested in railroads during an 1828 trip to Baltimore to sell horses to the BALTIMORE AND OHIO RAILROAD.

One of his first inventions was a railroad car equipped with what he called 'friction wheels.' The wheels were fit firmly to the axles, which were projected into outside bearings called 'journal boxes.' The entire journal-axle assembly rotated as a unit. This mechanism, which greatly reduced friction, set the standard for railroad wheels for the next hundred years. Winans demonstrated that a 100-pound car equipped with his 'friction wheels' could be pulled along a track by a half-pound weight suspended over a pulley with string. He set up the demonstration on a small track laid in a corridor of a Baltimore build-

ing for the benefit of B&O directors. One of the directors, 91-year-old Charles Carroll, the last surviving signer of the Declaration of Independence, sat in the car as the released 8-ounce bob, suspended down a stair well, pulled the car along. Winans later demonstrated that the half-pound weight could move a 460-pound friction wheel-equipped car. He became an engineer for the B&O in 1829, assisting PETER COOPER in constructing the TOM THUMB.

Winans devised the first eight-wheel passenger car equipped with swiveling trucks, or bogies. The two four-wheel trucks made it possible for long coaches to negotiate the many curves of the B&O with much less chance of derailing than had been the case with fixed-wheel coaches. The prototype *Columbia* contained many features that were to become standard features of American coaches, such as open platforms and a central corridor. Winans brought suit against the Schenectady and Troy Railroad for copying his wheel design. He won this suit, but lost similar actions in England against copiers of the 'friction wheel.'

In 1843, he was asked to design cars for the projected Moscow–St Petersburg railway in Russia. Winans declined, sending his sons Thomas Dekay and William Winans instead.

In 1832 he designed an engine called the *Samson* for the Baltimore and Susquehanna Railroad. This locomotive was equipped with a guiding truck, which he may have copied from JOHN B JERVIS. Winans collaborated with PHINEAS DAVIS on an improved GRASSHOPPER locomotive called the *Traveller*. The major innotion in this locomotive was a mechanism that allowed power to be transmitted to either one or two sets of wheels. Disengaging the forward wheels reduced the bucking motion characteristic of these locomotives.

He formed a company, Gillingham and Winans, which was put in charge of the B&O's Mount Clare shop. In this capacity he spent the next 25 years inventing, improving and manufacturing railroad equipment and machinery. The agreement with the B&O specified that he and George Gillingham could build engines for other railroads during slack periods. Winans continued to build locomotives with vertical boilers even though the B&O management wanted horizontal boiler

locomotives larger than the small grasshopper-type engines favored by Winans. Among the vertical-boiler engines produced by Winans was a type called the 'Crab.' These engines had horizontal cylinders that greatly reduced the bouncing on similar engines with vertical cylinders. The name was inspired by the movement of the pistons, which seemed to be opposite to that of the locomotive. The last Crab was retired from the B&O in 1893.

Winans devoted considerable time to designing locomotives capable of operating in the mountains west of Cumberland, Maryland. He proposed using locomotives that either had axles with sufficient lateral play to accommodate the curves or using two sets of blind wheels, that is without flanges. The idea was to prevent binding on curves. This was a simple mechanism. Spring-loading and other methods for returning wheel shafts to central positions were at least a century away. Critics predicted that Winan's blind wheel locomotives would derail. However, they were fairly successful.

In 1844, Winans set up his own shop and started to build vertical-

boiler 0-8-0 locomotives, commonly called 'mud-diggers' because of their tendency to pound clay up from between the ties in wet weather. Engines based on the European Crampton and British 'Bloomers' called Carroll of Carrollton were less than successful. They were notable for being the first American locomotives with a four-wheeled trailing truck. This 4-2-4 locomotive was quite fast, but was never used in regular service.

Winans is perhaps best known for the line of locomotives called 'CAMELS.' These were 0-8-0 engines, which, unlike the mud-diggers, did not have gears. These engines had a distinctive appearance due to the cab being mounted on top of a horizontal boiler. First produced in 1848, these were powerful engines capable of pulling heavy loads up the B&O's '17-mile grade,' which rose some 2000 feet in that distance. Some 200 of these were made and sold to a number of lines including the B&O, New York and Erie, and PENNSYLVANIA railroads.

When, in 1857, the B&O decided to adopt 4-6-0 locomotives and phase out the Camels, Winans refused to submit a bid and wrote a pamphlet in which

Ross Winans designed the camel-class locomotive in 1848. In spite of its unusual appearance, it was one of the most powerful engines of its time, because of the weight placed on its drive wheels.

he praised the Camel and condemned the 4-6-0 as an affront to the stockholders and a potential source of ruin to the railroad. The B&O responded with its own pamphlet criticizing the Camel and praising the B&O. This conflict caused Winans to lose his business. In 1861, General Stonewall Jackson raided the B&O yards at Martinsburg, Virginia, destroying 42 locomotives and taking 14 for use in the South. When the B&O then tried to buy three Camels it knew were in Winans' shop, the embittered Winans refused to sell. This refusal may have been as much due to his southern sympathies as ill feeling toward the B&O.

During the war he experimented with a steam cannon, which was seized by Union troops. A member of the Maryland legislature, he was arrested twice during the Civil War, and released on both occasions. In his later years, he worked on a ship called the 'cigar-steamer,' a narrow-hulled vessel that presaged the modern ocean liner.

Wisconsin and Southern Railroad.
The Wisconsin and Southern operates on former MILWAUKEE ROAD track northwestward from Milwaukee to Oshkosh, Cambria, and intermediary points including Ripon, Brandon and Iron Ridge. The abandoned track was bought by the FSC Corporation of Pittsburgh with state and federal aid. Operations started in 1980. The SOO LINE uses a portion of W&S track between Rugby Junction and North Milwaukee.
Locomotives: 19
Freight cars: 420
Miles operated: 147

The York. This vertical-boiler locomotive was designed by PHINEAS DAVIS in 1831 in response to a competition sponsored by the BALTIMORE AND OHIO RAILROAD. It won the $4000 prize offered for the locomotive that the B&O judged best for use on its rails. According to B&O specifications, the locomotive was to weigh no more than 3.5 tons; be built on a four-wheel, suitably sprung undercarriage; be no longer than four feet from front to rear axle; and be capable of pulling a load of 15 tons at 15 miles per hour on level track. In the interest of safety, the B&O expressed a preference for operating pressures under 50 pounds per square inch. Davis, who became the B&O's first master mechanic, improved the *York*, after which he was awarded a contract for a larger locomotive similar in general design to his first effort. This engine, called the *Atlantic*, was the prototype of the GRASSHOPPER class of engine used for many years by the B&O.

Glossary

Adhesive weight. The total of the driving-wheel axle loads.

Air-brake. A braking system in which compressed air is the operating medium.

Alternating current (AC). An electric current which reverses its direction of flow at regular intervals.

Arch. A shallow, semicircular configuration, usually constructed of firebrick or similar material, placed in a steam locomotive firebox below the level of the tubes. It is intended to promote efficient fuel consumption and reduce smoke emission while protecting the flue tubes.

Articulated locomotive. A steam locomotive that has two sets of cylinders, each of which drives an independent set of wheels supporting two sets of frames joined by a hinged joint or pivot.

Automatic train control (ATC). Any of various systems which help the engineer to avoid misinterpretation of signals.

Axlebox. A metal casing that houses the axle bearing. Attached to the frame, the axlebox transmits the weight of car to the axle.

Bogie. The British term for truck (see truck).

Boiler. The part of a steam locomotive in which steam is produced.

Boxcar. A rectangular, fully enclosed freight car.

Caboose. A car, usually placed at the end of a freight train, in which the conductor has an office and living quarters. With increasing use of computer controls, cabooses are falling into disuse.

Catenary. Supporting cable for the conducting wire of an overhead electrification system.

Circuit breaker. A switch which automatically makes or breaks the circuit according to preset conditions.

Class I Railroad. A railroad line with annual revenues in excess of a figure set by the Interstate Commerce Commission, adjusted annually for inflation. The figure for 1983 was about $82 million.

Compound engine. A steam engine in which the exhausted steam is directed into a second set of cylinders.

Consists. The composition of a train.

Container on flat car (COFC). A freight system in which a container that can be lifted intact from the car is carried on a flat car.

Direct current (DC). An electric current that flows in one direction continuously.

Direct drive. A system of power transmission in which there is a direct connection between the engine or

This Baldwin-built Mallet articulated 2-6-8-0 belonged to the Great Northern Railway.

motor and the driving wheels of the vehicle.

Doubleheading. Using two locomotives at the head to haul a train.

Exhaust pipe. A vertical pipe attached to the cylinder casing of a steam locomotive inside the smoke box in line with the smoke stack. It carries away the exhausted steam and the combustion products from the cylinders, producing a partial vacuum on the smoke box and draft on the fire.

Firebox. The section of a steam locomotive boiler in which combustion of fuel takes place.

Fireman. The member of a locomotive crew who feeds fuel into the fire.

Flatcar. A freight car with only a flat deck and no side rails or walls.

Force. See tractive effort.

Frame. The foundation or chassis on which a steam locomotive is constructed.

Frequency. The number of times per second an alternating current reverses its direction.

Frog. A type of rail crossing allowing two sets of running rails to cross each other at grade level at an angle of less than 90 degrees.

Gas turbine. A rotary internal combustion engine driven by expanding gases exerting force against vanes or similar structures mounted on a common shaft.

Gauge. The distance between the running edges of the rails of a railroad track.

Generator. A device that changes mechanical energy to electrical energy.

Headway. The time interval between trains running on the same line.

Hot box. An overheated axlebox bearing resulting from loss of lubrication between the bearing and the journal.

Intermodal transport. Combination of rail transport with another form of transportation such as ships or overland vehicles.

Journal. The part of a shaft or axle supported by a bearing.

Link motion. See valve gear.

Main line. The major line or trunk route used by the fastest, long-haul trains of a railroad.

Monorail. A railway in which the train runs on a single rail.

Motion. A moving mechanism on a steam locomotive.

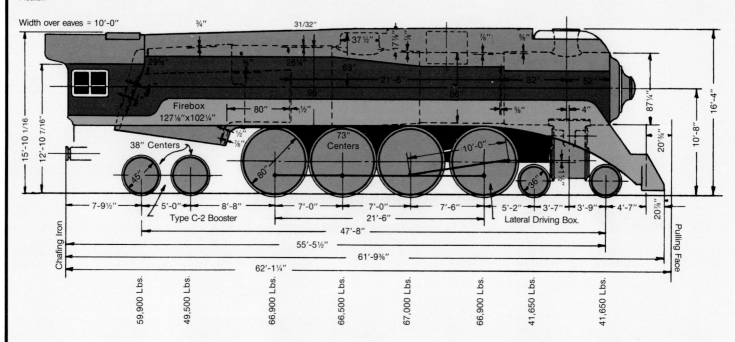

Equipped with No 5 SA
Worthington Feedwater
Heater.

Class GS-3, GS-80 26/32 267/B-109 - SF
Boiler Pressure 280 lbs.

Width over eaves = 10'-0"

Firebox
127⅛"x102¼"

38" Centers

Type C-2 Booster

Lateral Driving Box.

Chafing Iron

Pulling Face

59,900 Lbs. 49,500 Lbs. 66,900 Lbs. 66,500 Lbs. 67,000 Lbs. 66,900 Lbs. 41,650 Lbs. 41,650 Lbs.

Specifications for the GS-2 and GS-3 Steam Locomotive Classes

	GS-2	GS-3		GS-2	GS-3
Weight in Working Order, Pounds			**Boiler**		
On drivers	275,700	267,300	Diameter	OD front 86"	OD front 96"
Engine truck	81,300	83,300	Pressure	300 lbs	280 lbs
Trailer truck	118,000	109,400			
Total engine	475,000	460,000	**Cylinders**		
Tender 2/3 capacity loaded	313,730		Diameter	25½"	26"
			Stroke	32"	32"
Tractive effort			Diameter driving wheels	80"	80"
Main cylinders	64,760	62,800			
With booster	79,660	76,650	**Wheel base**		
			Driving	21' 6"	21' 6"
			Engine	47' 8"	47' 8"
			Engine and tender	96' 3"	96' 3"

Class GS-3

Driving axle journals-main	13" × 14"	Length of boiler tubes	21' 6"	Heating surface-evaporating	4890 sq ft
Driving axle journals-front	12" × 14"	Number of boiler tubes	49' 2¼" and	Heating surface of super-heater	2565 sq ft
Driving axle journals-others	12" × 14"		198' 3½"	Heating surface-combined	7455 sq ft
Engine truck journals	7½" × 14"	Heating surface of boiler tubes	4502 sq ft	Boiler capacity	102.3%
Trailing truck journals	front 7" × 14", back 9" × 14"	Heating surface of firebox	388 sq ft	Tractive effort to adhesive wt	.235

Above: One of the 20 new Southern Pacific 4-8-4 locomotives, in red, orange, black and silver livery, ordered from the Lima Locomotive Works. Early in 1937 Southern Pacific placed in service its first streamlined GS (General Service) locomotives, numbered 4410 through 4415, the GS-2s. These mighty engines were designed especially to power the luxury trains, including the *Daylights* on the coast run because they needed high speed for fast schedules, sufficient tractive effort for the 2.2-percent grade near Santa Margarita and flexibility to negotiate curves up to 100 degrees. Engine 4411 developed 4500 horsepower at 55 mph and had a top speed of 90 mph, although 75 mph was the highest operating speed allowed. Later

that year, Southern Pacific acquired GS-3 locomotives numbers 4415 to 4429, which were exactly the same as the GS-2 in appearance. However, the boiler pressure was stepped up to 280 pounds and nickel steel was used in making the boiler. Tractive effort delivered to the drivers was 62,800 pounds and another 12,300 pounds was developed by the booster engine. The GS-4 locomotives were placed in service in 1941 and were the last in this series of a great breed of engines before being eclipsed by the age of diesel. The GS-4s were assigned to haul freight after World War II.

Below: The boiler inside the engine of the GS-2 locomotive.

Multiple unit. Two or more locomotives or powered cars coupled to run in line or as a train, operated from one locomotive or unit.

Narrow gauge. A railway track narrower than the standard gauge.

Nose-suspended motor. A traction motor mounted on bearings on an axle that is driven via a flexible connection attached to a cross member on the truck. The gear on the axle is in constant mesh with the pinion on the armature shaft.

Pantograph. A device mounted on the roof of an electric locomotive or powered car which comes into contact with an overhead wire for picking up and transmitting electric power to the motors.

Pendular suspension. A suspension system allowing the body of the vehicle to tilt on curves allowing greater speed.

Pickup shoe. A device for picking up electric current from a third-rail system.

Piggyback. A system of carrying truck trailers or similar containers on flat cars.

Rail car. A self-propelled passenger rail vehicle.

Running gear. All the components involved in the movement of a rail vehicle, such as wheels, axles, axle-boxes, springs and frames.

Sleeper. British term for tie (see Tie).

Smoke box. The section of a steam locomotive boiler at the front which houses the main steam pipes to the cylinders, exhaust pipe and stack.

Stephenson valve gear. See valve gear.

Superheater. A device for raising the temperature and volume of the steam after it leaves the boiler barrel through the application of additional heat.

Tender. The car attached immediately to a steam locomotive and which carries fuel and water.

Third rail. A continuous nonrunning track placed alongside the running tracks to supply electric current for trains on the running tracks.

Tie. A member made of wood, steel or concrete placed between the rails

to keep the rails at correct gauge and to distribute the weight of the load on the track.

TOFC. A trailer on flatcar system of intermodal transport in which truck trailers are carried on flatcars.

Tractive effort. The energy a locomotive exerts at the point of the driving wheel treads.

Truck. A swiveling set of wheels mounted at either end of a rail car.

Trunk. A main line or route of a railroad from which other lines branch off.

Turbine. A rotary engine consisting of blades or fans attached to a central shaft which are turned by hot, expanding gases.

Unit train. A freight train consisting of one type of freight car, usually hopper cars for carrying coal or grain. Unit trains are seldom, if ever, broken up, and tend to operate continuously from loading to unloading point.

Valve gear. The mechanism that controls the movement the steam distribution valve of a steam locomotive.

Stephenson valve gear (link motion) A valve gear in which the steam lead is greatest at mid-gear and greatest at full forward.
Walschaert valve gear
A valve gear in which the lead is constant at any position of the reversing gear.

Union Pacific locomotive No. 768 was built by the Rogers Works of Patterson, New Jersey, in 1887. Rogers produced large numbers of the 4-4-0 locomotives, notable for their long configuration.

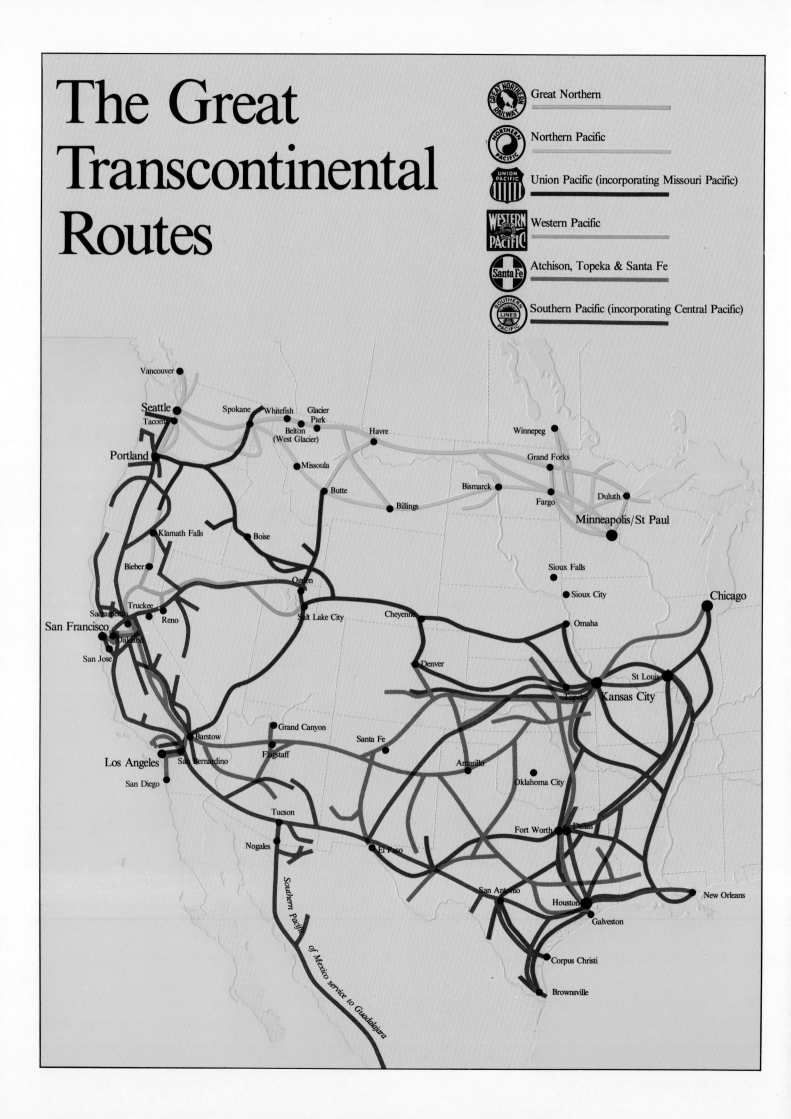

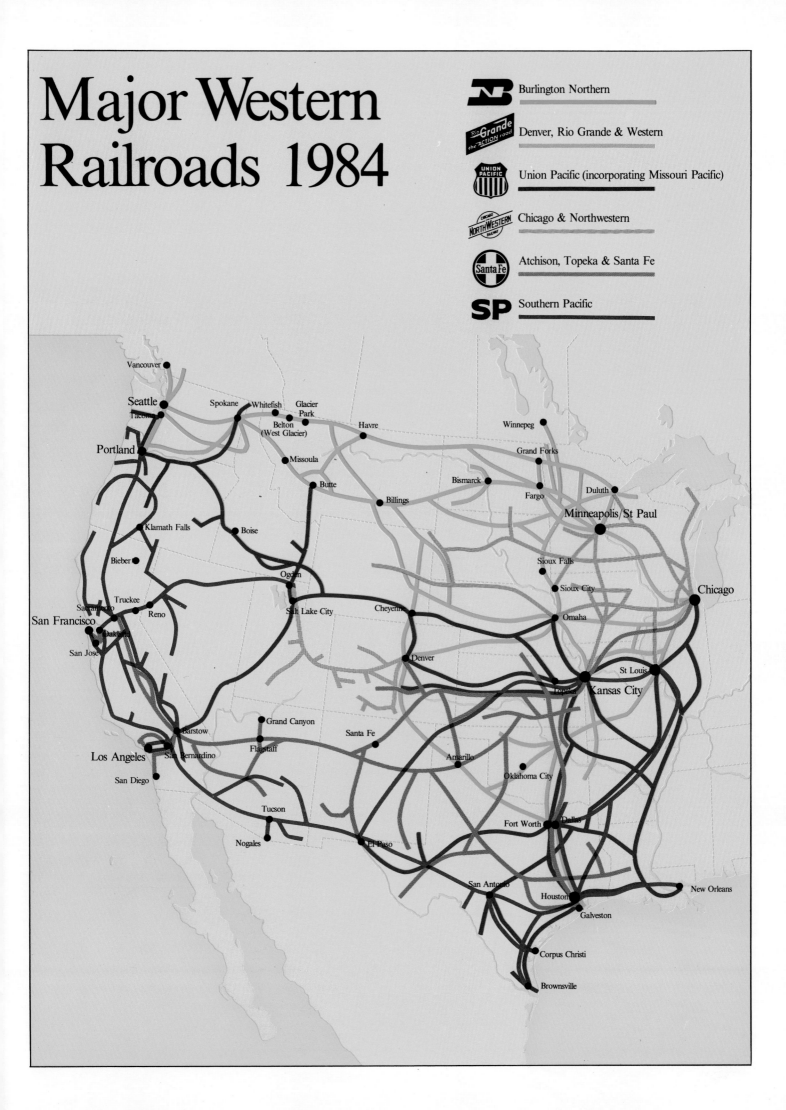

Major Western Railroads 1984

Burlington Northern

Denver, Rio Grande & Western

Union Pacific (incorporating Missouri Pacific)

Chicago & Northwestern

Atchison, Topeka & Santa Fe

SP Southern Pacific

Vancouver
Seattle
Tacoma
Spokane
Whitefish
Glacier Park
Belton (West Glacier)
Havre
Winnepeg
Portland
Missoula
Grand Forks
Butte
Bismarck
Duluth
Billings
Fargo
Minneapolis/St Paul
Klamath Falls
Boise
Bieber
Ogden
Sioux Falls
Truckee
Sacramento
Reno
Salt Lake City
Cheyenne
Sioux City
Chicago
San Francisco
Oakland
Denver
Omaha
San Jose
St Louis
Kansas City
Grand Canyon
Santa Fe
Barstow
Los Angeles
San Bernardino
Flagstaff
Amarillo
San Diego
Oklahoma City
Tucson
Fort Worth
Dallas
Nogales
El Paso
San Antonio
New Orleans
Houston
Galveston
Corpus Christi
Brownsville

The Eastbound Santa Fe *Grand Canyon* pulls alongside a freight train in Cajon Pass, where the main line crosses the coast range of mountains.